Enough Already!

Critical Media Literacies Series

VOLUME 4

The titles published in this series are listed at *brill.com/cmls*

Enough Already!

A Socialist Feminist Response to the Re-emergence of Right Wing Populism and Fascism in Media

By

Faith Agostinone-Wilson

BRILL

SENSE

LEIDEN | BOSTON

All chapters in this book have undergone peer review.

The Library of Congress Cataloging-in-Publication Data is available online at
http://catalog.loc.gov

ISSN 2666-4097
ISBN 978-90-04-42452-4 (paperback)
ISBN 978-90-04-39126-0 (hardback)
ISBN 978-90-04-42453-1 (e-book)

This book is printed on acid-free paper and produced in a sustainable manner.

CONTENTS

Introduction: An Urgent Situation 1

Chapter 1: On the Relevance and Necessity of Socialist Feminism 5

Introduction 5
Feminisms 7
Key Issues 14
"It Goes without Saying": Against Brocialism 25
Conclusion 29

Chapter 2: Fascism and Right-Wing Populism: Similarities, Differences, and New Organizational Forms 31

Introduction 31
Conceptual Overview 32
Shared Characteristics of Authoritarian Populism and Fascism 35
Differences 53
New Forms 56
Cautions 59

Chapter 3: Who Is the Real Working Class? Moving beyond the Construction of the White Male Industrial Worker as a Marker of Authenticity 61

Introduction 61
Neoliberalism's Effects 63
Constructing Capitalism through Race and Gender 70
Diversity of the Working Class 80
Conclusion 89

Chapter 4: Bernie Breakdown: Challenges Facing the Left in the Wake of the Sanders Campaign 91

Introduction 91
The Sanders Campaign: Lessons Learned 93
Conclusion 110

Chapter 5: Well, Actually: Cyber Sexism and Racism within Online Settings and the Enabling Discourse of E-Libertarianism 113

Introduction 113
E-Libertarianism 115

Forms and Functions of Trolling   125
Cyber Organizing   131
Conclusion   145

Chapter 6: Abortion through the Lens of Fetal Personhood: Social
Meanings and Functions   149

Introduction   149
Abortion: An Overview   151
Fetal Personhood: Ideology & Law   155
Oppressive Outcomes of Fetal Personhood   159
Conclusion   170

Chapter 7: In Defense of Science, the Press and Expertise for the
Public Good   173

Introduction   173
Attack on Expertise   175
Pseudoscience   179
Fake News   184
Both-Sides-Ism   188
Conspiracy Theories   193
Conclusion   201

Conclusion: Enough Is Enough   203

References   205

Index   219

INTRODUCTION

An Urgent Situation

This is not a hopeful or optimistic book. It is instead a sober assessment and wake-up call for the left as a whole, including centrist liberals. Likewise, this book is not going to spend the majority of time engaged in critique and then try to wrap up with a general plan for how to address the situation we are in. Such actions mean little when the critiques themselves are often fundamentally naïve and flawed to begin with. We are only beginning to realize the nature of the problem. In presenting a retrospective of Andrea Dworkin's work in *The New York Review of Books*, Blair (2019) features one of her more famous quotes:

> This book is an action, a political action where revolution is the goal. It has no other purpose. It is not cerebral wisdom, or academic horseshit, or ideas carved in granite or destined for immortality. It is part of a process and its context is change. (p. 28)

In a similar manner, this book is meant to serve as a form of cultural criticism where socialist feminism is used to read media texts. These texts track a growing problem of authoritarian populism and fascism that fails to be confronted in an organized, coherent, and meaningful way. When it is common to have mainstream media outlets entertain the thought of inviting fascists or climate deniers to "debate the issues," it should be apparent that the gravity of the situation has not yet taken hold.

Two primary questions drive this book. First, what is behind the rapid rise of strongman authoritarian populism and fascism, not just in the United States, but globally? Second, what leads these movements to always incorporate misogyny as part of their ideologies? In addressing these questions, this book is not going to spend the majority of its content critiquing the Democrats or other centrist groups. It is not going to devote two or three token sentences acknowledging the danger of far-right views, and then proceed to foster "both sides are equally bad" thinking that often masquerades as hard-hitting critique on the left. Though it should be acknowledged that centrists have facilitated our current situation, their contributions pale in comparison to what right-wing movements as a whole have done and are continuing to do.

In advancing a Marxist feminist analysis, this book unapologetically prioritizes minorities, women, and the LGBTQI working class. This means not hesitating to include the white working class as a target of critique when necessary. The focus of this book is confronting fascism and authoritarian populism along with the groups and ideologies that sustain it. We are well past the time on the left where we can skirt around the problem of the white working class' receptivity to racism and misogyny

© KONINKLIJKE BRILL NV, LEIDEN, 2020 | DOI: 10.1163/9789004424531_001

by conveniently sweeping it under the "false consciousness" rug. Along these lines, this book will not insert "not all men" or "not all white people" every time racism or sexism is mentioned. Sociological generalities will be used as this book deals with sociological concepts. If you can't paint with a broad brush where needed, the painting won't get done.

Further, I argue that the left's current approaches are insufficient for effectively confronting authoritarian populism and fascism. Rather than being in a "rough patch" that the next election will cure, what we are seeing is deeply systemic, enabled by a social media architecture, the enormity of which we are only starting to grasp. As Bello (2017) soberly warns us, "progressives must squarely face the fact that these movements are either in power or on the threshold of power—and once they get power, through elections or other means, they have no intention of relinquishing it" (para. 27). Hopes that Trump and other administrations will somehow play themselves out when people realize their sheer incompetence ignores the historical reality that the left once thought the exact same thing prior to the Nazis coming to power (Ulrich, 2016).

With few exceptions, the left is extremely naïve about the intentions of the far-right as well as the reliability of mainstream conservatives when it comes to their own enabling for opportunistic reasons. As Sefla (2017) warns,

> To build the kind of activist movement so the left can win future battles, it will have to learn key lessons in the skirmishes today. The first of these is that the existing institutions of this society can't be relied upon to stand up for our rights…it's a dangerous illusion to think that the courts will side with justice and freedom absent mass pressure from below…it's an even more dangerous illusion, echoed in some liberal circles, to think that certain parts of the military or security apparatus will tame Trump's excesses. (p. 7)

Indeed, the aftermath of the Mueller investigation demonstrates that concepts such as a sitting president cannot be indicted only highlights the tenuous loopholes that have held the system together up to this point. Trump's conduct has laid bare the fragility of Constitutional protections, and have seemed to taken us by surprise, if not unawares.

This naivete extends into ineffective media and academic practices such as assuming that facts alone will be enough to fight the far-right, that having a hands-off open marketplace of ideas will somehow facilitate people in selecting the best ones, or that the media owes fascist views an equal hearing (Camacho, 2016; DiMaggio, 2017; Sedillo, 2017). Hamilton (2016) sums up nicely the situation we are now in, where the media remains wedded to both-sides-ism and reinforces the right wing:

> Facts and truth are suddenly unrelated. Power no longer implies responsibility. Legitimacy and decency are now somehow passengers on separate ships. In this dynamic, *People* magazine can champion both the perpetrator and the

victim and see no contradiction or betrayal. Lilla can use the victory of a campaign steeped in identity politics to highlight the ineffectiveness of identity politics. And Lerner can argue that a campaign "advanced" by sexism, racism and xenophobia can tell us much about the targets of that bigotry, i.e. that they need to behave differently, but little about the supporters of that campaign. (para. 6)

Through the analysis presented in this book, it is hoped that readers will gain a sense of the scope and intensity of organizing on the right. Accurately comprehending their ideological components and strategies of discourse are essential for developing an effective response. Further, grasping how the media—intentionally or unintentionally—assists in the promulgation of authoritarian populism and fascism is required, especially in light of a move away from traditional journalism to online distribution of information. Most critically, there is a need to dialectically investigate the source of the willingness in the media to stretch the bounds of legitimacy to accommodate the actions of right-wing populists and fascists.

CHAPTER OVERVIEW

Each of the chapters in this book can be read in isolation without disrupting the overall flow of the text. Taken together, they present an unveiling of the problem of authoritarian populism and fascism. Chapter 1 establishes the need for using socialist feminist analysis to fully understand the current situation we find ourselves in. This chapter asserts that feminism and Marxism by themselves are insufficient for comprehending authoritarian populism and fascism, precisely because of their shared interest in misogyny. Different forms of feminism are briefly discussed, along with highlighting some of the activism happening around issues like reproductive rights that have introduced renewed energy into the Left.

Building on the foundation presented in Chapter 1, Chapter 2 dissects authoritarian populism and fascism by first examining shared characteristics between the two movements. This is followed by presenting key differences, important in the context of Hitler comparisons commonly seen in the mass media. This chapter asserts that while vigilance is important, misapplication of the fascist label can serve to hinder the ability to confront the current situation.

Chapters 3 and 4 then move to de-centering the white male working class, a key construct utilized in the media in its framing of economic policy. Chapter 3 deconstructs the white, straight, male, industrial sector worker which has for too long served as a stand-in for the working class as a whole, on both the left and the right. This chapter makes the case that in using the white male working class as a universal construct, the actual diversity of the working class is ignored and along with it, actions that can benefit all of the working class. Chapter 4 breaks down some of these problematics associated with Bernie Sanders 2016 presidential campaign, including destructive tendencies on the left that end up assisting, not hindering, the right-wing.

Chapter 5 takes on the problem of authoritarian populism and fascism within online contexts, including harassment of women and minorities. The ideology of e-libertarianism is critiqued as creating an enabling climate for right-wing movements. In particular, the discursive and organizational strategies of the alt-right are presented, along with the cultivation of the troll persona as fundamental for recruitment. The chapter concludes with a look at the manosphere and its impact on online contexts.

Because of its regular reappearance as a touchpoint for controversy, Chapter 6 examines abortion from a Marxist feminist framework. The social and legal constructs of the fetus represent a strategic move on the right from which to attack not only women, but the working class as a whole. This chapter argues that far from being a fringe issue or identity politics as is often portrayed, abortion and contraception are fundamental for the survival of the working class. The coverage of these issues is designed to create solidarity wedges between women, building on the historical power of sexual repression and shame.

Chapter 7 mounts a defence of science, reason, and the press, all of which have been under intensified assault since 2016. The mass media's approaches have enabled the right-wing to the point where fascism has become normalized as yet another issue. By framing anything outside of the tribal belief system as "fake news," authoritarian populists have successfully created impenetrable bubbles around themselves. The consequences of this situation are only beginning to play out, as the conclusion of the book addresses.

CHAPTER 1

ON THE RELEVANCE AND NECESSITY OF SOCIALIST FEMINISM

INTRODUCTION

After the 2016 election, there has been a dramatic increase in mass organizing around women's issues and gender equality not seen since the activism of the early feminist movement. This activism has also been able to harness the power and reach of social media to rapidly coordinate participants both online and on the street with unprecedented results. On inauguration weekend, January 21, 2017, close to four million people from 680 locations joined the Women's March, in the United states and across the globe (Smith, S., 2017, p. 12; Roesch, 2019, p. 8). In what started as a Facebook announcement after the 2016 election, this march surpassed the size of the demonstrations of the 1960s, making it the largest US protest turnout to date (Sefla, 2017; Roesch, 2019). In major cities, one out of every 100 US citizens marched, many of them never having attended a protest before (Sefla, 2017, p. 2). Not only were the numbers boundary-breaking, but the marchers themselves represented a "broad cross-section of women: urban and rural; white and of color; middle class and working class; more liberal and more radical" (Roesch, 2019, p. 9). Further, many of the leadership roles were occupied by women of color.

The march, considered the opening salvo of a "global woman's rebellion" was not only a direct repudiation of Trump and the right-wing he represents, it extended much further, to bring to the forefront "issues such as gender violence, wage inequality, reproductive rights, and women's reproductive work, as well as sexual liberties, at the center of the political and cultural debate of every country hit by the mobilizations" (Roesch, 2019, p. 8). Just one week after the march, protestors occupied major airports, in support of people from Muslim-majority countries who had been included in Trump's executive order banning refugees and citizens from entering the US (Sefla, 2017). Six weeks later, the globally planned "A Day Without A Woman" resulted in street and workplace demonstrations as part of the International Women's Strike, held on International Woman's Day (Roesch, 2019; Kumar et al., 2019; Fierro & Vasco, 2019). As with the Women's March, these actions were coordinated by minority women and "added demands for legal abortion, gender wage inequality, and the recognition of unpaid domestic work to the established demands against gender violence" (Fierro & Vasco, 2019, p. 35).

What these mobilizations have revealed is that what often starts out as a single-issue campaign quickly widens into larger, intersectional social demands regarding

© KONINKLIJKE BRILL NV, LEIDEN, 2020 | DOI: 10.1163/9789004424531_002

gender, sexuality, and the economy, providing the potential for on-the-ground, radical analysis. This is exemplified in the growth of the testimonial-based #MeToo and #TimesUp campaigns, which draw together diverse coalitions of women and men. As Schulte (2018) points out, while the awareness of #MeToo may have been due to celebrities and other prominent people with media access, "it had the potential to provide a platform for other women to tell their stories—including working-class and poor women who face harassment and assault on the job at alarming rates" (p. 17).

#MeToo quickly had reverberating effects within Congress, when California Representative Jackie Speier first released a video on social media which recounted her own experiences with sexual harassment at the hands of a chief of staff. Then, other female politicians added their own accounts. Within a few months, six Democrats and Republicans had been pressured to resign because of these sexual assault allegations (Schulte, 2018, p. 18). This is in addition to more than 20 women who have accused Trump himself of sexual assault, resulting in the Democratic Women's Working Group in the House drafting a letter calling for an investigation into the allegations. Eventually the letter garnered over 100 signatures, including from male signatories (p. 19).

However, these significant actions have not just been the result of the 2016 election, and have been building for some time. Actions such as the Ni Una Menos mobilizations in Mexico around femicide and sexual harassment, Women United Against Bolsonaro's street actions and Facebook Page with 4 million followers; Poland's mass protests of the country's abortion ban, Argentinian activism around femicide and abortion, and Ireland's mobilizations concerning the repeal of the Eighth Amendment which prohibits abortion are all the result of organizing over time and across different coalitions (Brum, 2018; Fierro & Vasco, 2019; Roesch, 2019). Most of these have built onto earlier mass actions from the 60s, 70s, and 80s.

In 2015, Argentina's Green Handkerchief mobilizations around abortion rights "spread like wildfire throughout the country" with supporters showing their solidarity by wearing green scarves featuring the movement's logo (Fierro & Vasco, 2019, p. 34). The handkerchief was an accessible and effective way to show strength in numbers, with even older rural men seen wearing them. Demonstrations in the hundreds of thousands stretched across 80 cities, putting pressure on Latin American governments to do something about femicide, gender violence, and reproductive rights (p. 35). In the US, McDonalds employees coordinated a mass strike across 10 cities, and Marriott workers participated in a two-month strike in seven states, both connecting the issue of sexual harassment, gender, and low-wage labor (Roesch, 2019, p. 10). The two things that all of these actions have in common are (a) they involve both social media and street action and (b) they are led by working-class women of color, contradicting the myth that feminism is only relevant for white, older, middle-class women.

This chapter is designed as an opening for the rest of the book, by making the case that socialist feminism is both relevant and necessary for confronting the growth of authoritarian populism and fascism. Neither feminism nor Marxism in isolation are sufficient for conceptualizing the current situation we find ourselves in, because the global spread of authoritarianism also harnesses economic, racial, and gendered factors under capitalism. The chapter, organized in three major sections, first opens with a presentation of broad forms of feminism, asserting that there is no single version of feminism and that it is shaped by different coalitions. This is followed by an overview of key issues impacting women and LGBTQ people, which are taken up throughout the rest of the book in more detail. Finally, a critical examination of brocialism, or sexism within leftist spaces, is framed as a unique challenge and a primary threat to solidarity within activist movements.

FEMINISMS

One of the primary challenges (as well as the exciting features) of feminism is that it can represent a variety of concepts, identities, philosophies, and interests, especially in media contexts. This section posits that there are several forms of feminism, which can be broadly organized into liberal feminism (within which there are different strands, beyond the scope of this section), postmodern theorizations (including Third Wave), conservative forms (neoliberal/imperialist and right-wing), and Marxist/ socialist alternatives, which are the most appropriate for confronting and fighting authoritarian populism and fascism.

These forms can often be distinguished by how proponents view origins and sources of oppression along with strategies for fighting it, with liberal feminists often locating oppression in sexist politicians and laws, postmodern feminists pointing to modernist constructions of identity and movement activism as problematic, conservative feminists rejecting collectivism in favor of individualism and the market, and Marxist feminists' location of oppression within capitalism (Goodman, 2016). Leavy and Harris' (2019) apt definition of feminism prioritizes its broad coalition building while also remaining clearly anchored to liberation and justice:

> Beginning with the status of girls and women, but not ending there, feminism is an engaged human rights position that seeks to expose and remedy gender inequities. The study of gender, as a starting point for approaching feminist research, cannot be understood without consideration of other aspects of human existence that influence the ways in which human beings interact socially, including race, physical ability, class, geolocations, and sexuality. We are not bodies that are only gendered, but rather, we simultaneously occupy race, ethnicity, social class, sexuality, and other positionalities. (p. 4)

This definition is inclusive of liberal, postmodern, and Marxist feminism but not neoliberal or right-wing conservative forms, which illustrates why one size does not fit all when it comes to feminism.

When examining media forms, one quickly sees that feminism has been coopted to serve a range of political purposes, not all of them centered on humanism, anti-racism, or liberation. For example, the history of the women's movement in the US is inextricably tied to that nation's colonial status as a white settler state, genocide and forcible displacement of indigenous groups, along with slavery and immigration controls, all occurring alongside the patriarchal domination of women's bodies (Tax, 2017; Theweleit, 2010a). Capitalism itself would not have been possible without accompanying colonization (Bohrer, n.d.). Feminism has been used by Europeans and Americans since the 1800s to buttress imperialism, the notion being that women in regions such as the Middle East, Africa and Asia needed (and still need) to be rescued from backward practices (Aftab, 2017; Kumar et al., 2019). Acknowledging this history along with current incidents is critical for conceptualizing the field of feminism as whole, along with understanding why there are conservative forms that coopt the superficial trappings of empowerment, only to further entrench white supremacy.

Conservative forms of feminism often emerge from cynicism and backlash, including among younger people, as Richards (2017) found:

> The fact of the matter is; feminism is not the majority worldview. When talking to young university students about feminism there is an overwhelming discomfort with a movement that should inspire enthusiasm. Both boys and girls do not want to be associated with it, do not want to hear about it, and do not have any legitimate understanding of what feminism is or does. (para. 4)

This reaction can be partly attributed to liberal feminism's initial failure to include the perspectives and interests of minority women and women from working-class backgrounds (Roesch, 2019). Many of the younger women, lesbians and transgender people who make up feminism's Third Wave have also found mainstream feminism to be limiting, exclusionary, or irrelevant to their needs, while still rejecting conservative feminism (Goodman, 2016). These feminists often draw on postmodernism for "reframing the theoretical framework of feminism" when addressing key issues like reproductive rights, rape, domestic violence, the environment and inequality (p. 219).

Neoliberal feminism represents the outer boundary that demarcates the separation between mainstream liberal feminism and conservative forms of feminism. What makes neoliberal feminism distinct is that it uses progressive sounding discourse to shift activism away from larger collective solutions like changing laws and policies—which liberal feminism advocates for, albeit in limited fashion—and instead moves this to the individualistic realm in the form of self-improvement (Rottenberg, 2018). This would include the growth of concepts like "leaning in," "achieving work-life balance," mindfulness, decluttering/simplicity movements, and changing one's attitude or outlook rather than insisting on significant social change. The message is to adapt to one's existing conditions as a way to foster one's liberation. Climate change represents the limits of neoliberal thinking, where capitalists can visualize a dystopian end to the world as we know it, but they simply can't comprehend that capitalism will end. Therefore, any solutions they attempt to craft has to be contained within the market, like changing personal consumption habits or recycling (Terzakis, 2018).

Imperial feminism, essentially neoliberal feminism on an international scale, incorporates three characteristics. The first is it being market-centered, with the market promoted as the primary means to liberate women. This relates closely to the second characteristic of the appropriation of feminism used to offset domestic labor onto non-Western women in the wake of massive privatization. Finally, imperial feminism emphasizes the role of corporate-sponsored NGOs in tamping down activism. As with all forms of conservative feminism, the neoliberal form also accelerates the "insourcing" of labor to minority and immigrant women so as to free the professional (often white) woman from the constraints of unpaid labor (Rottenberg, 2018). Aftab (2017) presents the example of Nike's social media marketing of their Pro Hijab as a form of feminist messaging in support of empire:

> Why did an image of a woman in a headscarf appeal to the American masses so much? Perhaps what made it so palatable was that it turned protests and marches into feel-good events for white people. Perhaps it circulated so widely because it helped to deflect attention from the atrocities that the United States is actively committing abroad, allowing Americans to revel only in the benevolence of US liberalism. At times, visibility or diversity projects do the opposite of what they claim to be doing—in this case, demonstrate how they can include the faces of hijab-clad Muslims while remaining actively complicit in structures that harm this very community. (p. 35)

Another powerful form of conservative feminism incorporates right-wing ideologies. It is important to note that this form does not fit the definition of feminism presented at the start of this chapter—which necessitates centering on human rights and liberation. Yet enough women utilize feminist-sounding discourse or even identify as feminist to make this its own category. Traister (2018) notes the historical continuity between the involvement of white women in maintaining segregation during the Jim Crow era and those who regularly call the police to report black people doing innocuous things like eating or walking, providing an apt reminder that "women's anger certainly isn't always progressive" (para. 27). Because of their association with white men, white women occupy a social position that simultaneously allows them to participate in regressive movements, while being framed as feminist. As such, women like Phyllis Schlafly have been active in pushing against the Equal Rights Amendment and LGBTQI rights during the 1970s, utilizing "protecting the children" and "family values" discourse, and participating in anti-choice movements, all claiming to promote traditional values that are under threat (Goodman, 2016).

Kimmel (2017) addresses the irony of conservative Tea Party women who work outside the home, often as the lone breadwinner, while vocally rejecting the working mother role. He views their position as the parallel to white men's sense of aggrieved entitlement:

9

> These working women do not—cannot—embrace the traditional roles that
> the party might have envisioned for them…they want to. The women of the
> Tea Party believe themselves entitled to live in a traditional, conservative
> household. Their sense of aggrieved entitlement runs parallel to the men's:
> they want their men to be the traditional heads of households, able to support
> their families. They want to be moms, not 'women.' (p. 65)

Similarly, during the Kavanaugh hearing, women who supported the Supreme Court
nominee created social media groups centered around prioritizing how husbands and
sons could be victimized by rape accusations, totally overlooking their own, their
daughters', or their sisters' greater potential for victimization (Roesch, 2019).

Indeed, the 2016 election revealed that 45% of women holding college degrees
voted for Trump (McClaren, 2016, para. 13). Even though most women ended up
voting for Clinton, 61% of white women who did not have a college degree voted
for Trump, "a man who bragged about grabbing women's genitals without consent"
(Windham, 2017, p. 10). In some cases, conservative feminism can extend beyond
the electoral sphere into white supremacist organizations, where women regularly
coordinate picnics, camping trips, parties, children's events and other activities
to create a sense of community cohesion around whiteness. For Kimmel (2017),
conservative feminism represents an additional way to reinforce nostalgia and a
restoration of white rule:

> Feminist in practice, antifeminist in theory, conservative feminism hopes
> to secure the economy so that women can return to their families and their
> homes and leave the labor force…the Tea Party mobilizes angry white women
> alongside angry white men, wannabe stay-at-home moms alongside wannabe
> domestic patriarchs, looking back to a long-gone era in which white men went
> to work, supported their wives and families, and all the government programs
> that enabled and supported that…were paid for invisibly, so it appeared that
> they had built it all by themselves. (pp. 66–67)

An alternative to liberal, postmodern and conservative feminism is Marxist or
socialist feminism. For the purposes of this chapter and book, the terms are used
interchangeably, as they address the same questions: "how is the political economy
gendered in late capitalism? And, how does the social reproduction of people
and communities renew capitalism, rather than support anti-capitalist praxis?"
(Armstrong, 2020, p. 7). However, this form of feminism is often overlooked or
dismissed as being irrelevant or consigned to history. For example, a common
misunderstanding about socialist feminism is that its association with Marxism
means that it automatically employs a colorblind class analysis when the growth of
this form of feminism was itself in response to more reductionist approaches to class
being used among the male-dominated left (Bohrer, n.d.; Goodman, 2016). Enough
time has passed to allow a mixture of corporate cooptation of and forgetting that
International Women's Day was first held in 1909 by the Socialist Party of America

to commemorate garment workers striking in New York. Not long after, the Russian Revolution had women on the front lines. Therefore, "it is not novel to tie socialism and feminism together; they are inextricably linked as movements and always have been" (O'Hagen, 2019, para. 5).

Likewise, a common critique of Marxism is that it rejects intersectionality, itself a concept claimed by postmodernists but that originated from a socialist feminist perspective of women of color dating back to Sojourner Truth and Anna Julia Cooper, along with the later Combahee River Collective:

> In its most basic form, then, intersectionality is the theory that both structurally and experientially, social systems of domination are linked to one another and that, in order both to understand and to change these systems, they must be considered together. Intersectionality thus critiques theories that treat forms of oppression separately, as well as attempts to locate one axis of oppression as primary. (Bohrer, n.d., para. 3)

As Bohrer reminds us, the "call to extend Marx's analysis beyond its original scope is precisely the project that all Marxism since the nineteenth century has taken up," even if some leftist men refuse to recognize this (para. 35). In other words, socialist feminism advocates for an extension of Marx's ideas, not a rejection of them. Both intersectionality and socialist feminism are compatible (Camfield, 2013).

Debates around the positioning of identity have long surrounded feminism as a whole, particularly the relationship of identity to the capitalist system (Bohrer, n.d.; Goodman, 2016). Marxist feminists, while supporting the aims of liberal feminism, disagree with mainstream feminism in terms of how to most effectively address oppression. Liberal feminists, to varying degrees, approach equality as achievable within the existing system, whereas leftist feminists assert that due to the relationship of gender with other aspects of identity such as race, a fundamental restructuring of the economy is essential in order to achieve full liberation (Burns, B., 2017; Tax, 2017). For that reason, one cannot solely use class analysis to account for the historically interconnected role of race and gender:

> Economic class structure is merely one part of a complex and multifaceted system of domination in which patriarchy, white supremacy, colonization (both direct and indirect) and heterosexualism are fundamental...This approach does not de-emphasize more traditional class analysis but follows the key insights of intersectionality in arguing that class, race, gender, sexuality, colonization and imperialism are constituted in and through one another in such a way that class cannot be considered the master-term of capitalist accumulation and antagonism. A truly adequate analysis of capitalism, both theoretically and historically...treats capitalism as the original synthesis of these systems of dispossession. (Bohrer, n.d., para. 39)

Socialist feminism therefore opposes the concept of class reductionism, especially when it comes to issues of gender and social relations under capitalism, known as social reproduction and including the concept of unwaged labor (Bohrer, n.d.). A more nuanced way of looking at gender in capitalism is that gender, along with race, just so happens to be one of several ways through which capitalism manifests itself as a totalizing system, in its process of constantly adapting (Theweleit, 2010a). An example of this is the patriarchal family form since the emergence of class-based societies, which underwent a massive restructuring from centuries of the extended family model, to the nuclear family. Changes we are now seeing regarding the eroding centrality of marriage to family formation represents a more recent manifestation of the interconnectedness of sociological factors under capitalism. As with other feminisms (except for conservative forms), socialist feminism has significantly revised its 1960s-1980s conceptualizations of the family from assuming a default white, heteronormative, and two-parent forms to an expansion of the notion of family itself (Bohrer, n.d.).

What socialist feminism does is add the dimension of economics to liberal feminist issues such as sexual harassment, which are often framed within patriarchy. O'Hagen (2019) provides the example of how sexual assault is typically connected to power and patriarchy, encapsulated in the statement, "rape isn't about sex, it's about power." However, often there is not much analysis of what structural societal features comprise such power, that leads to women being targeted for violence, such as being overrepresented in low-wage, non-unionized work, which is further tied to bosses controlling multiple aspects of their lives. Additionally, the lack of affordable housing, universal childcare, parental leave, a strong social safety net and limited access to health care often create situations where women are afraid to speak out against harassment and domestic violence. This also acknowledges that while more affluent professional women do experience sexual harassment, the brunt of the economic consequences fall on poor and minority women. Taken to a global scale, climate change hits those who have the fewest resources the hardest, because of women's historical exclusion from land ownership and ability to shape policy (Burns, B., 2017).

In addition to postmodern critiques, the concept of fusing intersectionality within socialist feminist analysis has often been rejected by the Marxian left itself, in a form of calling for "socialist, not feminist" politics (not unlike the calls for the Democratic Party to reject identity politics in order to win over the white working class) (Bohrer, n.d.). This significantly underestimates the distinct connections that patriarchy has with capitalism that would result in thin analyses if this were not taken into account (Camfield, 2013). As O'Hagen (2019) asserts, "it's complacent for any socialist to argue that ending capitalism will simply erase sexism from existence…Sexism persists because it is propped up by a deep-rooted set of beliefs and stereotypes that imagine women as inferior" (para. 6). At the same time, the necessity of understanding the need for feminist analysis within Marxism also underscores the necessity of socialism, "because women can't fight against sexism as a whole if they're too busy trying to keep their heads above water in an economic system that exploits them" (para. 6). For this reason, women's-only spaces—such as the Zapatistas—can be an essential component of organizing and need to be respected (Camfield, 2013).

Socialist feminism also provides one of the best ways to read the recent exciting rise in global activism, which shares the five traits of more radicalized demonstrations with the participation of young people; international cooperation; multi-movement coalitions; critiques of capitalism and patriarchy and a growing class consciousness happening within different demographics (Fierro & Vasco, 2019). These traits are critical because, "class struggle is how workers change themselves, realize their own social power, dramatically raise their class consciousness, and recognize the commonality of interests across divisions and the solidarity needed to win" (Blanchard, 2018, p. 25). Indeed, in looking historically at periods of leftist growth and radicalization of the working class, a common denominator has been feminists and leftists recognizing their shared experiences and priorities (Tax, 2017). More powerfully, many of the most successful movements incorporate intersectional leadership (Burns, B., 2017):

> *Actually-existing* socialist organizing and politics aren't the ideal that these socialists talk about. They exist within patriarchal societies. As a result, the actions and thinking of socialists will inevitably be limited and deformed by the patriarchal gender relations that we're committed to uprooting. So, socialists need to develop our politics by learning from the *actually-existing* struggle against patriarchy (as well as learning from history). To do this we need feminism. (Camfield, 2013, para. 7)

Marxist feminism offers one of the most effective means to address the various ways that women in particular experience alienation, in the form of their labor being produced for others' needs; being alienated from labor processes via automation—again for the benefit of profit and not people; alienation from others via competing in a framework of scarcity, and alienation from the environment (Terzakis, 2018). Capitalism can often feel overwhelming because it not only determines our experiences of the present, but it reconstructs history itself: "no past class conflict or gender relation will ever be wholly dead…as long as the capitalist mode of production remains able to create the conditions for reintroducing it within the diverse territories of its own domain of power" (Theweleit, 2010a, p. 359). This creates a feeling of hopelessness, where "the present stretches on into infinity," that change will not ever happen, or that it is futile to try (Nowak & Prashad, 2016, para. 35). A revolutionary response therefore becomes necessary, with wider—not narrowed—demands as socialist feminists in Argentina demand:

> We are antipatriarchal, anticlerical, anti-capitalist and internationalist feminists and dissidents. We want legal abortion, a completely secular state, comprehensive sexual education with a gender and dissidence perspective, a dissolution of the Senate, and much, much more. We want everything and will

go for everything. And, as our young activists sing during every mobilization, "We will overthrow patriarchy, and with it, capitalism!" (Fierro & Vasco, 2019, p. 45)

KEY ISSUES

As Goodman (2016) notes, "the election of the misogynist, racist, xenophobic billionaire Donald J. Trump handed women's liberation its most direct and malicious challenges in more than 100 years" (p. 258). In particular, people in the US are realizing that rights that were once thought of as guaranteed by law, such as access to legal abortion, are now under threat. Those in Western democracies are also becoming aware of the fact that the political oppression they have only begun to see has been the reality for the majority of the world's population. At the same time, events like the Kavanaugh Supreme Court hearing and the backlash against sexual harassment awareness remind us that we have never been in a post-feminist era. We are now confronting the fact that people hold contradictory perspectives on issues they filter through their "common sense," but this is not the Gramscian form of common sense that works toward liberation (Nowak & Prashad, 2016). Instead, it is an aggressive and regressive common sense that seeks to entrench the status quo with a vengeance.

While it can be profoundly demoralizing come to grips with the fact that a significant minority of the population never ceases in their attempts to roll things back at least 100 years, our collective awakening to the interconnected nature of key issues provides the foundation for lasting resistance. Traditional conceptualizations of key feminist issues have only alluded to the intersection of gender with class, race, age, ability and other identities whereas now we are seeing a widening, more nuanced dialectical analysis of how these issues connect to each other under capitalism:

> The profit-logic of capitalism, with its necessarily consequent ideas about reason, labour, race, gender and sexuality created both the metropole and the colonies simultaneously, and subjects on both sides of this divide were constructed, through systems of domination and exploitation, in the image of what capitalism needed to survive. That capitalism requires multiple kinds of exploitation, multiple forms of dispossession, and multiple kinds of subjects in order to gain global hegemony is corroborative evidence for Marx's fundamental diagnosis of the system's simultaneous resilience and its ultimate fragility. (Bohrer, n.d., para. 50)

Through this emerging understanding we can see how power operates through capitalism in relational ways, creating different experiences depending on one's position in society. For example, while poor and minority women bear the brunt of sexism under capitalism, even more privileged women are not immune from its effects as we saw with the media's treatment of Hillary Clinton during the 2016 election.

This section examines key issues that require both a Marxian and a feminist approach in order to comprehend what is happening. These include rape and assault, which also encompasses domestic violence; issues related to labor; the double standard in terms of media representation of female politicians; and the objectification of women within the media. It is important to note that while these issues are discussed in turn, they also overlap, as in the example of sexual harassment being a regular aspect of labor for many women in the workforce or how violent discourse and imagery impact how women are represented as sexual objects.

Rape and Assault

According to Carter (2014), over one third of women across the globe have been documented victims of violence, whether physical or sexual and most of those incidents are at the hands of intimate partners (p. 143). When considering unreported cases, this number is likely much higher, with a majority of women having been the victim of some sort of sexual harassment, rape, or domestic violence. The workplace in particular represents a space where women are likely to experience sexual harassment along with assessments of their abilities routinely based on their appearance and age (Paquette, 2017). This manifestation of sexism only adds to the climate where harassment is fostered. Recent activism around sexual harassment and rape have brought things like this to light, as Roesch (2019) notes:

> One is the way in which women's oppression continues to pervade and distort the most intimate aspects of their lives. In a move that has prompted discomfort as well as a potential backlash, the conversation has expanded beyond clear acts of harassment and assault to a deeper reexamination of sexual relations. (p. 10)

Socialist feminism is especially relevant for framing rape and assault because of its intersectional dimensions. For the most vulnerable, including poor, working-class women and transgender women, rejecting a man's sexual demands can mean violence or death. As an example, the primary cause of non-accidental death for Black women is murder, the majority of which is committed by intimate partners (Gallant, 2018, p. 39). After Hurricane Katrina, displaced women, who were already facing barriers to childcare and housing, had to contend with increased vulnerability to sexual assault—an important impact of the effects of climate change which makes this an environmental issue as well (Sanders, 2017).

Activism around rape and sexual harassment have also revealed that women who work in public and low-wage sectors are far more vulnerable. For example, close to 80% of women agricultural workers have experienced harassment, abuse and rape (Schulte, 2018, p. 17). Because the majority of these workers are undocumented, they fear the consequences of deportation and loss of income that their families depend upon. In the US military, of the estimated 26,000 incidents of sexual harassment, fewer than 3,200 were reported and 300 prosecuted, representing just over 1% of cases (Carter, 2014, p. 48). Roughly one third of female veterans stated they were victims of rape while in the military, with rape by colleagues being a primary contributor to PTSD in women (p. 49). Further, "US appellate judges have ruled in several cases that female victims, after release from the military, are not eligible for financial help for psychiatric or other damages unless they had reported the crime immediately after it occurred" (p. 48). Because the commanding officer holds the decision whether to move forward with prosecution for rape, victims are hesitant to report.

The #MeToo and #TimesUp campaigns have highlighted not only the egregious acts of men in positions of power, but the systemic protections that shield them from the consequences of their actions. Additionally, the experiences of those victimized by rape and sexual assault repeatedly demonstrate that "the rules that claim to be in place to protect women from abusers are there to protect the institutions from women's complaints of abuse" (Schulte, 2018, p. 20). This happens through the design of the criminal justice system that serves to discourage all but the most determined and well-resourced women to report sexual harassment and rape cases. If a case makes it to trial, the focus turns to the actions of the victim, with personal and often unrelated details laid out for all to see through virtually unlimited cross-examination by defense lawyers (Carter, 2014; Nicol, 2016; Schulte, 2018). Even if a group of women testifies against a single perpetrator, any inconsistencies between their accounts, which is often common in cases of sexual trauma, is used to create the perception that the victims are unreliable witnesses (Nicol, 2016). Sociological and psychological research about victims of sexual assault is not taken into consideration. Essentially, a woman "can be raped with impunity because she is not a believable witness" (Nicol, 2016, para. 32).

Rape and sexual harassment are unique in that the status of the victim in terms of *her* innocence is immediately the focus. This is due to the patriarchal construct of the "perfect victim," where, in order to meet this standard, a woman must have absolutely no sexual history whatsoever attached to her (Nichol, 2016). Instead of assuming that the perpetrator is innocent until proven guilty as one would with robbery or even murder, the default position is that the woman is lying or has somehow "misinterpreted" the intent of the perpetrator (Loofbourow, 2018; Nichol, 2016). Loofbourow (2018) explains:

> We don't question the particulars of someone's account of their mugging, but rape inspires people to start panning the story for possible "misunderstandings…"
> The painful experiences claimed by women make no impression at all on a certain kind of man's sense of reality. Her perspective is as unreal as it is inconsequential to him. Result: His and her story can be, in a limited and horrifying sense, equally true. (para. 13)

Loofbourow provides the example of Kavanaugh's friend Mark Judge, who Christine Ford asserted was in the room at the time of her assault when she was a teenager. It is indeed possible that Judge had no recollection of witnessing the attack, not because he was deliberately lying, but, more frighteningly, the event didn't even register as significant enough for him to remember.

What lies beneath patriarchal assumptions regarding rape and sexual harassment is the double standard, or the notion of "boys will be boys," more recently encapsulated in Trump's dismissal of his past assault of women as "locker room talk" (Weida, 2017). However, these sayings go beyond merely excusing men's behaviors or even naturalizing them, to fully stating that white men in particular are *entitled* to what they consider to be "youthful indiscretions" without any sort of consequences or controls on their behaviors (Loofbourow, 2018; Traister, 2018). Further, it is not enough that women are supposed to endure these behaviors, they are expected to openly forgive and absolve their perpetrators so as not to "ruin their lives." Solnit (n.d.) sees this as a way to invert the important gains of #MeToo and #TimesUp as more men are finally facing the threat that women have had enough:

> The follow-up story to the #MeToo upheaval has too often been: how do the consequences of men hideously mistreating women affect men's comfort? Are men okay with what's happening? There have been too many stories about men feeling less comfortable, too few about how women might be feeling more secure in offices where harassing coworkers may have been removed or are at least a bit less sure about their right to grope and harass. Men themselves insist on their comfort as a right (para. 18)

Solnit points to the example of Larry Nassar, the gymnastics physician who abused girls, and then complained that the testimonies of his victims made him uncomfortable.

The televised Kavanaugh hearing as a whole presents a case study of white male entitlement in live time. Traister's (2018) account of Republican responses to vocal protests during the first day of the hearings described a parade of privilege and dismissiveness, which was only a sign of things to come. When one of the female protestors accused Republican politicians of how cutting health care would lead to her death, Orrin Hatch responded, "We shouldn't have to put up with this kind of stuff" (para. 5). Ben Sasse insisted that "maybe the ladies should all just calm down" and stop the hysterics of exaggerating about the impact of health care cuts (para. 5). Then came Christine Ford's testimony of her assault at the hands of Kavanaugh when she was a teenager, which was a powerful indictment of not only Kavanaugh, but the Trump administration as a whole:

> With Ford's story came the explicit acknowledgment of what all those demonstrators had been working to convey for weeks: that this fight has been against an administration with virtually no regard for women, for their rights, or for the integrity of their bodies, either in the public or private sense. (para. 4)

The impact of Ford's testimony was immediately apparent, with even Trump concerned that she sounded very credible. Because of her status as an upper-middle class white woman, Republican politicians couldn't use their usual discursive weapons to deny her experiences as they did with Anita Hill during the Clarence Thomas hearings in the 90s. Something bigger would have to do, in the form of presenting a united white male grievance front. This involved taking the focus off of Ford and her believability—which they knew they had no chance of fighting— and placing it onto *their* supposed victimization. Aside from Kavanaugh's red-faced, tear-filled angry tirade at even having to hear Ford's testimony, there was Lindsey Graham's resentful declaration of, "I'm a single white male from South Carolina, and I'm told to shut up, but I will not shut up" (Beauchamp, 2018b, para. 2). Beauchamp notes that this quote marked the moment when the stakes of this hearing were elevated beyond just Kavanaugh and Ford:

> It's about beating back the challenge from feminists and people of color demanding a seat at the table; it is about showing that white men in power are not going anywhere—that they will not listen, will not budge, and will not give ground to #MeToo or the Black Lives Matter movement. (para. 3)

In particular, Graham's statement inverts a key assertion by women and minorities that "white men in positions of privilege don't have direct experiences with hostile sexism or racism, and should listen to the people who have" (Beauchamp, 2018b, para. 12). Indeed, during the hearings, one of the White House lawyers expressed concern that if Kavanaugh could be "brought down" by such accusations, then "every man certainly should be worried," a statement echoed by other conservative politicians and pundits (Loofbourow, 2018, para. 3). The idea that Supreme Court Justice, one of the most powerful and permanent positions in government, isn't automatically granted to a nominee, but said nominee is held to scrutiny is considered an affront too difficult for an oppressed white male to bear:

> "I will not shut up" is a perfect mantra for Trumpian backlash politics. There is no risk that white men are, en masse, going to be silenced: They occupy the commanding heights of power in every walk of American life. The demands that they be quiet at times are a response to the overrepresentation of their voices, that they understand what life is like for more vulnerable people and then change the way they act accordingly. (Beauchamp, 2018b, para. 13)

Ultimately, rape and sexual harassment are manifestations of a misogyny that is not outside the norm, but built directly into the structures of institutions and relationships. Much of this is religiously informed as well, with women cast as inferior and subservient to men (Carter, 2014). In commenting on the doubling down of prominent politicians after the Kavanaugh hearing, Loofbourow's (2018) sober assessment effectively sums up the realizations of many women just waking up to the authoritarian populism and fascism in their midst:

> It is now clear, and no exaggeration at all, that a significant percentage of men—most of them Republicans—believe that a guy's right to a few minutes

of "action" justifies causing people who happen to be women physical pain, lifelong trauma, or any combination of the two. They've decided—at a moment when they could easily have accepted Kavanaugh's denial—that something larger was at stake: namely, the right to do as they please, freely, regardless of who gets hurt. Rather than deny male malfeasance, they'll defend it. Their logic could not be more naked or more self-serving: Men should get to escape consequences for youthful "indiscretions" like assault, but women should not—especially if the consequence is a pregnancy. (para.15)

Labor

Since capitalism depends on the labor of women, including unpaid domestic and emotional support work, it is not possible to separate women's inequality at work from the discrimination they face outside of it (Penny, 2011; Roesch, 2019). Globally, women are responsible performing two thirds of all work, yet 70% remain in poverty and 66% are illiterate due to lack of access to education or having to work to support their families, even as children (Carter, 2014, p. 86). Climate change also more dramatically impacts women, who are often displaced after weather events due to inability to afford housing in less affected regions:

It's the women and children who increasingly have to go further and further from their homes to get water or face the daily threat of drought who do not have the luxury of being in denial about climate shifts. In fact, climate-change policy debates and ideological wars are a luxury that only men...and people of color with privilege can afford. The real, unfortunate truth is that the world's predominantly female poor will feel the effects of any and all attempts to soften, silence, or deny climate change. (Sanders, 2017, p. 20)

As Weida (2017) observes, "it seems there is no resume solid enough, no political pedigree pure enough to overcome sexism and misogyny in America" (para.16). Though capitalism has adopted neoliberal feminist discourse in shaping workplace policies within more prosperous democracies, gender inequality is an inherent feature of the workplace. Despite women making up nearly 50% of the workforce in the US and receiving more college degrees than men, women who work full time still earn just over 76% of what men do (Carter, 2014, p. 168). Older women often face additional employment discrimination (Paquette, 2017). Even in more "liberal" and privileged job sectors, such as postsecondary education, women only hold 28% of professorships at the highest rank and earn 80% of male professors of similar rank (Carter, 2014, p. 170). Within attacks on K-12 education, a combination of funding cuts and privatization has targeted women, in particular "mass layoffs of teachers of color" along with increased policing of black students through the school-to-prison pipeline (Blanchard, 2018, p. 12).

Massive sociological changes within a short period of time have shaped the composition of households, with women often placed in the role as sole income earner or, at the very least, vital to the survival of a two-income-earner household. Currently, 44% of mothers who work outside the home are the only income earner in their families, with 25% co-breadwinners who contribute one fourth to half of their household's income (Roesch, 2019, p. 14). Black women provide over 86% of their household's income, illustrating the impact of race and gender on labor (p. 14). This is in sharp contrast to 1950, where 93% households consisted of married people with children (p. 13). By 2017, just over 20% of children live in single-mother-headed households (p. 13). As the median age for marriage approaches 30 along with more people opt out of marriage, this is continuing to shape the formation of the family.

Labor also involves the harder-to-track but far more ubiquitous forms of unpaid labor or reproductive work, which includes things like household maintenance (itself a vast category of work), child care, care for older relatives, agricultural work, extra errands at work, and the like (Burns, B., 2017). This is borne out by the astounding statistic that of all goods sold in developed countries, 80% are purchased by women (Penny, 2011, p. 1). Often this unpaid labor is accompanied by the labor of emotional support that often falls on women who are already employed full time, as Piepzna-Samarasinha (2017) aptly sums up:

> They're going to ask you to listen, do a favor, do an errand, drop everything to go buy them some cat food or crisis counsel them. Manage logistics, answer feelings emails, show up, empathize, build and maintain relationships. Organize the childcare, the access support, the food. Be screamed at, de-escalate, conflict resolute. They're going to say, "Can I just pick your brain about something?" and then send you a five-paragraph email full of pretty goddam complex questions. It'd be real nice if you could get back to them ASAP. They're going to ask if you can email them your PowerPoint and all your resources. Some of them will be people who are close to you; some of them will be total strangers. Do you have a minute? For free. Forever. And you know what's going to happen? You're going to do those things. Because you do, indeed, care. (p. 21)

Even though more affluent women perform such reproductive and emotionally supportive labor, they are often able to offset it by paying poor and minority women for maid service and child care, at often poverty-wage levels. Penny (2011) links this to "western women's despair at the very point of asking our male relatives to do their bit, our unwillingness to challenge the system at its root" where "an entire generation has been willing to simply hand down their oppression to poor, migrant, and ethnic minority women" (p. 61). Essentially, exploitation through reproductive labor is now shifted onto a specific segment of the population who are also women. This is reflected in women making up three fourths of the top ten lowest wage jobs, with much of that work in service industry occupations (Roesch, 2019, p. 15). This type of work is also associated with higher rates of sexual harassment, with 50% of all women who work in food service reporting unwanted sexual advances (Sustar, 2018, p. 38).

In examining issues related to labor and gender, it is clear that "working-class women are valued less by just about every measure—wages, benefits, housing, education" and that this isn't an accidental development (Schulte, 2018, p. 23). It is of benefit to the capitalist class to disrupt any form of solidarity between men and women, especially to reinforce the idea that women are gaining too much power at the expense of men. At the same time, the capitalist class is all too aware of the consequences of women themselves coming together and saying "no":

> Female power of refusal is the single most scary, most horrifying, most insistently phobic thing facing any society, ever. Women could, in theory, refuse to cook and clean and care and keep society running. Women could refuse to fit themselves out in conformity with the patriarchal proclivity not just for staid, acceptable sex, but for social order. (Penny, 2011, p. 62)

Media Representation

Female politicians represent an important case study that is worth examining concerning the double standard inherent in media representation. Dittmar (2016) analyzes how female candidates' appearance and mannerisms are more of a media focus than their intelligence or policy positions, where coverage "includes more attention to hair, hemlines, and husbands" (para. 12). Common examples include an intense analysis of voice and inflection, as in critiques of Carly Fiorina and Hillary Clinton for being "shrill, whiny, or unnecessarily angry or nagging," all age-old sexist stereotypes applied to women (para. 10). Right-wing blogger Matt Drudge created a front-page headline and feature story on his website speculating on if Clinton wore wigs or not and *Slate* noting that she dressed like a lesbian, even if she wasn't one herself. While all critiques of female politicians like Clinton are not inherently sexist, people rarely seem to ask, "am I judging this woman candidate in ways that no candidate could ever measure up?" (Wilz, 2016, p. 357).

A key component of differential treatment of female politicians in the media includes the requirement that they be "likable." This includes having to walk a fine line between masculine and feminine performances and involves behaviors like not talking too loudly, smiling more and certainly never openly confronting sexism (Penny, 2011; Wilz, 2016). Even after being subjected to three years of Trump's public conduct, the media continues to speculate on the likability of 2020 presidential candidates like Elizabeth Warren and Kamala Harris. It is clear that male candidates can adopt any manner of masculine posing, and still be within the realm of acceptability and relatability, as with Trump's treatment during the entire runup to the 2016 election as a candidate with equivalent viability. Another example includes Clinton and Sanders advocating the same policy positions, but Sanders' positions seen as more viable because of his particular populist masculine presentation style (Wilz, 2016).

In this sense, Hillary Clinton represents the apex of unlikability, not only due to her serious demeanor, but because she doesn't let a sexist remark go unnoticed. During a 2015 debate with Clinton, Bernie Sanders rebutted her questioning his record on gun control by stating, "all the shouting in the world" wouldn't stop gun violence (Dittmar, 2016, para. 11). The very next day, Clinton referred to Sanders' statement at a political appearance, noting, "I've been told to stop, and I quote, 'shouting about gun violence.' Well, first of all, I'm not shouting. It's just, when women talk, some people think we're shouting" (para. 11). The media continued to dismiss Clinton's policy positions—as well as the concerns of millions of female voters—by focusing on unfounded conspiracies about emails, fueled by Wikileaks' distribution of Russian sources: "over and over again, Clinton voters watched the media ignore a woman's experience in both foreign and domestic matters and her extensive, well thought out platform in favor of chasing the titillating shadow of her alleged misconduct" (Weida, 2017, para. 18).

A more extreme example of likability applied to Clinton was Meet the Press's Twitter critique of her as being "over-prepared" when there was no comparison to Trump's ill-prepared performance (Kellner, 2017). Apparently, a woman being prepared is too alienating and unfriendly, as Weida (2017) explains,

> When given a choice between a blatantly sexist, incompetent man who spewed violence at every turn and a calm, controlled woman who had steered our country through troubled waters for the better part of a decade, 46.4% of the voting populace pulled the lever for the nightmare we are currently living. The threat of nuclear war, racism in the White House, and the slow bleed out of Constitutional Rights was more palatable than a woman who didn't "smile enough" and seemed "too prepared." (para. 22)

The double standard of media treatment applied to female politicians also takes on social class dimensions. Washington Examiner media writer Eddie Scarry shared a photo on Twitter of Representative Alexandra Ocasio-Cortez in office attire, with the caption "I'll tell you something, that jacket and coat don't look like a girl who struggles" (Del Valle, 2018, para. 4). This remark was an attack on Ocasio-Cortez's embracing of her background as a working-class Latina, open solidarity with her younger, multi-racial constituency, and her direct critiques of the capitalist class. As Del Valle explains, "the underlying message in Scarry's tweet is clear: if people are really from working-class backgrounds, they can't afford to look well put together or elegant" (para. 9). Scarry's remark also alludes to the common conservative talking point that people aren't really be poor if they have a television or cell phone; therefore, "people who can't afford things like health care or housing are blamed for their inability to do so" (para. 19).

Because women candidates are often vocal supporters of issues like reproductive rights or equal pay, this automatically "feminizes" these issues and frames them as less important compared to "real" policy, touted by male candidates (Dittmar, 2016; Wilz, 2016). Hillary Clinton took on the notion of "playing the gender card" by replying, "if calling for equal pay and paid leave is playing the gender card, then deal me in…if helping more working parents find quality, affordable childcare is playing the gender card, then I'm ready to ante up" (Dittmar, 2016, para. 17). Indeed, constant criticisms of female supporters of Clinton took the form of accusations of "vagina voting," implying that the only reason women voted for her was because of their shared gender. The irony is that male voters continually express gender affinity through their voting patterns, but often get to hide behind party affiliation as well as men nearly exclusively running for office since the founding of the United States. Dittmar discusses exit polling from 27 Democratic primaries where Clinton earned 60% of the female vote compared to 49% of the male vote (para. 18). In contrast, Sanders gained 38% of female voters and 48% of male voters (para. 18).

Objectification

Closely associated with the double standard in terms of how women are portrayed within the media is their hostile objectification and sexualization without their consent, as a form of diminishment and gender policing. Wilz (2016) points to the example of search engines, where typing in the name of a male politician, like Trump, Cruz, or Sanders along with the word "porn" yields far fewer graphic results than doing the same with Clinton, Pelosi, or Palin. This form of pornification carries over into the daughters of female politicians, as a way to censure the audacity of women seeking public office:

> Pornification highlights sexuality in contexts that otherwise are not normally sexualized and, through the use of crude humor or gender-based parody, disciplines individuals who do not conform to traditional gender norms. Furthermore, because women candidates perpetually combat the double bind between femininity and competence, media frames that cast them as sex objects undermine their credibility as leaders in ways that the same frames do not undercut male candidates. (p. 358)

Not just limited to more prominent women seeking office or celebrities, objectification is saturated throughout all forms of media and extends into everyday life. As soon as a woman is perceived to have stepped "out of line"—in other words, going about her daily life in public—they are immediately disciplined through being called a slut or other sexual slurs, nearly always paired with the words "ugly" and "fat." Penny (2011) asserts this is a form of backlash against the legal gains that women have made under feminism. The increased policing of women's bodies, which has accelerated under neoliberalism, includes intensified monitoring of any kind of fat, in any form, and is tied to men's fears of women gaining power:

> Cellulite, saggy bellies, fat around the arms, natural processes which affect all female bodies, even the leanest, after puberty, are particularly loathed… the threat that patriarchal birthright will be "swallowed up" or "suffocated"

by gender equality is made manifest in the fear of female fat, and that phobic response to the reality of physical femaleness has been internalized by women and men across the western world. (Penny, 2011, pp. 32–33)

Trump himself regularly demeans women through attacks on their appearance, as in his connecting Fox News host Mika Brzezinski's facelift to her lack of intelligence (Paquette, 2017). Many women could relate to this because of how they are regularly judged based on their appearance, which is directly connected to age and gender discrimination in the workplace. During a 2016 rally, Trump referred to his debate with Hillary Clinton: "I'm standing at my podium and she walks in front of me, right. She walks in front of me, and when she walked in front of me, believe me, I wasn't impressed" (Kellner, 2017, p. 5). Transgender bodies are also constantly surveilled, as in 2015 when Mike Huckabee, in a speech to a religious broadcasters convention, flippantly remarked, "I wish someone had told me that when I was in high school I could have felt like a woman when it came time to take showers in PE" (Dittmar, 2016, para. 7). Here, we see this feeble attempt at humor used to diminish transgender identity as a matter of flippant decision-making. With this type of comment, Huckabee and others also employ sexism to "present masculinity and sexuality as mutually reinforcing, so that masculine dominance relies upon heteronormativity" (para. 7).

A major contribution to the use of objectification as a form of backlash is the legalization of oral contraceptives in 1965 (Penny, 2011; Mason, 2016). This marked the moment when women's sexual activity could be separated from pregnancy and, more importantly, placed that decision squarely into the hands of women. The arrival of the pill, along with other forms of contraception, has been one of the single biggest contributing factors to the growth of women participating in the paid workforce. Women could determine when and how far apart to space having children, assuming they even elected to have children in the first place. As a result, the "post-Fordist capitalist control of women's gendered labor needed to be extended beyond the sexual and into the substantive, nutritive, and the semiotic architecture of gender and physicality itself" (Penny, 2011, p. 4). The monitoring of women's bodies had to move into other aspects of daily life.

In particular, capitalism feeds on two powerful, gendered insecurities: discontent with one's appearance and responsibility to meet men's needs, both aspects of women being expected to keep themselves in check (Penny, 2011; West, 2016; Solnit, n.d.). Both of these insecurities have spawned massive profit in the cosmetics, lifestyle coaching/counseling, fitness, household maintenance, boutique foods, and other related industries. As West (2016) notes, women are exposed to constant media messaging, which has become internalized and reinforced through interactions with others. This "steers humanity toward conservatism and walls the narrow interests of men, and keeps us adrift in waters where women's safety and humanity are secondary to men's pleasure and convenience" (p. 19). An example of this is Stormy Daniels' interview with Anderson Cooper regarding her past involvement with Trump, where she explained, "I had it coming for making a bad decision for going into someone's room alone…well you put yourself in a bad situation and bad things happen, so you deserve this" (Solnit, n.d., para. 14). On the flip side, Solnit notes how the media also portrays Daniels as an opportunist because of her financial success.

Finally, while the media superficially conflates 24/7 surveillance of the female body with liberation, what is actually happening is that objectification has become a form of alienation under capitalism. As Penny (2011) notes, "we live in a world which worships the unreal female body and despises real female power" (p. 22). This is reflected in how men's suffering—defined as not getting what they feel entitled to at that very moment—is viewed as more significant than "a woman in pain who has never been told that what she wants might matter" (Loofbourow, 2018, para. 10). Ultimately, by remaining fixated on what women need to do to improve their bodies, this limits the scope of our political expectations to highly individualized things like weight or lifestyle fixes, as a form of personal responsibility, which then becomes the flippant go-to solution when presented with larger social problems (West, 2016).

"IT GOES WITHOUT SAYING": AGAINST BROCIALISM

One of the more challenging problems that socialist feminists confront is sexism and racism on the part of leftist men. This ranges from regular dismissal of the importance of acknowledging the need to include feminism as part of Marxist analysis and organizing, to condescending forms of communication, to exploiting the characteristics of patriarchal constructions of leftist organizations to sexually harass and rape women (Goodman, 2016; Morris, 2010). "It goes without saying" refers to the usual opening response of leftist men when socialist feminists raise important issues related to gender, race, and sexuality, as in, "it goes without saying that these are major problems, but once capitalism has ended, these problems will as well." Women are supposed to sacrifice their political interests for the larger aims of the group so as not to be "divisive." Often this takes the form of "mansplaining," where males will assume a condescending tone in online settings, to lecture women about things like what makes someone a real feminist or what is or isn't racism. A more dramatic example of mansplaining took place in an online comment that went viral where someone identifying as male told women they were overinflating the estimated cost of tampons by not using them correctly (Khan, 2019).

A more recent social-media-based term for sexist leftist men is *brocialist*, combining characteristics of "bro" behavior (immature, fraternity culture, centered on male bonding/joking around) with socialist or left-progressive beliefs. *Manarchist* and *manarchism* are similar terms, referencing the anarchist community. The accompanying ideology—brocialism—advocates for a more aggressive insistence on colorblind Marxism, often using "edgy" and ironic discourse via social media, usually commenting rapid-fire in groups. When confronted about their sexism, they will immediately point to their progressive credentials, as if they cannot possibly be misogynistic:

> Brocialists are quintessentially anti-intersectional…they dominate spaces, manipulate women, and dismiss identity politics as "divisive." Typically, they are privilege-blind cishet white men, often significantly above the poverty line…who refuse to acknowledge oppression and privilege, intersectional or otherwise, outside of classism and socioeconomic status…brocialists refuse to accept that within their own movement (as within society more broadly) there may be misogyny, from mansplaining to rape threats; resorting instead to the No True Scotsman fallacy by accusing feminists and other critics that they must be speaking to the wrong so-called "socialists." (SJWiki, para. 3)

Morris (2010) provides an example of a meeting organizer who would dominate gatherings by speaking loudly, using difficult vocabulary to shut people out of the discussion and talk down to those he considered less intelligent. If anyone pointed this out, "he would feign ignorance…and complain of being infantilized" when he was the one patronizing the members (para. 13).

Though Sanders himself is a vocal supporter of women's rights, a segment of his brocialist followers, dubbed "Bernie Bros" were described as "flustered, shouting white guys" who regularly dismissed feminism while aggressively touting a colorblind class analysis (Dittmar, 2016, para. 18). During the Democratic primaries, comments from Bros included "their vaginas are making terrible choices," referencing the stereotype of women only supporting Clinton because of her gender, along with regularly using "bitch" and "cunt" to describe both Clinton and her supporters (McMorris-Santoro, 2016, para. 5). The comments of the Bros seemed to advance a nostalgic view of past elections without female candidates being gender neutral and not cluttered up with identity politics, when "gender dynamics have been at play in all US presidential elections to date" (Dittmar, 2016, para. 1).

Sensing that the online harassment was beginning to negatively impact Sanders, his campaign officials reached out to the Clinton campaign to apologize and try to more intensely monitor Facebook and Twitter pages for "Bro-y" posts (McMorris-Santo, 2016, para. 3). Male Sanders supporters responded by either asserting that the Bernie Bro persona was a fictional media construct meant to attack Sanders or distancing themselves by calling out the Bro behavior. As McMorris-Santo describes, "online Sanders supporters always stress in conversation that the vast majority of Sanders supporters aren't Bros—and they claim many of the so-called Bros can in fact regularly be found posting in conservative forums" (para. 39). Indeed, much of the Bro posts ranged in style from a detached mansplaining, to angry accusations of Clinton supporters trying to bring Bernie down, "a style of discourse that's anathema to the progressive, feminist quarters of the internet that share many of Sanders' policy views" (para. 29).

The foundation of misogyny and racism within leftist spaces is the refusal of socialist men to acknowledge the need for intersectional Marxist analysis. A recent example was the 2016 World Conservation Congress failing to directly acknowledge women or gender within the motions brought to the membership (Burns, B., 2017).

Because of insisting on automatically "folding in" the issues of women and minorities into socialist organizing by never directly using the term "feminism," this creates a climate where sexism can occur unchallenged as well as making it more difficult for women who have been harassed and assaulted to come forward (Camfield, 2013). Accounts of leftist women have included organizations ignoring or covering up instances of patronizing behaviors, intimidation, domestic abuse, sexual harassment, and rape (Morris, 2010; Wrigley-Field, 2019).

As Morris (2010) points out, rather than being an anomaly, sexism is built into the functioning of many leftist organizations as well as representing a major reason these organizations often collapse because of their vulnerability to infiltration by informants. In recounting her experiences with leftist men within socialist organizations, the failure to address misogyny is apparent:

> Despite all that we say to the contrary, the fact is that radical social movements and organizations in the United States have refused to seriously address gender violence as a threat to the survival of our struggles. We've treated misogyny, homophobia, and heterosexism as lesser evils—secondary issues—that will eventually take care of themselves or fade into the background once the "real" issues—racism, the police, class inequality, U.S. wars of aggression—are resolved. There are serious consequences for choosing ignorance. Misogyny and homophobia are central to the reproduction of violence in radical activist communities. Scratch a misogynist and you'll find a homophobe. (para. 4)

Morris discusses the activist accounts of Assata Shakur, Elaine Brown, and Roxanne Dunbar-Ortiz who all noted that the same organizations that were easily infiltrated by informants also happened to be spaces that regularly overlooked gender violence.

It is also worth examining that the political trajectories of many older far-right spokesmen such as Irving Kristol, David Horowitz and Michael Savage, once involved memberships in New Left groups and movements from the 1930s to the 1960s (Nagel, 2017; Packer, 2016). These movements were typically rigid, ultra-doctrinaire and relegated women (assuming they were part of the organizations) to service-oriented positions. More contemporary alt-right figures like Andrew "Weev" Auernheimer once participated in the Occupy actions and "now regularly posts anti-Semitic and anti-gay rants on YouTube, has a swastika tattoo on his chest and was the self-appointed president of a trolling initiative called the Gay Nigger Association of America" (Nagle, 2017a, p. 16). The discursive tone within these New Left groups (both online and in-person) is often indistinguishable from the right-wing ones they now occupy.

Ghomeshi (2018), a Canadian journalist who was accused (and later acquitted) of sexual assault by multiple women, provides insight into the ability of sexist men to take cover in leftist organizations:

> At some point, when it came to women, I began to use my liberal gender studies education as a cover for my own behavior. I was ostensibly so schooled in how sexism works that I would arrogantly give myself a free pass…before

> 2014, it was unimaginable that I would become a poster boy for men who are assholes. I had not been a network boss or an executive with institutional power; there had been no formal complaints at work that I was aware of over the years. (p. 29)

Ghomeshi also catalogues an extensive list of activities that provided him progressive street cred, including wearing the right slogans on his t-shirts, speaking at liberal events, participating in marches, and supporting various social justice causes.

Organizational structures and their insistence on handling things "in-house" (because law enforcement is an arm of the capitalist class) also provide cover for sexual predators. Morris (2010) recounts several sexual assaults experienced by female and transgender volunteers from Common Ground one year after Hurricane Katrina. These assaults were committed by white men, but the leadership of the organization "shifted the blame to the surrounding Black community," in the form of distributing warnings to female activists to not be out alone at night, building on racist stereotypes of the Upper Ninth Ward being a "dangerous place" (para. 9). Essentially, it was "easier to criminalize Black men from the neighborhood than to acknowledge that white women and transgender organizers were most likely to be assaulted by the white men they worked with" (para. 9). One man was finally reported to the police, but only after he assaulted three women in the span of one week. The more recent example of the dissolution of the International Socialist Organization after it surfaced that the group mishandled an accusation of sexual assault is another example of the organizational structure providing cover for gender violence to continue (Wrigley-Field, 2019).

A subset of brocialist also openly supports authoritarian regimes like Putin or Assad, simply on the basis of them being considered enemies of the US. Known as *tankies*, these individuals will employ whataboutism to reference the imperialism of the US as a way to make excuses for oppressive rulers, similar to apologists for Stalin (SJWiki, n.d.). One of the more prominent tankies is Julian Assange, often celebrated for his self-styled whistleblower journalism through WikiLeaks. Originating with a specific focus on anti-war activism through releasing videos of the US military committing war crimes, eventually Assange's efforts moved in a more disturbing and far-from-social-justice-oriented direction. In massively dumping documents with no vetting in the name of "transparency,"

> WikiLeaks also posted links to a set of huge voter databases, including one with the names, addresses, and other contact information for nearly every woman in Turkey. It also apparently published the files of psychiatric patients, gay men, and rape victims in Saudi Arabia. Soon after that, WikiLeaks began leaking bundles of hacked Democratic National Committee e-mails. (Halpern, 2017, para. 12)

Halpern goes on to recount how Assange refused to disguise the identity of Afghani civilians in the Manning leak, with the blanket response, "Well they're informants. So, if they get killed, they've got it coming to them. They deserve it" (para. 9).

Assange has also been tied to alt-right and nationalist figures like Nigel Farage, former head of the UK Independence Party (UKIP) and Israel Shamir, anti-Semitic associate of Putin who shared documents from the Manning leak with Belarusian President Lukashenko, who then used the documents to "imprison and torture members of the opposition" (Halpern, 2017, para. 8). More recently, there is the example of Russian intelligence efforts to influence the US election through the WikiLeaks hack (Halpern, 2017; Kellner, 2017). It is also telling how Assange expresses open contempt for feminism. Silverman (2017) reviews footage of Assange responding to allegations of sexual assault by two women:

> Assange's own lawyers seem exasperated with him at times, particularly during a scene where he blames "radical feminists" for his legal problems. As the scene continues, Assange mulls how one accuser might be ripe for character assassination, but he decides it's far harder to torpedo the reputations of two accusers. Going public with their accusations could be difficult for the women, Assange proposes, implying that WikiLeaks supporters would make their lives miserable. Perhaps, he says, adopting a vague, conditional tone, he could apologize for whatever hurt he may have somehow caused. Later in the film, he states his belief that these accusations actually brought him and his organization valuable attention. (Silverman, 2017, para. 7)

Ultimately, the sheer amount of resources and energy that misogyny takes from activist movements slowly erodes the solidarity that is necessary to confront oppression under capitalism. While we can expect right-wing spaces to be patriarchal, authoritarian, and racist, the fact that leftist groups and leaders can harbor the same ideologies is demoralizing. Time that should be spent on organizing and community outreach is instead devoted to addressing sexual harassment and assault, assuming that those are even acknowledged. Because of the marginalized status of leftists in countries like the US, instances of gender violence are often assumed to be false constructions by the capitalist class to divide the movement (Wrigley-Field, 2019). This creates a default cover for misogyny to flourish. As Morris (2010) stresses:

> We have a right to be angry when the communities we build that are supposed to be the model for a better, more just world harbor the same kinds of antiqueer, antiwoman, racist violence that pervades society. As radical organizers we must hold each other accountable and not enable misogynists to assert so much power in these spaces. Not allow them to be the faces, voices, and leaders of these movements. (para. 22)

CONCLUSION

Socialist feminism is relevant and necessary for confronting authoritarian populism and fascism. It advocates an intersectional analysis, which is critical because of the multifaceted nature of oppression within capitalism. Power operates in a variety of ways, and is experienced differently depending on one's position in society; understanding this allows us to respond accordingly. As Camacho (2016) concludes, "we will have to utilize all of the legal, political, economic, activist/organizing, artistic, and religious means available to us (para. 9). Socialist feminism allows us to deal with the many contradictions inherent in people's common-sense formation of their understanding of the world, changing common sense into "the good sense of our times" (Nowak & Prashad, 2016, para. 12).

It is also clear that though there have been important gains within the past few decades, the current political system is not meeting the needs of the working class, and of women in particular. The fact that much of political discourse and policy— whether liberal or conservative— remains mired in a nostalgic past prevents the ability to enact a dialectical materialist vision:

> The time of the present is over, and the time of the future is at hand. What this means is not that we are on the threshold of a breakthrough, but that the managers of our world order are not capable of solving our problems. That means that the present has no solutions for us. We need to seek our solutions from the future, from a different way of ordering our needs and our luxuries, our excesses and our scarcities. (Nowak & Prashad, 2016, para. 41)

What is needed is to build a militant, unified movement across the global working class that is focused on meaningful change (Goodman, 2016). Socialist feminism can provide a foundation for that vision and a strong enough one for confronting the growing threat of authoritarian populism and fascism.

FASCISM AND RIGHT-WING POPULISM

Similarities, Differences, and New Organizational Forms

INTRODUCTION

Historical parallels between today's political events and pre-WW2 Germany are a common sight on social media, whether in meme or op ed form. This ubiquity has reached such heights that the memetic concept of Godwin's Law was created, positing that as a comments thread on an Internet site gains activity, the probability of someone comparing said topic to Hitler or the Nazis approaches 1 (Godwin, 2018). Anyone who brings up Hitler is then deemed as having lost the debate. Initially meant as a satirical way to characterize online discourse, Godwin's Law has taken on new relevance after the 2016 election, where even Godwin himself acknowledged it was no longer hyperbole to compare Trump, the alt-right, or Bolsonaro to Hitler (Mandelbaum, 2017).

Within liberal and leftist discourse, calls for vigilance regarding fascism and the political climate are ever-present, evidenced by the viral spread of posts such as Lawrence Britt's (2003) *Fourteen Defining Characteristics of Fascism*. Even though he was referred to as "Dr. Britt," Britt himself emphasized that he was not a historian, and had written the list in response to the George W. Bush administration post-9/11. Since then, the list has been used by various liberal and conservative groups to make a point in online arguments across cyberspace, whenever rhetorically useful. In particular, the enduring popularity of this list has taken on a life of its own, often shaping how the left conceptualizes fascism and attempts to confront it, most often unsuccessfully.

Following the defeat of Nazi Germany, it was highly stigmatizing to the right to label its associated movements as fascist. However, since then, much of the right's activities has moved into the electoral arena, so it becomes less effective to apply the fascist label. As Renton (2019) asserts, it creates an image of leftists as the ones always "fixated on the past" (p. 88). Much like color blind racism (Bonilla-Silva, 2018) has resulted in the right wing claiming they aren't racist because Jim Crow laws have been overturned, it no longer carries the same sting to call conservative politicians and voters fascist. They will just claim they aren't fascist and accuse the left of hyperbole, often applying Godwin's Law in the process. Added to this is the conundrum of only 6% of Americans endorsing far-right positions about sexual

© KONINKLIJKE BRILL NV, LEIDEN, 2020 | DOI: 10.1163/9789004424531_003

harassment, immigration, and Muslims while rightist political parties in the US and globally consistently poll high among party supporters (Renton, 2019, p. 79).

Liberals, in particular, tend to portray Trump and the alt-right as sudden, local aberrations, failing to connect their rise to neoliberal economic policies, replacement of leftist analysis with centrism, and decades of coordinated right-wing messaging such as Fox News (Beauchamp, 2016; Fraser, 2017; Kellner, 2017). Achar (2018) explains that we are now in a period of "fertile ground" where the turn has not been so much toward socialism as much as toward the far right:

> The rise of the latter typically happens when traditional bourgeois rule starts losing legitimacy (consent, hegemony) on a backdrop of socioeconomic crisis while the anti-capitalist left is not yet strong enough to take the lead of the people (the nation). As with the "infantile disorder" of radical left politics, the far-right disease of bourgeois politics can take the shape of mass movements, but also engender terrorist fringe activities when the former fail to arise (p. 35)

The election of Trump also connects to similar global events that represent an international authoritarian populist and fascist backlash to the secular dimensions of neoliberalism, with some signs of interest in socialist ideas in the mix (Fraser, 2017). These events include the outcome of the referendum on Brexit, Le Pen's National Front, insurgent candidates like Bernie Sanders, and Bolsonaro's victory. Trump is often portrayed as ushering in this trend, but the election of Putin in 2000, Orban's 2010 rise to power in Hungary, Hindu nationalist candidate Modi's win in 2014, and Duterte—whom Trump openly admires—illustrates that this series of events extends further back and far beyond the US (Bello, 2018, para. 2). This is the result of new forms of right-wing messaging and organizing, both across the globe and within nations, such as electoral alliances between the Five-Star Movement and Northern League in Italy along with the far-right Alternative fur Deutschland gaining seats in the German legislature.

Because of the prevalence and complexity of concepts surrounding fascism and authoritarian populism, this chapter is organized into broader themes, with a focus on current media and political discourses. After an initial overview of both fascism and authoritarian populism, key similarities between the two will be presented. These include conservative enabling, enforcement of capitalism, rationalizing violence, rejection of liberalism, enforcement of masculinity, and rampant corruption. These similarities are followed by differences that are important to keep in mind when attempting to draw historical parallels between fascism in the past and today. An analysis of new forms of organizing among the right concludes the chapter, followed by a cautionary note regarding the current state of matters.

CONCEPTUAL OVERVIEW

It is estimated that 3.3 billion people are subjected to autocratic rule of some kind, with less than 5% of the world's population living in what can be classified as a "full democracy" (Der Spiegel Staff, 2018, para. 6). With this in mind, it should be no surprise that authoritarian populism and fascism make recurring appearances. It is also important to acknowledge the links between neoliberalism, fascism, and authoritarianism, which involve the dismantling of democracy. Miocci and DiMario (2017) assert that "capitalism as we know it" utilizes the same political ideas as fascism, such as the notion of a natural or organic society, limitations of human rights, particularly labor organizing, and privatization/corporatization (p. 2).

Next to its sheer prevalence, what makes unpacking the Right challenging is that there are different factions, which can be classified "in terms of how far each is willing to go in the defense of capitalism" (Renton, 2019, p. 85). These include general conservativism, which is tied more to the electoral system, fascism, and the non-fascist far right, which includes populists of the Trump supporting variety, also working within electoral systems. Renton asserts that each of these factions has specific goals, including maintenance of the status quo (conservatives), restoration of a lost past (far right populists), and counterrevolution (fascists).

Populism is a broad political philosophy that positions "the people" against "the elite," the elite serving as a catch-all term for often contradictory constituents, such as the ultra-wealthy and minorities dependent on welfare. For Fletcher (2016), authoritarian populism represents "a revolt against the future" (p. 11). Its ideology and discourse are obsessed with a lost past which must be restored. Within the US, this is nearly always tied to white supremacy and Christianity, which presents white Christians as "authentic" Americans, positioning others as illegitimate to some degree and a threat to the restoration of lost values (Connor, 2018; Renton, 2017; Resnikoff, 2017). What is interesting about populism is that its terminology used to be more closely associated with *demagogue*, but since 1970 the term *populist* is now used at a ratio of 9:1 compared to *demagogue* in the Google Books search engine (Connor, 2018, para. 4). Renton (2017) alludes to these demagogic qualities in defining populism:

> A populist is someone who says that the whole people supports them. But, no politician in history has ever been universally popular. A populist is, therefore, someone who deals badly with the issue of dissent. Because they are by their own definition popular, therefore any protesters are somehow outside the category of "the people" and since they are not fully human, they are entitled to be repressed. Populists, in other words, are suspicious, vulnerable to conspiracy theory and authoritarian. (para. 13)

Authoritarian populism draws its power precisely from its ability to build alliances with segments of the white left, because it represents itself as defending the common person, along with providing an acceptable electoral outlet for dealing with distrust of elites, fear and resentment (Connor, 2017; Resnikoff, 2017; Renton, 2017). However, rather than leftist ideas penetrating into populism, typically the reverse happens, where followers are exposed to white nationalism, thus "changing the nature of both left and right politics in the process" (Resnikoff, 2017, para. 8).

Indeed, such populist movements have come and gone throughout US history with examples including Andrew Jackson, the Know Nothing Party in the 1850s, William Jennings Bryan's campaign, the America First movement during the 1920s, and Barry Goldwater's 1964 campaign (Connor, 2018).

Fascism carries forward the tenets of authoritarian populism, with the aim being a full consolidation of state power and capitalism, including all cultural apparatuses. Theweleit (2010b) conceptualizes fascism as "revolution's negative image" that "takes the whole living social reality and forces it to approximate an image in negative" (p. 382). This can also be thought of as fascism being about "anti-production," compared to the "living labor" of human-centered activities (p. 216). The very concept of a fascist state is totalitarian by default, the goal being "to repress and discipline the population, while protecting and promoting capitalist property relations, profits, and accumulation, and laying the basis for imperial expansion" (Foster, 2017, para. 13). This seizure and holding of absolute power are essential components of fascism, with sheer existence being the only justification required to hold power (Theweleit, 2010b). Moreover, fascists are often able to easily maneuver the more plutocratic tendencies within liberal democracies in order to establish themselves (Foster, 2017; Ulrich, 2016).

Even though fascism also draws from authoritarian populism's notion of restoration of an imagined past in its discourse and imagery, it takes things further with the aim of destruction for the purpose of ushering in a rebirth of a nation and its unified people (Muirhead & Rosenblum, 2018; Ulrich, 2016). The unity of the people involves the illusion of an erasure of social class or political parties, to be replaced with the nation as an organizing construct:

> What the fascist understands by the term "unity" is a state in which oppressor and oppressed are violently combined to form a structure of domination. For him, unity denotes a relationship not of equality, but of domination. Equality is considered synonymous with multiplicity, mass—it is thus the precise opposite of unity, since unity rigidly fuses these baser elements with what is "above them," "interior" to "exterior"…the concept of nation can be seen, then, as the most explicit available foundation of male demands for domination. (Theweleit, 2010b, p. 87)

For Theweleit, fascists contrast themselves against the "mass," or what "belongs below" using concepts such as culture, nation and race, where "the "individual" carves out a place for himself as the bearer of "culture": a handful of (male) "individuals" constitute the "few"—who determine and sanction definitions of "culture" (p. 45).

Finally, *neofascist ideology*, as promoted by alt-right figures like Steve Bannon, represents a troubling blend of authoritarian populism and fascism (Foster, 2017; Renton, 2017). These include acknowledging the failure of neoliberalism, but this is narrowly framed as opposition to corporations or globalization from a nationalist perspective. Related to this are targeted attacks on immigrants and refugees from specific regions such as central/south America or the Middle East. This anti-globalization narrative asserts that both China and Islam are expanding to assert global dominance. In response, the United States and the restoration of Christianity are necessary to stem this tide. Bannon sees the alt-right's rise in the US as the "Fourth Turning," the other three turns being the Revolutionary War, the Civil War, the Great Depression and WWII (Foster, 2017).

The most dangerous hallmark of neofascism is the global scope of its organizing, which Renton (2017, 2019) discusses in depth. The problem, of course, is attempting to pinpoint the specific moment when liberal democracy, with the assistance of authoritarian populism, moves into a fascist phase, or more specifically, from neoliberalism to neofascism, indicating that fascism may not be as much of an aberration as usually presented (Foster, 2017; Theweleit, 2010b).

SHARED CHARACTERISTICS OF AUTHORITARIAN POPULISM AND FASCISM

This section outlines some of the key shared characteristics of authoritarian populism and fascism while acknowledging there are important differences in degrees of adherence to specific ideological aspects. These include (1) conservative enabling; (2) enforcement of capitalism; (3) rationalizing violence; (4) rejection of liberalism; (5) enforcement of masculinity and (6) rampant corruption. These characteristics constantly interact with each other, making specific boundaries challenging to discuss. For example, free market ideology (enforcement of capitalism) is often combined with appeals to racism (rationalization of violence) in discussing corporate globalization while misogyny (enforcement of masculinity) is used to call for a restoration of a unified, non-secular past (rejection of liberalism). Brecher (2017) notes how authoritarian populist and fascist politicians both "combine charismatic leaders, traditional conservative forces, and multiple forms of political repression" to steer the working class away from a dialectical understanding of their situation (p. 44).

Conservative Enabling

By far one of the most prominent shared characteristics of authoritarian populism and fascism that contributes to the relative ease of their ability to establish power is the enabling of these ideologies by conservatives. Whether considering Hitler's electoral trajectory or media messaging leading to the Brexit referendum outcome, the utter facilitation by conservatives cannot be overlooked. Conservative enabling happens in three ways. First, conservatives seek permanent political power in any way they can obtain it. Second, closely related to this, is the delusion that "we can contain him/them" which always accompanies the rationalizations of more reluctant conservatives who are willing to overlook all manner of disturbing events in order to maintain power (Brecher, 2017). Authoritarian populists and fascists can often pull more centrist liberals or "undecided voters" into the orbit of this thinking, particularly during uncertain economic times. Third, this is made possible by a retreat of the left, which creates the vacuum needed for such consolidation of power.

First, as Renton (2019) astutely notes, "If anyone is expecting the mainstream right to be an ally in the fight against fascism, they are likely to be disappointed" (p. 87). Fascism and authoritarian populism have always been extremely useful tools for conservatives to maintain permanent political power. The example of conservative accommodation to the Nazi party platform in order to suppress the spread of Marxism and worker uprisings is illustrative (Ulrich, 2016). Hindenburg paved the way for Nazi rule by invoking emergency powers, making it easy for appointed chancellors to move to a system of autocratic decrees rather than by majority votes (Browning, 2018). It is more accurate to say that National Socialist leadership opportunistically used *characteristics of the existing system* (put in place by conservatives) to their advantage more so than Hitler being a master of strategy (Ulrich, 2016). This created reciprocal benefits for various conservative constituencies:

> The Reich chancellor could now concentrate on crushing the political Left and bringing German society as a whole into line with Nazi ideals without any fears of military intervening. The military leadership in turn had received a guarantee for its monopoly position and was assured that its concerns would enjoy the highest priority within the new government. (Ulrich, 2016, p. 417)

In a similar manner, Trump and his populist coalition have managed to take advantage of Republicans' desire to maintain permanent power by playing on shared policy goals like privatization, cutting taxes for the wealthy, appointing anti-worker Supreme Court justices, repealing the *Affordable Care Act*, targeting of immigrants and refugees, increasing the military budget, and voter suppression (Browning, 2017; Sefla, 2017; Taibbi, 2018). This has been further enabled by Trump managing to earn the votes of 90% of Republicans who turned out in 2016, many of whom were uninspired by traditional conservative messaging (Renton, 2019, p. 82). Rather than seeing him as a liability, Republican politicians such as Mitch McConnell have viewed Trump as a clear path to permanent political power and have not deviated from their support, nor are there any signs of this changing any time soon (Browning, 2018; Beauchamp, 2018a; Kellner, 2017).

Second, conservatives and even some moderates and liberals enable authoritarian populism and fascism by maintaining the illusion that either they can contain far-right excesses or that the system will somehow serve as a series of checks on more extreme actions. Hindenburg and other conservatives assumed they could gain the benefits of Nazi party policies to buttress his already eroding support while asserting they could control Hitler at the same time (Browning, 2018; Ulrich, 2016). Thinking that they have a handle on the situation, conservatives fail to imagine the culmination of their enabling, as Gropnik (2016) explains:

> To say "Well, he would not *really* have the power to accomplish that" is to misunderstand the nature of thin-skinned authoritarians in power. They do not

arrive in office and discover, as constitutionalists do, that their capabilities are more limited than they imagined. They arrive, and then make their power as large as they can. (para. 3)

Another way of rationalizing riding the far-right train as far as it will go involves minimizing the actions of authoritarians by continuously moving the bar of normalization until it is no longer recognizable (Gropnik, 2016; Sykes, 2017). Sykes (2017) likens this to conservatives claiming that such-and-such has to happen before we need to act, when "whatever people have said has to happen, has, in fact, already happened, over and over again, and the GOP has swallowed it anyway" (para. 12). By allowing increasingly extreme behaviors, the GOP has now created a situation where there is little to differentiate themselves from Trump. This includes mainstream conservative writers who situate themselves as "intellectuals," attempting to "impose some coherence and substance on Trumpism" while "attributing to Trump an ideological lucidity that seems little more than a projection of their own wishful thinking" (Heilbrunn, 2017, para. 32). Sykes (2017) holds up the example of Mitt Romney, who is lauded for speaking out against Trump one day, then turns around and eats a reconciliation dinner with him the next, locked in a "relationship of morbid co-dependency" (para. 7).

Even disillusioned voters who once supported more liberal or leftist candidates feel they can safely support authoritarians, assuming that the system in place will protect them or that it will weed out more extreme elements while still retaining aspects of what they want. This was evidenced in Bolsonaro's election, where Bevins (2018) provides several examples of voters who were against most of his policies, but justified their votes with, "I don't think he will be great, necessarily, but he's what we need right now" (para. 18) or the resentment-infused rationale, "I'm against the program to pay criminals in jail even more than I make" (para. 19). Another voter asserted that "he won't be governing alone, and he won't be able to do everything he wants" (para. 16). Taibbi (2018) notes how the ousting of Steve Bannon, an action much-celebrated in the media, encapsulated conservative thinking that they had been able to contain the situation when all the while they "overlooked who put Trump in power in the first place" (para. 6).

Third, none of this is possible without the additional assistance of leftists going into retreat, creating a vacuum that enables authoritarians to consolidate power. A major factor contributing to Hitler and Mussolini's rise were the Communist parties in those countries deciding that social democrats were the real threat, while minimizing the fascist parties as an irrelevant fringe element (Browning, 2018). Instead of banding together to focus on confronting fascism, the liberal and leftist parties fought each other, as Gopnik (2016) outlines:

The militant left decided that their real enemies were the moderate leftists, who were *really* indistinguishable from the Nazis. The radical progressives decided that there was no difference between the democratic left and the totalitarian right and that an explosion of institutions was exactly the most thrilling thing imaginable. (para. 6)

While the left was divided, conservatives and other right-wing parties unified, a situation that seems to be playing out today in a similar manner (Browning, 2018). When the left faced continual defeat, they "withdrew, demoralized, into private niches," while "those sections of the middle classes that had previously kept their distance hastened to embrace the National Socialists, with flags flying" (Ulrich, 2016, p. 431).

The retreat of the left today has manifested itself in different ways, such as electoral shifts among the working-class turning to nationalist political parties who hold out economic promises wrapped in racist discourse (Der Spiegel Staff, 2018; Alfonso, 2017). Another manifestation is that rather than directly confronting authoritarian tendencies in government, liberal parties "default to bureaucratic mode," as if existing laws will somehow serve as a deterrent to future actions (Gessen, 2017, para. 9). A prime example of this was the outcome of the much-anticipated Mueller report, which rationalized not taking action against Trump for obstruction of justice by citing existing Department of Justice policy that a sitting president could not be indicted (Waas, 2019). Centrists also enabled Bolsonaro's rise by supporting the impeachment of Rousseff and soon found themselves quickly engulfed by a miniscule political party that backed Bolsonaro (Bevins, 2018). Ultimately, the space created by leftist retreat is also an outcome of conservative enabling of fascism and authoritarian populism:

> Today, it's self-evident that we have a failed liberalism (neoliberalism) wherein the system politicians have lost legitimacy and are increasingly hated…And it is precisely at such a moment, when the liberal and conservative bourgeois order is increasingly unstable and untenable, that fascism becomes a clear and present danger. (Draitser, 2017, para. 28)

Enforcement of Capitalism

Despite the ever-present use of "common man" discourse and promises of "overturning the system" or "draining the swamp," fascists and authoritarian populists are all about enforcing the capitalist system, though it is a more nuanced relationship than is often portrayed by the left. The irony is that many of their preferred policies are destabilizing for capitalism, such as deportation of immigrants and nationalist positions on trade. Davidson (2017) captures this contradiction:

> Here we see emerging a symbiotic relationship between one increasingly inadequate regime response to the problems of capital accumulation and another increasingly extreme response to the most irrational desires and prejudices produced by capital accumulation. (p. 63)

For Davidson, the right wing as a collective uses three approaches to capitalism: direct support, backing ideologies that support capitalism, or destabilization, either intentional or unintentional. This played out in the case of Nazi Germany where capital was needed to enact the National Socialist vision. Yet capitalists themselves didn't require anti-Semitism, but were fine with its utilization in their efforts to control labor. Put simply, "German capitalism did not need Auschwitz, but it needed the Nazis, who needed Auschwitz" (p. 64).

Authoritarian populists and fascists share three aspects of capitalist enforcement in its ideology and policies. The first includes having a solidly middle-class base, with parts of the working class drawn in. This, in turn, impacts the type of discourse used to gain support for such policies. A second aspect is messaging around the mythology of individualism and the free market, though within a collectivist authoritarian context, or "explaining collective events by the initiative of individuals" (Sartre, 1976, p. 26). Finally, the third way capitalist enforcement occurs is through the suppression of labor, such as targeting dialectical organizational strategies like unions. This represents a delicate balancing act, as Kimmel (2017) outlines:

> The extreme Right faces the difficult cognitive task of maintaining their faith in America and in capitalism and simultaneously providing an analysis of an indifferent state, at best, or an actively interventionist one, at worst, and a way to embrace capitalism, despite a cynical corporate logic that leaves them, often literally, out in the cold. (p. 254)

First, middle class support, in addition to support of the wealthy is a universal trait of authoritarian movements, whether in Brazil, India, or the US (Bevins, 2018; Bello, 2018; Renton, 2017). The strongest support for the Nazi party came not from the working-class, who were more likely to reject their messaging, but from the middle-class (Ulrich, 2016). Much of this middle-class support involves a fundamentally irresolvable contradiction, as Daher (2017) outlines concerning the growth of rightist Islamic movements:

> Just like the petty bourgeoisie in general, Islamic fundamentalist organizations are pulled in two directions—toward rebellion against existing society and toward compromise with it. Either way, their reactionary project offers no solution to sections of the peasantry and working class that are attracted by it. (p. 96)

This contradiction is stark within the US, where one of strongest segments of Trump's middle-class support is represented by police unions, including the Border Patrol (Myerson, 2017).

The mobilization of middle-class support involves presenting their position as being squeezed by both the "ruling elite" or "global corporatists (often liberal, secular) and the undeserving poor (those on welfare, ethnic scapegoats) (Daher, 2017). The middle class is an ideal target for authoritarian messaging during economic crises because they typically have some degree of prosperity compared to the rest of the working class, and they often have accompanying defensive beliefs emerging out of fear of loss of status (Sartre, 1976). Fascists and authoritarian populists will play on the fears of the middle class as losing their way of life at the hands of the government, who enact preferential policies for minorities and other "deadbeats" (Ulrich, 2016). Aware of this, some fascist programs promise voters a social safety net, but only through welfare chauvinism, with benefits limited to the native (usually white) population (Bello, 2018; Resnikoff, 2017). In the US, this is similar to Trump supporting subsidies for farmers, but cuts for food stamp recipients.

Second, though varying in storytelling structure, capitalism is enforced by a prominent free market messaging. Ulrich (2016) recounts how the Nazis did not fundamentally alter existing capitalist structures but simply re-interpreted capitalist relations where "men's social existence was not to determine their consciousness, as Marxist teaching had it: their consciousness was to determine their social being" (p. 536). Labor was presented instead as a way to earn dignity in support of a larger social project rather than a way for workers to organize together. This ideological re-alignment was necessary in order to defeat the Marxist parties standing in the way of the National Socialists. In the end, however, nothing approaching significant change was ever accomplished, even though Nazi propaganda could convey "a feeling of social equality" with Hitler as "messianic savior" (p. 545). Similarly, Trump presents himself as a populist opponent of global trade, when what he and his supporters reject are the multicultural/global aspects of neoliberalism, not capitalism itself (Fraser, 2017).

Free enterprise is also presented as a pure vision that has been tainted by globalization and corporatization, which explains the fetishization of the small business owner in much nationalist and white supremacist discourse (Kimmel, 2017; Stan, 2017). This has been facilitated by the failure of neoliberalism to fulfill its promises of financial growth and stability in the face of "social dislocation, rapid demographic changes, a decline in the life expectancy of white women, and the election of America's first black president" which "added spark and fuel to…a whitelash" (Resnikoff, 2017, para. 26). In many ways, the rejection of neoliberalism has not translated to leftist critique so much as attracting voters to white nationalism. Within the US, figures like Steve Bannon promote deconstructing the administrative state, deregulation, tariffs (even though there is not enough manufacturing infrastructure to offset costs), and isolationism in a quest to obtain the purest essence of capitalism, even though this vision totally overlooks capitalism's global nature (Stan, 2017).

Third, the enforcement of capitalism also requires suppression of labor, either overtly, as through legislation or violence against unions or more indirectly, through insisting on sacrifice or in promoting the idea of workers being entitled to their position. Fascists are often associated with overt violent acts against leftists and workers, but usually those measures are not necessary. Instead, various carrot and stick strategies can be used, such as eroding worker solidarity with the promise of even greater fulfillment to come (Ulrich, 2016). In particular, fascists will often invoke the idea of there being no meaningful differences between social classes and therefore no need for labor unrest so long as everyone gets behind the vision (Theweleit, 2010b).

Theweleit (2010b) points out how higher-ranking Nazis commonly insisted on workers making sacrifices, but this only referred to those beneath the top strata. An interesting psychology then takes place among the crowd who is expected to make continual sacrifices for the nation:

> The audience listening to the man above the crowd must surely sense his absolute unwillingness to make sacrifices of his own. For this very reason, they follow him gladly, in the hope that remaining with him will bring deliverance. What he means when he says, "We must all make sacrifices" is always "We (the group to which I belong) must stand fast together and sacrifice others." (p. 92)

To pull off this major feat of false consciousness by breaking apart worker solidarity, authoritarian populists and fascists often dress their discourse up in leftist trappings by defending entitlement programs that have mostly white recipients, invoking nationalism by promising to bring back American jobs, or deporting immigrants (Alfonso, 2017). This enables capitalists to gain the support of the very workers who they are actively harming. However, the ultimate outcome remains the suppression of the greatest impediment to authoritarianism: a united working class who rejects racism and sexism (Foster, 2017).

Rationalizing Violence

To varying degrees, both fascism and authoritarian populism make ready use of violent and eliminationist rhetoric and actions (Bello, 2018; Stan, 2017). Further, these ideologies provide several justifications for violence, often portraying the proponents of such violence as victims in an attempt to project blame and establish false equivalences between racist protest and when oppressed groups protest (Wise, 2016). The core motivating force behind this violence is sheer revenge and there is no limit to its size and scope:

> Fascist revenge is vast and expansive; it devastates the earth and annihilates human beings by the millions. Fascism may not have offered "justice" to the masses, but it did offer them the power to take revenge...these forms should be seen instead as orchestrating direct incursion by the fascist macromasses into the part of the earth which the fascists—quite simply by their own existence— considered their own. (Theweleit, 2010b, p. 367)

For Theweleit, fascists simultaneously occupy a position of self-assertion and allegiance to systems that require absolute compliance—they feel the illusion of power but only within the limits of hierarchy. Further, the delicate balance between legitimate and illegitimate violence often means that authoritarians, such as Putin and Duterte, will delegate more overt forms of repression to vigilantes in law enforcement (Gessen, 2017).

The authoritarian populist and fascist rationalization of violence (whether actual or discursive) shares three characteristics, the first being deployment of racism and xenophobia in support of ethnocentrism, cultural superiority, and nationalism (Bello, 2018; Mishra, 2018). A second characteristic is the prioritizing of emotion and feeling over material reality. This is closely linked to the third characteristic, freedom from the responsibility of one's actions, or permission to oppress others. Taken together, far from perceiving themselves as repressed or limited under authoritarian regimes, violence provides an intoxicating, freeing experience for supporters who seek power at all costs:

> When Richard Spencer argues that America belongs to whites because "we conquered this continent" and no matter how bloody the process, ultimately "we won," he reduces all complex moral and philosophical arguments, both for his side and against it, to a simple equation of "might makes right." At that point, winning itself becomes the only necessary and sufficient standard upon which to rest a claim to power of any kind. (Wise, 2016, para. 10)

The first characteristic of both authoritarian populism and fascism's rationalizing of violence involves the construction of a nationalist identity through the use of racism (targeting minority groups) and xenophobia (attacks on immigrants and refugees). Both racism and xenophobia serve to reinforce the cultural superiority of "real" citizens as compared to those who don't belong, as a way to cement national identity. It doesn't matter if these concepts are rooted in reality; what matters is the creation of such an ideal (Ulrich, 2016). This is often done through utilizing metaphors of purity juxtaposed against contamination, such as Hitler's positioning of the Jews as parasitic or Hindu supremacists in India using pseudoscience to justify different castes (Mishra, 2018). Rather than being an aberration, the agendas of many of the leaders and political parties associated with authoritarian populism and fascism have long been building their rhetoric and actions to this global convergence (Resnikoff, 2017). More recent examples of this are Trump's false equivalence between the actions of racists and protestors at the Charlottesville march and his pardoning of former Arizona sheriff Joe Arpaio (Gessen, 2017).

In terms of racism, state-sanctioned violence by police against minorities serves as an overt way to intimidate communities, as well as create an association in whites' minds between crime and certain minority groups readily distributed by the media (Giroux, 2016; Stan, 2017). Trump's initial appointment of Jeff Sessions as attorney general reinforced this messaging. Even when limited to discursive violence, phrases such as "America first" and "make America great again" directly invoke intentions to do whatever it takes to force minorities to submit to white supremacy (Sefla, 2017). Assertions about criminality and immigrants are not borne out sociologically, but the point of such propaganda is to leave just the smallest shred of doubt (Hamilton, 2016). Additionally, older anti-Semitic conspiracy theories are often woven into anti-immigrant discourse, as in the case with Trump and his followers constantly invoking George Soros or "international banks" being connected to Mexican investors who were supporters of Hillary Clinton's campaign (Kellner, 2017).

Particular targets also include immigrants from Muslim countries as well as Muslim citizens within European countries and the US. Beauchamp (2018) provides the example of Hungary, where Orbán presents himself as the only barrier between citizens and being taken over by Muslims, even though only a fraction of the Hungarian population was born in another country. Because of its location, Hungary is often a stop for migrants due to its EU membership, a situation that Orbán exploits to stoke fear in his supporters. This islamophobia is reflected in Trump's administrative pick of John Bolton, who advocates the "clash of civilizations" thesis between the West and the Middle East (Giroux, 2016). Other examples include the France's National Front, the Northern League in Italy, UKIP in Britain, Wilder's Party for Freedom in the Netherlands, and the Finns Party, all who use racist and xenophobic messaging to advocate the restriction of non-European immigrants (Alfonso, 2017; Resnikoff, 2017). These leaders and political parties advocate solutions such as border walls, deportations, and the construction of detention centers to house immigrants and refugees.

Smith and Hanley's (2018) analysis of the motivations of Trump supporters reveal important findings regarding the relationship to race. The authors find that Trump's predominantly white base, "is more readily found among voters who want domineering and intolerant leaders than among voters of any class background" (p. 197). Attitudes regarding authoritarian leadership were the primary forms of distinction between those who voted for Trump and those for other candidates. Additionally, these voters more strongly agreed that whites were discriminated against when minorities received benefits they felt should be theirs, what the researchers call the perception of "line cutting": "The defiant wish for a domineering and impolitic leader, which is strongest among Trump's most fervent supporters, coalesces here with the wish for a reversal of what his base perceives as an inverted moral and racial order" (p. 198). This goes beyond simple racial resentment into a desire to reassert the principles of white dominance, a wish that Trump appears to promise to fulfill.

This leads into the prioritizing of emotions and perceptions over experience or reason, the second characteristic involved with rationalizing violence. As Theweleit (2010a) explains regarding the affirmations that fascism offers:

> What fascism allows the masses to express are repressed drives, imprisoned desires...fascism teaches us that under certain circumstances, human beings imprisoned within themselves, within body armor and social constraints, would rather break out than fill their stomachs; and that their politics may consist in organizing that escape, rather than an economic order that promises future generations full stomachs for life. (p. 432)

Using his media-created position as a political outsider who will make things right, Trump, himself resentful, mirrors his supporters' resentments in a self-reinforcing prioritizing of emotion (Kellner, 2017). Likewise, Bolsonaro embodies self-truth, where "the content of what he says doesn't matter: what matters is the act of saying it" (Brum, 2018, para. 10).

Truth is therefore transformed into a mere personal choice, to be assigned to the person you agree with. Whatever Bolsonaro or Trump might say is determined to be honest and sincere, while their critics are dismissed as having ulterior motives. Authoritarian populists and fascists are quite comfortable with emotion over consistency and it serves as a major source of their power, especially when conveying violent messages (Connor, 2018). Followers are drawn to a demagogic figure like Trump, Putin, or Bolsonaro, "not by a belief in the efficacy of his policies but by the emotional satisfaction they experience in his presence" (para. 28). For Connor, demagogy is itself a "form of expressive politics," and is incredibly difficult to counter because this emotional attachment to a leader can often endure their failure to follow through with promises (para. 30). Anti-revolutionary social bonds are further consolidated over collective anger, with members mirroring each other's resentments while being contained and absorbed by the crowd (Sartre, 1976). This is the key distinction between harnessing anger among leftist movements and right-wing ones: meaningful change is subdued by self-expression and the status quo remains (Burton, 2018a).

The third and perhaps most powerful characteristic of rationalizing violence is that authoritarian populists and fascists give permission to their followers to participate in various levels of enacting such violence, or, they are promised freedom from the responsibility of their actions (Theweleit, 2010b). Jacobs (2018) points out that a common misconception is that all authoritarians are submissive and seek approval from those they perceive to be strong or that they prioritize respecting authority. Instead, Jacobs notes that Trump supporters prefer "a belligerent, combative approach toward people they find threatening" over more conventional values such as traditional respect for authority and obedience (para. 5). In other words, "authoritarianism in the Trump era is not the wish to follow any and every authority, but, rather, the wish to support a strong and determined authority who will crush evil and take us back to our true path" (para. 15). Understanding this distinction is an essential component in fighting fascism and authoritarian populism.

This dominant totality of being (Theweleit, 2010b) requires the element of establishing superiority where the needs of others are viewed as a threat to the freedom from responsibility and the right to violence. Ethical and moral constraints are out the window, encapsulated in Trump's comment that he could stand in the middle of Fifth Avenue and shoot somebody, and still not lose voters. Giroux (2016) concludes that "Ruthlessness, narcissism and bullying are the organizing principles of Trump's belief that only winning matters and that everything is permitted to further his own self-interests" (para. 8). This carries over into hostility toward public institutions that adhere to principles of diversity with a preference for a vigilante-oriented police force and self-styled militia groups (Gessen, 2017).

Ultimately, the sheer audacity of unaccountability drives violence to repeat the unthinkable and escalate the next time around. Yet, it is important to understand that freedom from responsibility never applies to everyone, just the authoritarian populist or fascist who is entitled to free reign of their emotions and desires (Sartre, 1976). The very notion of being held accountable is a major affront. What contributes to their perceived immunity is the relative lack of accountability of past perpetrators. Brum (2018) and Bevins (2018) provide the example of Bolsonaro openly celebrating past Brazilian and other South American dictators' acts of torture and murder. He feels free to do this precisely because of the Brazilian government's unwillingness to hold people accountable for those actions. As Theweleit (2010a) concludes:

> that explains the enormous attraction of fascist celebrations and their overwhelming impact on participants: "I can't believe my eyes…what in the world are they doing?" and then the liberating thought, "but everybody's doing it…my God, they are actually *doing* it!" (in the name of the law, too). (p. 430)

Against Liberalism

Though the forms and degrees may vary, another commonality among those who hold various populist and fascist ideologies is an opposition to liberal democracy and secularism (Bello, 2018). After decades of progress-centered messaging about technology, civil rights, global connectedness, education, and science—albeit from a neoliberal framework—it seems jarring to see "a slide back into the age of authoritarianism" on a world-wide scale (Der Spiegel Staff, 2018, para. 5). The embracing of populist and fascist ideas builds on a form of cynicism that is disconnected from social action with people seeking emotional validation from violence, nostalgia, and scapegoating versus meaningful change. For Ulrich (2016), the conditions leading to Hitler's rise reflected a similar erosion of belief in government which had been building for a long time:

> Those in power appeared to have no solutions to the crisis, and the more helpless they seemed to be, the greater the demand became for a strong man, a political messiah who would lead Germany out of economic misery and point the way towards renewed national greatness. (p. 223)

Authoritarian populists and fascists channel their opposition to liberalism in the form of attempting to lay claim to and enforce a specific conceptualization of culture onto the population. Liberalism and secularism represent a degraded culture against which order must be restored. Theweleit (2010b) outlines the notion of "the mass" and the threats it represents, which have been enabled by multicultural permissiveness and/or lack of religiosity. In particular, war culture, whether talking about the military, policing or vigilante-based enforcement, permeates the opposition to liberalism as it is considered the highest cultural form (Giroux, 2016; Theweleit, 2010b). This is encapsulated in common Internet memes which assert that the military or Second Amendment is what protects the First, or the Blue Lives Matter flag stickers meant to send a message that police violence is always justified, especially against minorities. Trump himself regularly invokes anger toward liberal institutions at his rallies, prompting his supporters and politicians to threaten civil war if Trump would ever be impeached (Coutts, 2017).

It is no coincidence that authoritarian populists and fascists are against the press, and view any sort of investigative journalism as an affront to their untouchable status. This has gone as far as calls for criminalizing acts of journalism that are viewed as hostile to authoritarian leadership, including within the US. By building a sense of distrust in the press, truth then becomes a matter of which point of view you follow, not the facts:

> When citizens favor blatant propaganda as their primary source of information about the world, there is little hope that they will be able to separate themselves from reactionary, officially-endorsed fascism. The cult of Trump will provide cover for an administration that has long expressed contempt for freedom of the press, and is now indicating its support for fascist policies aimed at criminalizing journalists for reporting on classified intelligence the Trump administration would prefer be kept secret. (DiMaggio, 2017, para. 8)

Polling of Trump supporters has revealed extreme hostility toward the media (other than right-wing outlets like Fox News, of course), with close to half of Republicans endorsing the idea that the government should shut down outlets that broadcast "biased or inaccurate" information (para. 7). Nearly 66% of Republicans state they trust Trump as a source of news more than CNN, *The New York Times* and *The Washington Post* combined (para. 7).

Authoritarian populists and fascists also show their opposition to liberalism by invoking nostalgia as a way to weaponize the past, feeding into notions of what Kimmel (2017) calls aggrieved entitlement. Right-wing movements are rarely future-oriented, and when the present is discussed, it is always as a form of contrast to an idealized past, highly gendered, with the past being a time when men ran things, "the way it was supposed to be." Liberalism is therefore associated with femininity and weakness (Davidson, 2017; Kimmel, 2017). As Davidson (2017) emphasizes, "the political goal is to always push popular attitudes and legal rights back to a time before the homogeneity of "the people" was polluted by immigration…usually at some undetermined period before WWII" (p. 61). Conservative think tanks and groups such as the Claremont Institute advocate that the principles of government have been eroded by policies that have enabled dependency on welfare and rampant political correctness (Heilbrunn, 2017). Only a return to the "rough and ready" American spirit and originalism of the Founding Fathers can stop such societal decline.

It is important to note that while both Marxists and right-wing movements utilize the past as part of their ideologies, there is a critical difference. The Marxist use of dialectical materialism involves the past being employed as a form of historical analysis and a way to confront the normalization of the status quo. With right-wing movements, nostalgia is weaponized as a way to enforce a mythical past bound up in racist and sexist discourse, all in the service of capitalism. Giroux (2016) discusses how fascism can be opposed by such use of the past in order to "protect the present and the future against the damage now forgotten" (para. 2). In contrast, the call to "make American great again" keeps Trump supporters not only locked into a past, but one that never existed (Kellner, 2016).

Enforcement of Masculinity

Though often not discussed in relationship to fascism and authoritarian populism, gender plays a pivotal role through an enforcement of a specific vision of white supremacist masculinity. Both share the characteristic of hyper-masculinized discourse which saturates their ideologies and reveals important contradictions:

> It is through a decidedly gendered and sexualized rhetoric of masculinity that this contradiction between loving America and hating its government, loving capitalism and hating its corporate iterations, is resolved. Racism, nativism, anti-Semitism, antifeminism—these discourses provide an explanation for the feelings of entitlement thwarted, fixing the blame squarely on "others" whom the state must now serve at the expense of white men. The unifying theme is gender. (Kimmel, 2017, p. 255)

Gender essentialism, which extends to homophobia and transphobia, is a matter of absolutes and fits in nicely with right-wing movements, especially the notion of needing to get back to the correct order of things when men ruled. Popular figures like Jordan Peterson use flawed principles of evolutionary psychology and mythology to posit that if men simply took control, the West could be brought back into line in a world where "the clear borders of culture have been dissolved" (Burton, 2018a, para. 3).

Specific interpretations of mythology and mysticism (including religion) often appear within such discourse, with "the theme of intense male comradeship nourished by violence and at odds with bourgeois family life" (Lyons, 2017, para. 13). This brings to mind earlier 1980s and 1990s incarnations of the mythopoetic men's movement where group events like primitive camping retreats were meant to promote bonding through a reconnection with a lost masculinity. Peterson relies heavily on Jung's archetypes, asserting that order and culture are primarily male, with chaos and the unknown being female (Mishra, 2018). Any form of opposition to male dominance is portrayed as going against the natural order of things, reflected in support for figures like Putin, who "embodies the longing for an unbroken, unambiguous identity that seems to have gone missing in pluralistic, heterogenous

47

societies" (Der Spiegel Staff, 2018, para. 45). Wolff (2018) speculates that a figure like Steve Bannon, who also advances similar views, could once be harmlessly considered a rugged antihero with a working-class background but now is dangerous considering the political climate. We are currently in a situation, Wolff asserts, where "the American man story is a right-wing story" (p. 57).

Enforcement of masculinity within authoritarian populist and fascist ideologies involves the three components of first, misogyny; second, women and the feminine (including homophobia) being positioned as threats; and third, the contradictory persona of man as simultaneously warrior and victim. Lopez (2017) points out the important distinction between more traditional, paternalistic forms of sexism among conservative and even liberal voters and more aggressive manifestation of misogyny, the latter being closely correlated with support for Trump. This reflects a more deliberatively misogynistic outlook toward women than simply wishing they would occupy more traditional roles, as is often theorized about the right wing.

In comparing the Christian right with the alt-right, Lyons (2017) finds a coming together around such rampant misogyny:

> The two movements agree on several key points: that gender roles are based on innate differences between males and females and need to be aggressively enforced for the good of society as a whole; that it's natural and right for men to hold power over women; and that women's main functions in society are to provide men with support, care and sexual satisfaction, and to bear and raise children. (para. 7)

Common positions taken by the alt-right, especially in online forums, is that women should not be allowed to vote and should have major restrictions imposed upon them in terms of reproductive policies (Nagel, 2017). Though there may be some women who identify themselves members of the alt-right, the majority of the movement makes it pretty clear that they are hostile to women, at the very least labelling them as irrelevant to their overall aims.

Alt-right discourse is filled with misogynistic and homophobic language, with those labeled weak as "cucks" or "fags" as well as receiving graphic threats of rape (Romano, 2016; Lyons, 2017). Racism and misogyny are fused together within the alt-right, to advocate not just for white supremacy, but "more specifically white male supremacy," the sexism of which often serves as a recruitment tool from misogynistic online groups to white supremacist ones (Lyons, 2017, para. 2). Indeed, some of the men's rights and pickup artists blogs regularly assert that western civilization is collapsing because of women's reproductive and economic freedom as well as immigration and interracial marriage (Nagel, 2017).

An interesting contradiction emerges within fascist discourse in particular regarding the family. In many cases, the family represented a form of order which reflected the ideal fascist state, beginning with the authoritarian father at the head of the household who expected unquestioned obedience, and the use of harsh punishment to police the ego. Fascism requires the family in order to acclimate people to its requirements. However, the family also served as a challenge to establishing fascism in that feelings of care and self-preservation could interfere with establishing total loyalty from citizens (Theweleit, 2010b). To deal with this contradiction in Nazi Germany, families ceded control by registering their children in the Hitler Youth and Girls League, where children's obedience shifted from the parents to Hitler. This broke the final self-preservation bond of the family as "it became an organization for the terror of formal domination" (p. 252). This was also done through rendering women invisible, as Theweleit (2010a) found in analyzing the diaries and memoirs of Friekorps members where wives were hardly mentioned:

> Relationships with women are dissolved and transformed into new male attitudes, into political stances, revelations of the true path, etc. as the woman fades out of sight, the contours of the male sharpen; that is the way in which the fascist mode of writing often proceeds. It could almost be said that the raw material for the man's "transformation" is the sexually untouched, dissolving body of the woman he is with. (p. 35)

A second manifestation of the enforcement of masculinity in authoritarian populist and fascist discourse and actions is through positioning the woman or the feminine as a threat. The most recent political examples of woman as threat includes violent reactions to Congresswomen Alexandria Ocascio Cortez and Ilhan Omar, as well as Hillary Clinton, perhaps the original ultimate figure of cosmopolitan liberalism and male displacement that has sustained conservative anger for over 30 years (Fraser, 2017). Figures such as Clinton serve as a stand-in for blame about immigration and economic loss because of her association with feminism even though she is a more centrist political figure.

Where Theweleit (2010a) found that Friekorps members were silent regarding their wives, there was no shortage of descriptions of Jewish or communist women and the depravities they represented, encapsulated in the persona of "the proletarian woman" who served as a focus of male bonding over the use of violence to rid society of her presence:

> The proletarian woman is shameless…is a whore…The women are threatening, because, among other reasons, they are not virgins. The sexual experience that nationalist soldiers sense in them seems to release a particularly powerful fear. That fear is brought into association with the word "communist" (p. 68)

Theweleit posits that contributing to this personification of women were dramatic social changes brought on by the economic conditions of the post-WWI era. Women were now more visible, often the single heads of households, joining in labor actions, becoming vocal in the Communist parties, and creating disruptions around access to food and necessities—in other words, changing into an alien being from the Friekorp male point of view. Worse still was their perceived sexual freedom, which was directly connected to the leftist notion of solidarity, prioritizing connections with others over allegiance to the state. Today, both populists and fascists openly despise the transgressive figure of the poor woman, especially if she is black or Latina. Images of out-of-control sexuality are channeled into the stereotype of the welfare queen who is always having children and regularly summoned to buttress rage and resentment.

An additional aspect of the feminine-as-threat present in both authoritarian fascism and populism is homophobia, even though authors such as Lively and Abrams (2002) continually attempt to link homosexuality with Nazism as a way to both discredit LGBTQI rights and minimize the far-right's historical record of targeting the LGBTQI community with violence and discrimination. Theweleit (2010b) presents a complex analysis of the fascist framing of homosexuality, acknowledging that while some key Nazi party members were gay, knowledge of this fact was utilized in a strategic way by the upper echelon:

> In the first instance, the fascists feared the potential of permissible homosexuality to develop into forms of sexuality they could no longer easily organize and contain. Second, the legalization of homosexuality was seen as likely to eliminate one of the key areas of transgression into which the fascist had to be initiated and accepted, were he to gain access to the secrets that were the domain of a specific power elite. In other areas of social life, the Nazis were clearly denied access both to secrets and power: thus, homosexuality became all the more indispensable. It replaced access to social decision-making power with the freedom to do what was forbidden. (p. 339)

Similar to the phenomenon of Republican politicians who sponsor anti-LGBTQI legislation later being found to be gay themselves, if gay Nazi party members refused to follow orders, they would be faced with the threat of exposure. Therefore, the permission granted to higher-ranking officers to be gay was to further entrench a dependency on the fascist movement for political (and literal) survival. This created a constant, destabilizing dichotomy which Theweleit describes as, "thou shalt love men, but thou shalt not be homosexual…thou shalt do what is forbidden, yet still be punished" (p. 339).

The third and final aspect of enforcement of masculinity is the irresolvable pairing of man as both dominating warrior who establishes authority while also being simultaneously a victim of feminism, reverse racism, liberalism, and global corporatist capitalism. The warrior/victim dichotomy begins with a construction of the dominant white masculine persona, which is constructed by patching together "a theory that explains their plight—grafting together fringe elements of evangelical Christianity, traditional anti-Semitism and racism, and general right-wing paranoia into an amalgam that is loosely held together by a nostalgic vision of hardy, independent frontier manhood" (Kimmel, 2017, p. 248). This warrior persona is then set into a portrait of extreme victimization (the undeserving taking what is his), with his primary agenda being the restoration of the correct order of things.

The utilization of the warrior/victim dichotomy is aptly represented by DeVega's (2016) account of a professor who began to field questions from students who were concerned about what Trump's election would mean for them and their rights. However, the professor noticed that one white male student was happy with the election results, and would make obvious facial expressions whenever issues of race or gender were brought up in class. After the election, this same student insisted on bringing up the topic of the election, even though the class was addressing another unrelated topic. After the professor attempted to redirect the class to the topic at hand, the student

> stood up, taking off his belt and then putting it on her desk. Smiling, with a mix of threat and joy, he announced that "We won!" His point was made: This is "his" country—and by extension (at least in his mind) his classroom—now and again. For this angry young white man, America's natural order of things had been restored with the election of Donald Trump. (para. 4)

This dichotomy also allows for the insertion of shadowy figures, such as Obama, or "The Scary Jew," which enables a rhetorical "out" in allowing the victimized warrior to still support capitalism—which he cannot ever reject—while criticizing its "Jewish" or other excessive influences. As Kimmel (2017) explains, "it's not the capitalist corporations that have turned the government against them, but the international cartel of Jewish bankers and financiers, media moguls, and intellectuals who have already taken over the US state" (p. 262). Indeed, much of anti-Semitic propaganda promulgated today emerged during the same 19th century time-frame as most of the ideas continually recycled in authoritarian populist and fascist discourse by figures like Peterson: "responding, in the same way as Peterson, to an urgent need, springing from a traumatic experience of social and economic modernity, to believe—in whatever reassures and comforts" (Mishra, 2018, para. 9).

Rampant Corruption

The final shared characteristic between authoritarian populism and fascism is not only corruption, but corruption on a scale that far exceeds what is found in mainstream political organizations. This is highly ironic because right-wing leaders routinely run on a law-and-order platform of ending corruption, or, as Trump puts it, "draining the swamp" (Der Speigel Staff, 2018). In what Kellner (2017) calls Trumpland, corruption involves "an amalgam of private and public interests, encompassing the local, national, and global empire of a new world order" that is run on what can best be described as incompetent secrecy (p. 98). Russia's business practices are another example of the imbedded corruption in authoritarian regimes and they are fully connected to the United States through PR firms and foreign policy (Pomerantsev & Weiss, 2014). Nazi Germany itself was also rife with corruption throughout all levels of government (Ulrich, 2016). As in the case of the Republican Party not only excusing but protecting Trump, conservative enabling allows corruption to flourish, creating a double standard for those in power and ordinary citizens.

Corrupt regimes rely on lying as a strategy, which serves the function of covering the actions of authoritarian populists, but also creates a deliberately destabilizing climate where people are not sure who to believe, even if they are directly witnessing evidence in front of them (Alfonso, 2017; Gessen, 2018; Niman, 2019; Theweleit, 2010a). For Gessen (2018), totalitarianism requires the "continuous alteration of the past, and in the long run probably demands a disbelief in the very existence of objective truth" (para. 4). The past has to be reshaped on a regular basis in order to accommodate the constantly-changing present in the interests of the regime. Ultimately, it doesn't even matter if people believe the lies, they have to simply see the lies as the only viable option (Gessen, 2018). This mirrors the authoritarian populist and fascist leaders' own quest to challenge the concept of truth itself (Der Spiegel Staff, 2018).

Double-speak is a significant aspect of lying, where citizens are promised specific actions, but with no significant follow-through. Alfonso (2017) provides the example of Geert Wilders in the 2010 election where he promised not to raise the retirement age. Right after being elected, he said that he was open to considering raising the age. Yet this doesn't matter as long as the leader emotionally fulfills the desires of their followers and reframes the double-speak in some acceptable way. Incoherence is another strategic aspect of corruption, because to seek power at all costs means doing whatever it takes to preserve it:

> A demagogue can blow hot and cold, this way and that, adopt phrases or policies from one source one day and repudiate them the next. There may be nothing at the core except a vacuum that sucks into itself clichés, slogans, facts, factoids and fabrications, fragments of ideologies, policies developed by others, sometimes those others themselves—whoever and whatever might help him gain power at any given moment. Then, at his whim, he disgorges it all. The political vacuum at the core of demagogy, moreover, may correspond to, and perhaps derives from, a moral vacuum, the absence of concern for anything other than the self. (Connor, 2018, para. 26)

In order to pull all of this off, tribalism is required—the fascist or authoritarian populist leader relies on followers who elevate the leader to cult-like status who can do no wrong (McClaren, 2016). The growth of the Tea Party faction in the US is an example of harnessing dichotomous thinking to declare that there can be no middle ground (Jones, 2015). Even if a political party itself isn't popular, the status of the leader can be enough to revive or sustain it, as with Trump. Ulrich (2016) provides the example of how German citizens would speak highly of Hitler, but not those around him. Therefore, "the mythology of the Fuhrer served a compensatory function; it blunted dissatisfaction over the problems and shortcomings of the Third Reich by blaming them solely on Hitler's subordinates" (p. 520). In a similar manner, Republican politicians like Mitch McConnell consistently poll in the low 20s, yet they retain their positions because of their support of Trump, who maintains a high approval rating among Republican voters (Beauchamp, 2016). Any dissatisfaction that Republican voters might have with the GOP are thereby channeled onto state and national representatives, leaving Trump untouched.

DIFFERENCES

Despite sharing several characteristics, it is important to acknowledge that there are key differences between authoritarian populists and fascists. In order to effectively confront the growth of the right wing, it is essential to accurately frame what is currently happening, rather than indiscriminately assigning labels. By only using the fascist label to categorize anything remotely authoritarian, the "opposition culture consistently misses the boat on the populist lure of fascism, especially in its incipient phases" (Weinberg, 2010, para. 31). In her introduction to Theweleit's (2010a) examination of the psychology of the Friekorps, Barbara Ehrenreich notes how "fascism tends to become representational, symbolic" or that it is "really about something else" such as economic fears or repression (p. xi). The critical thing to understand is that the acts that Theweleit describes from Friekorps diaries and memoirs were things that actually happened, that their violent assaults and murders were not "mere gestures." In other words, "the fascist is not doing 'something else,' but doing what he wants to do…what he wants he gets" (p. xi).

The first important difference has to do with paths to power. Depressing as it may be to face, authoritarian populists like Trump simply use the existing electoral system without having to implement any significant changes, whereas fascists, though they can gain access electorally, immediately seize control of the government, including the military and police (Browning, 2017; Renton, 2017). While those in favor of labelling Trump a fascist might point out that Hitler also won electorally, he essentially came to power through a political party that took voters away from other conservative parties, combined with street violence. Trump easily assumed leadership of a Republican Party that had been well on the way to authoritarian populism for decades. By contrast, fascist regimes have "reactionary ambitions to uproot all elements of proletarian democracy within bourgeois society…these goals combined with the organization of a mass base, and the use of mass politics" (Renton, 2019, p. 85). In one example, Hungary's Fidesz party has assisted Orbán in reconfiguring the electorate by passing a law that granted citizenship rights to those of Hungarian ethnicity in countries such as Romania. Many of these individuals have never been to Hungary but they compose 10% of the electorate who supports Orbán's agenda close to 95% of the time (Beauchamp, 2018a, para. 40).

One could even argue that the authoritarian populist label doesn't even fully apply to Trump who routinely contradicts several of its assertions. Some examples include Trump's threats of military aggression against North Korea and Syria or supporting Russian sanctions which conflicts with populist principles of not getting engaged militarily in other nations or claims of Trump being an economic populist while pretty much following the typical GOP playbook with tax cuts that benefit the wealthy or cutting social spending (DiMaggio, 2017). In order to fully establish, at minimum, authoritarian populism, Trump would have to overcome a capitalist class who openly depends on the global nature of trade (Sefla, 2017).

A second important difference is that fascist regimes tend to reject the free market libertarian economics of authoritarian populists in favor of creating social programs within a nationalist bent, because they know they need more than ambitious rhetoric to gain support for what they plan to carry out (Ulrich, 2016; Renton, 2019). For example, France's National Front platform includes cutting taxes for the lowest income voters, price controls for utilities, keeping the 35-hour work week, and pension benefits (Alfono, 2017). This is done within an ethno-nationalist framework of welfare chauvinism where such benefits are exclusively for native-born citizens, common platforms of the Alternative for Germany and Sweden Democrats in addition to France's National Front (Resnikoff, 2017). Currently, existing US civil rights restrictions, regardless of how feeble they are, do not allow for similar discriminatory practices. Republicans in the US want to pretty much seek to cut all social programs across the board for everyone, though they have to be strategic in how they frame it.

Territorial ambitions and conquest represent a third distinction between authoritarian populists and fascists. Hitler's goal of "acquiring living space" in order to meet the economic needs of German citizens was an integral part of Nazi policies (Ulrich, 2016, p. 204). Likewise, advocating nostalgia for dictatorship is a regular aspect of Bosonaro's speeches, even as far back as 1999 when he declared on television: "Voting won't change anything in this country. Nothing! Things will only change, unfortunately, after starting a civil war here, and doing the work the dictatorship didn't do. Killing some 30,000 people…If some innocents die, that's just fine" (Bevins, 2018, para. 10). In contrast, though white nationalists such as Richard Spencer commonly call for the creation of a white ethno-state by using the phrase "blood and soil," when confronted by journalists as to how this would be specifically done, they readily retreat into avoiding the question of how an ethno-state be carried out without mass murder, such as claiming it could happen by "free choice" (Wise, 2016, para. 3).

A fourth distinction includes the larger ideological aims of authoritarian populism being about restoration of a lost past versus fascism's goal of total transformation, a form of starting over:

> The revolution of the right in both fascist Italy and Nazi Germany claimed to be using the state to socially engineer a new man and woman with new values. This is a project of transformation. The non-fascist far right however insists that the people are already the repositories of homogeneity and virtue…by contrast, the enemies of the people—elites and others—are neither homogeneous nor virtuous. Rather, they are accused of conspiring together against the people,

who are depicted as being under siege from above by the elites and from below by a range of dangerous others. (Davidson, 2017, p. 62)

This is reflected in the different historical conditions under which fascism arose in Germany and Trump's authoritarian populism. In the 1920s and 30s, Germany was grappling with the economy and continuing its WWI-era fight to establish rule in Europe. By contrast, Trump's "make America great again" policy—which came on the heels of the 2008 recession—is not so much about dominating specific nations, but about asserting imperialism through a rebirth of the US as a center of influence (Foster, 2017; Renton, 2017). Additionally, 19th century fascism faced a stronger, more militant left that it had to violently overcome through the establishment of fascist organizations. Today's left is so immobilized that the far-right is pretty much limited to aiming their opposition against secular democracy, as conservatives have been doing since the Enlightenment (Renton, 2017).

In summary, characteristics of non-fascist, far-right administrations involve working within existing electoral systems, including political parties; rejecting the concept of a strong, centralized state regarding the economy (but more authoritarian populist regimes might consider strategically employing welfare chauvinism); and they do not challenge traditional class alignments as fascism does (Renton, 2019). As with continually denying that they are racist, the bulk of far-right political parties openly reject the notion that they are fascist nor do they identify with Hitler, Mussolini or other 20th century figures (Weinberg, 2010; Renton, 2019). Likewise, while Hungary's Fidesz seeks to destroy democracy, the GOP in the US hasn't yet reached that stage because the existing system is too profitable (Beauchamp, 2018a). What we currently have is one of two major political parties that is "indifferent to the consequences of their actions" and hasn't really been able to accomplish much legislatively (para. 110).

However, this does not mean that fully-realized fascism isn't possible. What we are currently experiencing in the US could be an initial stage of downplaying or denying fascism, then slowly acclimating people to it. Neiwert (2017) asserts—and I concur—that Trump is a right-wing nativist populist, not a fascist. However, he regularly flirts with fascist and white supremacist *ideas*, at the very least promoting the notion that these ideas are "as equally bad" as leftist and social justice movements:

While it's not inevitable that Republicans will go further in this direction, it's easy to imagine them doing so as the American electorate becomes more diverse and more liberal: with more extreme gerrymandering, harsher voter restrictions, and more right-wing media consolidation and harassment of independent outlets. No single law or anti-immigrant speech would inaugurate a soft fascist regime. But a version of Hungary's system could plausibly take root without many Americans realizing it. (Beauchamp, 2018a, para. 111)

NEW FORMS

Conservatives have long relied on what Apple and Whitty (2002) characterize as a "power bloc" of different right-wing coalitions, including the religious right, neoconservatives, neoliberals, and libertarians. These groups will often unite, depending on the specific issue at hand. For example, religious fundamentalists often support neoliberalism or connect the concept of a free market to Christianity (Daher, 2017). There may be minor disagreements amongst the right, but those differences can be set aside, especially when it comes to limiting the civil liberties of women, minorities, immigrants and LGBTQ people or to cut taxes for the wealthy in order to restrict social spending.

Though these patterns of coalition-building are familiar, there are many new forms of ideological positioning and organizing happening within the right today. Browning (2018) posits that a newer form of authoritarianism, *illiberal democracy*, has become a significant means of consolidating power where "opposition parties can be left in existence and elections can be held in order to provide a fig leaf of democratic legitimacy, while in reality elections pose scant challenge to their power" (p. 16). As an example of this, Browning goes on to explain how the Electoral College in the US has essentially been weaponized:

> The fifty senators from the twenty-five least populous states—twenty-nine of them Republicans—represent just over 16 percent of the American population, and thirty-four Republican senators represent states with a total of twenty-one percent of the American population. With gerrymandering and voter suppression enhancing even more the systemic Republican advantage, it is estimated that the Democrats will have to win by 7 to 11 points in the 2018 elections to achieve even the narrowest of majorities in the House of Representatives. (p. 16)

Adding to this, the choice now comes down between illiberal democracy (the far right) or "undemocratic liberalism," represented with more centrist politicians; along with a fully marginalized left (Der Spiegel Staff, 2018, para. 15). This has also been referred to as "soft fascism," where the political system doesn't have to utilize extreme measures in order to engender compliance since the left as well as the mass media is effectively neutered (Bello, 2018; Beauchamp, 2018a).

The most pressing threat is the global scale of organizing and international cooperation on the right, especially through social media, where "far-right activists can draw on funds, infrastructure, and speakers from allied groups in other countries" (Renton, 2019, p. 79). A key example of this is the Free Tommy Robinson campaign after the alt-right celebrity pleaded guilty to contempt of court. Robinson had established strong connections with anti-Muslim groups outside of the UK, including Republican State Congressman Paul Gosar from Arizona. These alliances have been building over the past 20 years, such as Russian media actively hosting and promoting political figures associated with Brexit, anti-gay organizations such as the World Congress for Families, assorted white supremacists, anti-Semites and others who openly support Putin (Pomerantsev & Weiss, 2014). As different groups experience PR and electoral successes, they can then point to those as recruiting tools that their movement is strong and accomplishing things that governments cannot do alone. At the same time, these groups can distribute blacklists or mobilize attacks on social media against their perceived enemies.

Closely related to this global mobilization is the removal of obstacles related to gatekeeping that once faced more extreme-right candidates or those from non-political backgrounds (Renton, 2019; Sefla, 2017). Despite being primary enablers of authoritarianism and fascism, conservatives did once enact some sort of ideological check within their parties, as they did when David Duke ran for Senate in the 1990s. This is no longer the case. The election of celebrities like Trump are made possible by him fusing a direct relationship with the media and his base, in effect bypassing GOP lawmakers who scramble to keep up (Beauchamp, 2016). Media outlets like Fox News create an airtight propaganda bubble around Trump, keeping mainstream news organizations in check by turning them into "yet another political enemy around which to mobilize grievances and resentments of his base" (Browning, 2018, p. 16).

Currently, the majority of the energy around conservative organizing is through the Third Position movement (Resnikoff, 2017) of the alt-right, "a sanitizing term applied to a collection of hate groups and their leaders" who, using anarchistic tropes, openly advocate the usual line-up of white supremacy, anti-Semitism, Islamophobia, misogyny, and xenophobia (Stan, 2017, para. 2). What makes the alt-right somewhat distinct from authoritarian populists and fascists is that these ideologies are synthesized with the ironic discourse and attack-dog mannerisms of social media, which facilitates their growth and recruitment of members, as well as successful elections of candidates such as Trump (Romano, 2016; Nagel, 2017). Bevins' (2018) conceptualization of Bolsonaro's persona as "Operation Condor plus the Internet" is an apt description of the alt-right as a whole (para. 10).

The alt-right is also deliberately obscurantist, as with Richard Spencer claiming that "the left is right and the alt-right is the new left" (Nagel, 2017, p. 51). This is reflected in widely-shared Third Position authors like Aleksandr Dugin, who promotes the concept of a Fourth Political Theory, "a necessary collaboration between a bygone left (communists, socialists) and a bygone right (fascists)" where a rebranding effort of sorts is attempting to rise above traditional political categorizations like liberalism, socialism, or fascism (Draitser, 2017, para. 35). Alt-right figures like Steve Bannon regularly utilize the discourse of leftist critique as part of reinforcing white nationalism, such as framing the media as "corporatist" or "globalist" (Foster, 2017).

Marantz's (2017) account of alt-right conspiracy theorist Mike Enoch's pathway from libertarianism to white supremacy and fascism reveals how people are recruited into the movement due to the allure of the troll identity:

As a liberal, he had dealt with troubling facts—the achievement gap between black students and white students, say—by invoking the history of racial oppression,

57

or by explaining why the data didn't show what they appeared to show....But all those explanations were abstract at best, muddled at worst, and they required levels of context that were impossible to convey in a Facebook post. Now he was free to revert to a far simpler explanation: maybe white people had more wealth and power because white people were superior. After arguing himself out of every previous position, he had finally found the perfect ideology for an inveterate contrarian—one that presented such a basic affront to the underlying tenets of modern democracy that he would never run out of enemies. (para. 34)

Wolff's (2018) interview with Richard Spencer also reveals many key aspects of the alt-right, including it's overall "tear it all down" ethos and prioritizing of camp and disruption (Nagel, 2017). When Wolff (2018) asked Spencer about how to place Bannon and Trump on the right-wing spectrum, Spencer asserted that neither fit the definition of alt-rightists as he saw it, but that they regularly advanced alt-right talking points along with being "open to the people who are open to these ideas" (p. 138). Commenting on Trump, Spencer didn't hesitate to apply labels accordingly:

We are the Trump vanguard. The left will say trump is a nationalist and an implicit or quasi-racialist. Conservatives, because they are just so douche, say oh no of course not, he's a constitutionalist, or whatever. We on the alt-right will say, He is a nationalist and he is a racialist. His movement is a white movement. Duh. (pp. 138–139)

Ultimately, Spencer, like other alt-right figures, sees Trump as a gateway to further infiltration into mainstream US politics by first harnessing anti-immigrant sentiment, then escalating to mass deportations, which will finally result in a white ethno-state (Nagel, 2017).

The growth of the alt-right has also revealed that traditional avenues of conservative messaging, like think tanks, once thought to be impenetrable, are fast becoming obsolete. This is especially the case with those who have opposed Trump and his brand of populism. Though they retain some degree of influence among GOP politicians and their agendas, think tanks like the Heritage Foundation and the American Enterprise Institute are fast losing ground compared to Fox News, Brietbart and online alt-right media (Heilbrunn, 2017). This shift away from traditional conservative media and authors is connected to larger economic changes in the wake of the 2008 recession and the discrediting of neoliberal optimism regarding free trade, pluralism, and globalization (Der Spiegel Staff, 2018). As Taibbi (2018) notes,

The Grand Old Coalition is broken. Conservative intellectuals have gone from faux-praising the ordinary Joe to arguing that too much democracy is a bad thing when dumb people are involved. And the family-values set has not only been stuck with an oversexed thrice-married pig as president, but left to watch in horror as they've been replaced as national moral censors by the Social Justice Warriors of the Internet. In the Harvey Weinstein era, the Christian right doesn't even have a monopoly on bashing Hollywood mores anymore. (para. 20)

In effect, traditional conservatives have been rendered irrelevant in the wake of the alt-right and new forms of right-wing organizing. Their only choice is to follow suit and board the Trump train.

CAUTIONS

The ideological flexibility of today's far-right combined with the reach of a for-profit social media represents one of its more pressing dangers (Resnikoff, 2017). These groups are highly adept at self-presentation. For example, the American Freedom Party, a strong supporter of Trump's candidacy, recognized the need to tone down its white supremacist rhetoric—such as replacing the term "white nationalist" with "white advocate"—to make it "more palatable to moderate white voters" (para. 31). Likewise, anti-Muslim organizing provides a more subtle way to scapegoat an ethnic minority by claiming to be opposed to religion, not race (Sunshine, 2017). Often these groups utilize intersectional tactics, like using the support for LGBTQI rights to promote Islamophobia. Trump himself has no coherent political worldview other than strung-together talking points that are highly inconsistent, depending upon his current mood, need to protect himself, and permanent desire for attention (Browning, 2017). However, those he surrounds himself with, such as Steve Bannon and Stephen Miller, along with associated neoconservative generals, DO have specific ideological visions and see Trump's impressionability as a net gain.

In the past, conservatives had to distance themselves from their supporters' calls for violence. As Renton (2019) has noted, "We are living in a moment where the mainstream right wagers that by moving onto ground previously inhabited by the far right its own popularity will rise" (p. 84). Prior fears of appearing too supportive of authoritarian tendencies are eroding as conservative politicians are finding they need to join the alt-right train, or be left behind electorally (Lopez, 2017). The political calculus is clear, as DiMaggio (2017) remarks concerning Trump's response to the aftermath of Charlottesville's white supremacist march:

> Trump knows he can't afford to alienate racist elements on the right to get re-elected, and he doesn't want to alienate them, since he himself is a racist and a bigot. Hence the refusal to use clear language to condemn the murders. His political reasoning here is completely transparent, as he's spent his entire political career cultivating hate on the reactionary right. Although Trump eventually condemned the attack after receiving a large amount of negative press, his reversal is part of a broader trend Trump is known for, in which he initially signals to racists in his support base that he approves of their actions, thereby devaluing any later reversal as merely the product of political pressure, rather than principled opposition. The damage, of course, has already been done. Far-right fascists and racists know that the president supports their behavior when he goes out of his way to provide them cover. (para. 22)

We also have to be alert to the fact that "early fascism nearly always plays to populism" with its discourse about being on the side of the forgotten or the "little guy" and through a racist and xenophobic lens (Weinberg, 2010). Despite our current conditions being different than those of 1930s Germany and that fascism has potentially taken on new forms, we should never overlook that the overall aims are the same: "openly espousing racism, nationalism, anti-environmentalism, misogyny, homophobia, police violence, and extreme militarism" (Foster, 2017, para. 21). In his sobering analysis of white supremacist Richard Spencer, Wise (2016) reminds us that the answer isn't one of accommodating racism, but of opposing it:

> His is not a movement of intellectual and moral principle. It is a movement of conquest, domination and control, which seeks power for power's sake—an entirely fascist precept, incapable of existing side by side with any pretense to democratic norms or institutions. If we are to fight it, we must understand this. His is a movement that, unchecked, cannot lead to anything other than mass violence and the complete extirpation of those seen as standing in its way. If might makes right—and it does in the worldview of white nationalists—they cannot be expected to accept a partial victory (as they did in the past) and not see it through to the end. Their goals, however much they try and hide them, are genocidal. They must simply be stopped. (para. 20)

In this vein, traditional liberal approaches like calling for dialogue or counteracting fake news with factual information are not sufficient (Camacho, 2016). We are dealing with a right-wing that is either determined to restore nations to their former glory or to completely dismantle and replace them with a fascist governmental structure, both of which having minorities and immigrants in their sights as part of those plans. Evidence of the insufficiency of liberal-left responses includes the continuing influence of Brexit, and the global rise of right-wing nationalist and fascist parties in Europe, Eastern Europe, Australia, India, and South America, along with other regions (Resnikoff, 2017).

Renton's (2019) advice for confronting the right is prescient. First, it is critical to acknowledge that opposition needs to be aimed at what the right wing is doing *now*, not so much applying the fascist label to tie it to past actions or some future dystopian predictions of what could be. Instead, successful strategies are intersectional, such as highlighting the current harms of racist and sexist policies, as well as extending the fight to Internet spaces where the right likes to establish dominance. Second, the electoral right does far more damage in the long run than the street right, yet the street right is most associated with traditional fascism in its symbolism, language, and actions. While Antifa is busy confronting right-wing speakers on college campuses, they completely overlook cuts to Medicare happening in Congress. Third, and most important, is to "cleave apart the alliance between center- and far-right" (Renton, 2019, p. 89). We have to focus our efforts on breaking apart this coalition, whether in online spaces, electorally, or through organized action.

CHAPTER 3

WHO IS THE REAL WORKING CLASS?

Moving beyond the Construction of the White Male Industrial Worker as a Marker of Authenticity

INTRODUCTION

The 2016 election revealed the enduring nature of assumptions about the working class as white male manual laborers as well as appealing to the needs of the "middle class," also a stand-in for a specific type of white workforce (Winant, 2017). Even though overt racial language was rarely used in outlining the contours of class, it was pretty apparent in discourse surrounding the election that only some workers mattered:

> The common denominator of so many of the strange and troubling cultural narratives coming our way is a set of assumptions about who matters, whose story it is, who deserves the pity and the treats and the presumptions of innocence, the kid gloves and the red carpet, and ultimately the kingdom, the power, and the glory. You already know who. It's white people in general and white men in particular, and especially white Protestant men, some of whom are apparently dismayed to find out that there is going to be, as your mom might have put it, sharing. The history of this country has been written as their story, and the news sometimes still tells it this way—one of the battles of our time is about who the story is about, who matters and who decides. (Solnit, n.d., para. 3)

Shortly after the 2016 election, as people attempted to cobble together some sort of analysis of what exactly happened, a bipartisan narrative emerged of the beleaguered, economically targeted white working class who was driven to support Trump because the Democratic Party overlooked them in favor of lavish attention granted to minorities and women (Demeter, 2016; Walters, 2017; Mason, 2017). This only "reaffirmed the message that whiteness and the working class were the same thing and made the vast non-white working class invisible or inconsequential," including the idea that their economic suffering was apparently irrelevant (Solnit, n.d., para. 9). This mirrors what Resnikoff (2017) identifies as a hallmark of populism: that the white worker is part of a vanishing working and middle class, despite the fact that minorities have experienced the brunt of a capitalist economy. Even within socialist organizing, the white, male, heterosexual, manual worker has been presented as the universal stand-in for all of labor (Hill, Sanders, & Hankin, 2002).

Walters (2017) outlines how both the right and the left devoted endless time and bandwidth to folksy interview portraits of small industrial and rural towns in economic ruin and their Trump supporter residents. Taken together, these stories broadcast the message that "racism and sexism were unfortunate side effects of the real illness of economic vulnerability and insecurity" while identity politics also served as "so much elitist petulance that ignores the populist surge at the heart of Trump's victory" (para. 2). McAuley's (2019) analysis of the right-wing drift of the mostly white Yellow Vest protest movement in France finds that even though the protesters represent a minority of the country (with other demonstrations drawing much larger crowds around issues of climate change and women's rights), "the concerns of this minority are treated as universal by politicians, the press...working class whites command public attention even when they have no clear message" (p. 61).

Even two years after the election, the media remains focused on how Trump's policies have impacted his supporters, *not* on the non-Trump voters who comprehended the impacts of a Trump administration to begin with (Solod, 2017; Walters, 2017). Their narratives remain hidden because they are not considered part of the authentic working class. As Demeter (2016) points out,

> if we're paying attention to reality, most members of the working class would, by definition, be women and/or people of color. But that's not what people who talk about the politics of the "working class" mean. Women and people of color are engaged in ridiculed "identity politics," while white men who haven't done well economically are the sainted "working class." (para. 2)

For all of the media attention it receives, one would expect this authentic working class to be highly politically engaged and dominant from a demographic standpoint. However, in light of the overall population, Trump's base is essentially a minority. Maison (2017) provides the example of McDowell County, West Virginia, located in coal country which is highly supportive of Trump and other conservative candidates. Even though Trump won the majority of the county by 66%, less than 35% of eligible voters turned out, compared to other parts of the state with turnout at almost 60% (para. 6). McDowell County is not a unique phenomenon as many high-poverty regions of the US have low voting rates, which, of course, benefits Republicans. The problem is, that as long as the meme of the authentic working class persists, the solidarity of the working class needed for mass mobilization remains an impossibility (Winant, 2017).

An important aspect of understanding the problem of working-class solidarity is acknowledging that color and genderblind capitalism is not possible, especially in a colonial settler state like the US (McLaren & Farahmandpur, 2002; Cole, 2018; Stanley, 2018). Capitalism is intertwined with sexism, racism, homophobia and xenophobia. These are not mere "strategies" used by the ruling class used to control workers, or side effects of capitalism, as the common line of left reasoning goes:

> In the United States, the hold of racism on white workers has been a constant historical problem for working-class organization. It has been a barrier to union organizing and socialist class consciousness. There are many instances where white workers have actively rejected unionism, typically in the South, because it implied shared membership with black workers. Even in the face of utmost hardship, white workers have traded away economic improvement and class strength for illusory cultural privileges of whiteness. (Martinot, 2000, p. 43)

The left needs to confront the problem of racism within white workers and stop diverting it to the middle or ruling classes or minimizing racism and sexism as "just part of capitalism." It needs to let go of the "authentic working class" meme. This will require a dialectical historical engagement with the conditions that shaped white supremacy and patriarchy as part of the rise of capitalism.

This chapter addresses several concepts related to the persistence of the white male worker as "authentic working class," beginning with an overview of the impacts of neoliberalism. This then creates the conditions needed for backlash, which Trump and other authoritarian populists took advantage of during the election. Next, an examination of capitalism as constructed by race will include the historical development of white worker identity and why this remains a major barrier for socialist organizing. In particular, the strategic significance of white rural spaces will be analyzed along with a dialectical reading of what shapes those spaces. The chapter will conclude with a revised portrait of the working class as highly diverse, including more members than ever before due to drastic changes in the contexts of waged work. Examples of organizing drawing on these strengths will also be presented.

NEOLIBERALISM'S EFFECTS

Representing a specific form of capitalism, neoliberalism can be defined as "a corporate domination of society that supports state enforcement of the unregulated market" which includes limiting the rights of the working class, eviscerating the social safety net and shielding the capitalist class from the consequences of their actions (McClaren & Farahmandpur, 2002, p. 37). Also known as "socialism for the rich," or "third way," neoliberalism brings with it lower taxes for the top 1%, removal of environmental protections, and movement to financialization-based economies that trade in debt—a key factor contributing to the 2008 global recession (Collins, 2015). As A. Smith (2017) explains, neoliberalism replaced the older state infrastructure-funding philosophy of Keynesianism, which was in place from the New Deal era of the 1930s to the early 1970s. Reagan and Thatcher cemented the policies of neoliberalism in the 1980s, which continued through the Clinton administration in the 1990s, ushering in the politics of austerity that continue today (Fraser, 2017). Because it is supported by the capitalist class, neoliberalism can accommodate various presentation styles, from conservative and militaristic to multicultural and global cutting-edge.

Currently, a significant portion of the global white working class (in particular, the middle class), instead of resisting the neoliberal onslaught, has been drawn to nationalism with its attendant isolationism and economic protectionism. This has happened in the absence of viable left organizational alternatives such as rank-and-file unions (Post, 2017). Intensified targeting of minorities, refugees, LGBTQ, and women has been a feature of the platforms of the Republican Party in the US, the United Kingdom Independence Party (UKIP), Marine LePen's National Front in France, and the Five Star Movement in Italy, to name a few. This section will first present a picture of the current economic situation facing the working class under neoliberalism, with a focus on the philosophy of progressive and regressive neoliberalism and its impacts after the 2008 global recession. It is followed by an overview of the various forms of backlash and resentment discourse that shapes the ideologies of white workers, furthering their allegiance to authoritarian populism.

Current Economic Situation

Often brandishing the concept of "freedom," the United States has always had an extremely limited view of human rights, which has enabled capitalism to operate relatively unchecked (Surin, 2018). Essentials like education, environmental protection and shelter are not viewed as rights while "freedom is equated with a specific form of individualism that is shorn of responsibility" (Dolack, 2017a, p. 14). In other words, the US working class is "free to compete in a race to the bottom set up by capitalists" (p. 14). Neoliberalism as philosophy and policy gains its power from the unwillingness of the capitalist class to address poverty in any sort of meaningful way. At the same time, neoliberalism presents itself as emerging naturally in a global context, when it is in actuality the result of deliberate decisions regarding the prioritization of markets, buttressed by military force worldwide (Sefla, 2017, p. 3).

Brenner and Fraser (2017) note that as soon as social activism began to challenge capitalism on many fronts in the 1970s, neoliberal restructuring began, taking the working class by surprise. Struggling to remain relevant against the onslaught, resistance groups such as unions and feminist organizations began to immediately shift their focus to business unionism and liberal feminism, marginalizing more militant forms of organizing. Since its full implementation in the 1980s, neoliberalism has presented itself for over thirty years as a forward-thinking type of economics, emphasizing diversity and upward mobility as replacements for eroding social safety nets. During the Clinton administration, the full financialization of the economy occurred, with a shift toward Wall Street and deregulation of the banking sector (Fraser, 2017). This was reflected in the discourse of "self-sufficiency" applied to single mothers after welfare reform in 1996 (Brenner & Fraser, 2017).

Though portrayed as an oppositional figure, Trump in no way represents any sort of cessation of neoliberalism. It needs to be stressed that "what his voters rejected was not neoliberalism, tout court, but progressive neoliberalism" (Brenner & Fraser, 2017, p. 130). Trump and his supporters view progressive neoliberalism as a mix of Wall Street and the media on one side and globalization and "identity politics" movements on the other:

> Rejecting globalization, Trump voters also repudiated the liberal cosmopolitanism identified with it. For some…it was a short step to blaming their worsening conditions on political correctness, people of color, immigrants, and Muslims. In their eyes, feminists and Wall Street were birds of a feather, perfectly united in the person of Hillary Clinton. (p. 131)

In many ways, it was Obama's continuation of progressive neoliberalism's austerity and focus on individualized success that paved the way for Trump's authoritarian populism (Sefla, 2017).

One immediate outcome of Neoliberalism was the massive relocation of manufacturing from the United States to the global South, now representing close to 70% of production (Foster, 2017, para. 61). The wealth from this shift did not "trickle down" to workers, but has been continually hoarded and transformed into financialized assets (Collins, 2015). Sustar (2018) points out that the loss of manufacturing jobs in the US was not a result of offshoring or importing goods from other countries as economic nationalists suggest, but to productivity shifts including automation. Accompanying this production shift is extreme wealth disparity, such as the top 1% in the US increasing its wealth by a rate of 120% between 1980 and 2015 (Foster, 2017, para. 61). Essentially, the only significant growth experienced under Neoliberalism has been the capitalist class, the top 10% alone has over 70% of the wealth in the US (para. 61). Foster points out that six billionaires (four are from the US) hold more wealth than the poorest half of the world (para. 61).

In addition to the capitalist class re-asserting its hold on profits through wealth disparity, the other aspect of neoliberalism is mass privatization (Thier, 2019). The earlier tentative agreements between the working class and New Deal legislation were radically upended, resulting in austerity combined with deep cuts in social programs deregulation, and lack of access to health care. This has had several impacts, including the US now having the highest infant mortality and obesity rates among developed countries, a rise in disease incidents like the Zika virus, and conditions often associated with the 1800s, such as hookworm parasites in Alabama (Surin, 2018, p. 8). Currently, the US remains in 36th place for access to water and sanitation, as the crisis in Flint, Michigan illustrates (p. 8). One fourth of US youth live in poverty and the incarceration rate (heightened during the 1990s due to three-strikes laws) is the highest globally (p. 8).

Housing remains out of reach for many, with home prices outpacing inflation and rising by 60%, also impacting affordability of rent (Dolack, 2017a, p. 14). It is no longer possible in the US for a minimum wage, full-time worker to afford a one-bedroom apartment. For example, in West Virginia, a minimum wage worker would have to put in 49 hours a week to obtain a one-bedroom apartment, and 80 hours a week in the District of Columbia (p. 15). Much of this stems from the 2008 global recession which was caused by accumulating credit and debt, in particular rapidly rising home prices due to subprime mortgage speculation, immediately followed by the bottom falling out of the stock market and investment banks (Thier, 2019; Rasmus, 2018b). The consequences were over nine million foreclosures and eight million lost jobs (Thier, 2019, p. 92). At the end of 2009, 18% of workers (close to 30 million) faced unemployment, part-time work, or ceased to be able to find a job (p. 93).

While the 2008 recession impacted the working class as a whole, including the middle class, it was the poor who were hit the hardest. Thier (2019) notes that households in the lowest tier of income levels had the highest unemployment rate of 30%. By contrast, top earning households only experienced a 3% unemployment rate. When combined with underemployment rates, "half of the nation's poorest families experienced unemployment or underemployment during the recession" (p. 93). And while many Trump supporters fall into that category, African American and Latino/a workers were especially impacted (Sustar, 2018). For example, median household wealth of black families will, if conditions persist, become zero in 2053, with Latino/as hitting zero by the 2070s (p. 38). This makes the focus on the "authentic" white working class all the more puzzling in terms of economics.

In addition to the financial impacts of neoliberalism, traditional means of civic participation and organizing has been radically limited. In 2016, voter turnout was only 55.7%, making the US 28th in turnout compared to other countries who regularly average 75% (Surin, 2018, p. 8). While close to 100% of voters are registered in countries like Sweden and Japan, only 64% are registered in the US (p. 8). These numbers are kept low partly due to Republican voter suppression tactics like partisan gerrymandering, voter ID laws, and purging voter rolls (Wang, 2012). Unions represent another protective form of civic engagement and organizing for the working class, but membership has been on an ongoing decline since the 1950s, from 33% of private sector workers once unionized to just under 7% today (Sustar, 2018, p. 27). This demonstrates that the strategy of business unionism has only assisted in the demise of unions, not protected them as proponents asserted. Instead, workers have lost the ability to utilize unions as a way to leverage wages and quality of working conditions for all.

Backlash and Resentment

An inevitable result of neoliberalism's failure to deliver to the working class is an increase of backlash and resentment, particularly among whites. Racism has long served as a potent form of gaining the consent of the white working class to the austerity cycles that are built into capitalism. So long as people can see the ability in the long term to retain their social position and increase their economic gains— however minor—they will overlook the multiculturalism and diversity that is part of Neoliberal globalization. However, after the 2008 crisis, the deal was off, and blame easily shifted to a mixture of "global elites" and immigrants in particular (Der

Speigel Staff, 2018; Mason, 2016). Shenk's (2017) interview of author Katherine Kramer reveals this dynamic:

> When a substantial portion of the population perceives that they are not getting their fair share, and that this is the result of people in power giving their share to those who are less deserving, we are on fertile ground for a politics of "us versus them." Political actors can step in and validate that resentment and make promises to stop the flow of resources, power, and respect to the undeserving. Situations of economic and cultural insecurity seem especially ripe for the success of this kind of politics. (para. 3)

Forsetti's (2016) account of growing up in a white, rural fundamentalist Christian community reveals many key contradictory aspects of backlash and resentment discourse. These include being upset at the current state of the economy while continually voting for politicians that advocate for the very policies that cause economic collapse, or blaming government while accepting social security, welfare, farm subsidies, commodities insurance and other government protections. They see their own poverty through the lens of victimization, but refuse to allow that description to apply to non-white people who they claim are undeserving "moochers" (while also living in all-white communities far from diverse populations). Likewise, they reject relocating to where work is available while criticizing poor urban residents for remaining where they are, as in the aftermath of Hurricane Katrina. Drug addiction in rural communities is a "health crisis" while in urban areas it is a "character flaw." Outsiders are viewed with suspicion and denied business permits, or the community creates a hostile climate for diverse populations like LGBTQI people, but then residents complain that no businesses want to relocate to rural communities. All of this takes place within a global context of disrupted homogeneity in many of these locations, which is leading to the contradictory manifestations of white resentment (Der Spiegel Staff, 2018).

By far, immigration provides the most potent organizing point for this resentment and backlash, encapsulated in the demand to "build the wall." This reveals the profound irony of white workers blaming refugees and immigrants, who are the first-line victims rather than the causes of neoliberalism. Immigrants from Central America in particular have served as fodder for the Republican Party to gain support for Immigration and Customs Enforcement (ICE) raids, detention centers (including detaining of children), increased militarization of border patrol, eliminating the Deferred Action for Childhood Arrivals (DACA) college funding program and more recently, Trump's family separations (Bacon, 2018; Anderson, 2017). What is overlooked in these efforts is any kind of commentary on what has been driving migrants to flee those regions of the world, such as past and present US efforts in destabilizing governments. Essentially, migrants "are looking for economic survival in countries tied to the neoliberal economic model" (Bacon, 2018, p. 33). Worldwide, there are more than 50 million of these individuals who are perpetually scapegoated by the right (A. Smith, 2017, p. 44).

Much of the origins of xenophobic immigration policy is tied to the discourse surrounding the North American Free Trade Agreement (NAFTA) in the 1990s, which provides a case study of Neoliberalism's failed promises. When NAFTA was first presented, it was sold as a net positive for everyone, albeit in the racist, paternalistic frame of a more "advanced" country (the US) bringing a more "backwards" one (Mexico) into modernity (Simons, 2017). Much like today, Mexico was portrayed in the 1990s as a corrupt and criminal regime that could be safely contained through trade. Now that NAFTA has gutted the Mexican economy as well as impacted immigration, Trump and his supporters have revived discourse surrounding Mexicans being a criminal element, invading the borders, bringing disease and taking jobs. This represents further irony in that a wall and its associated draconian policies would only serve to *reinforce* an intimidated, low-wage labor pool for corporations, rather than discourage immigration (Chomsky, 2017).

This targeting of immigrants is happening at the same time when the visibility of Latino/as and Muslims have increased in terms of political activism and post-secondary educational attainment (Anderson, 2017; DeVega, 2018; Chacon, 2017). This has enabled "American exceptionalism" to be supplanted by narratives of "American victimization" in what can best be described as a massive national amnesia regarding the history of the US's involvement with Mexico and other countries (Simons, 2017). At the same time, the failure of earlier administrations to confront xenophobic immigration policies has in many ways paved the way for Trump's even more extreme proposals, as in Obama's DACA program creating a separation between "deserving" immigrant college students from less educated, poorer immigrants in order to win centrist support (Chacon, 2017; Chomsky, 2017). This includes Democrats' consistent framing of immigration in terms of "tough on crime" discourse, which only validates Republican talking points instead of challenging them.

Backlash and resentment also cluster around narratives about poverty, which relate to who is or isn't viewed as the "deserving poor." Kimmel (2017) discusses the concept of *aggrieved entitlement* as a central component of white resentment, or "the sense that those benefits to which you believed yourself entitled have been snatched away from you by unseen forces larger and more powerful" (p. 18). This is a form of reverse victimology, where whites see themselves as "helpless" against an incoming tide of women and minorities who are taking what belonged to them. Another powerful component of resentment around poverty is the *fundamental attribution error* or "natural tendency to see the behavior of others as being determined by their character—while excusing our own behavior based on circumstances (Szalavitz, 2017, para. 4). This is enormously beneficial to capitalism:

> For elites, pinpointing defective culture as an explanation for poverty deflects investigation and rationalizes political complacency, enabling capitalists and policymakers to scrutinize individuals rather than institutions. This trend is

most evident in the Republican Party, within which the trope of the undeserving poor is practically a mantra. (Stanley, 2018, p. 42)

An additional aspect shaping poverty is that its overall economic impacts are far greater in the United States compared to other democracies. In terms of risk factors, or what are commonly referred to in backlash discourse as "poor choices," Americans actually have fewer of these risk factors compared to 40 years ago or to those living in other democracies (Brady, Finnigan & Hubgen, 2018, para. 10). The penalties for risk factors are just higher in the United States. For example, a lack of a high school education increases the likelihood of one being poor by just over 15% whereas in other democracies it only increases the risk of poverty by less than 5% (para. 11). Backlash discourse also overlooks how the majority of people in poverty are employed, such as 78% of the families receiving Medicaid having at least one employed household member (Rader, 2017, para. 8). The majority of the working poor are simply employed in sectors barely paying a subsistence wage, with service industry jobs paying in the low $20,000s (para. 8).

In the US, welfare represents a particularly racialized and gendered form of backlash discourse (DeVega, 2018). Though blamed for poverty and moral decline, people living in single mother-headed households only represent a very small percentage of the larger population at 8.8% (Brady, Finnigan, & Hubgen, 2018, para. 4). For those receiving welfare, 90% have two or fewer children (S. Smith, 2017, p. 20). Coupled with the power of fundamental attribution error within conservative groups, "poor people tend to be the hardest on each other," especially white women who receive welfare harshly judging minority female recipients (Szalavitz, 2017, para. 14).

This also partly explains the tendency of Trump supporters to demand that Social Security and Medicare are left untouched, while they insist on resisting the Medicaid expansion or the Affordable Care Act, programs that cover more poor and diverse individuals (Thompson, 2017; DeVega, 2018). Smith and Hanley (2018) found that the economic pessimism of Trump supporters coupled with their willingness to sacrifice their own financial well-being in support of right-wing policies was due to racial resentment. Close to 40% of the economic policy differences between liberals and conservatives could be attributed to racial views alone (p. 206). Likewise, DeVega (2018) notes that the more that social programs were associated with minorities, white support for cutting those programs increased, even if they acknowledged this would harm white populations (para. 17). There is also a class dimension to this, as Kimmel (2017) observes that even among white supremacists, the groups they prioritize defending include *middle-class whites*, not poor ones, who are often described in the same demeaning terms as minorities. Conservative whites will fully support policies that primarily benefit the white middle class, like mortgage interest/property tax deductions and other tax benefits, for all intents and purposes forms of white welfare (DeVega, 2018, para. 6).

A final area of resentment and backlash discourse involves jobs and affirmative action. As with issues of welfare, the notion of who deserves sympathy and support revolve around notions of the authentic working and middle classes. For example, in the 1970s and 1980s, black inner-city unemployment reached crisis levels, but advice was blithely given for blacks to simply move or retrain for other jobs. Now that economic changes have impacted labor sectors where whites are heavily represented, a whole new talking point has emerged, such as the need for the government to prop up coal and manufacturing (Hamilton, 2016). Even though the likelihood of a white male having just a high school diploma making a living wage at the same job for life has disappeared, this mythology has persisted, along with adherence to the American Dream, transforming into resentment when it remains unfulfilled (Thorton, 2016; Kimmel, 2017). Notions of merit, encapsulated in discourse around affirmative action reflects the enduring assumption that minorities have taken spots from "qualified" whites, totally overlooking generations of legacy admissions at colleges and nepotism in hiring (Anderson, 2017).

For Traister (2018), resentment and backlash boil down to the consistent privileging of the anger of white men. As she notes, "their anger is revered, respected as the stimulus for necessary political change" (para. 12). At the same time, this anger is presented as coming from intellectual and rational spaces, the implication being that women and minorities are emotional and irrational or too fixated on identity politics:

> Think about how the anger of white men in the Rust Belt is often treated as politically diagnostic, as a guide to their understandable frustrations: the loss of jobs and stature, the shortage of affordable health care, the scourge of drugs. Meanwhile, the Movement for Black Lives, a response to police killings of African Americans initiated by women activists, is considered by the FBI to pose a threat of "retaliatory violence" and discussed as a "hate group." (para. 12)

CONSTRUCTING CAPITALISM THROUGH RACE AND GENDER

Alternative Marxist theorizing that specifically focuses on the composition of the working class includes Operaismo or Workerism and Open Marxism. In particular, Operaismo takes up the question of the impact of technology on workers and how the working class shapes the actions of capital (Hardt & Negri, 1994). Open Marxism seeks to widen the messaging of dialectical materialism, aimed at building coalitions within the working class (Bonefield, 1992). Both of these anti-authoritarian left approaches target industrial sectors of the working class, but have also been applied to the changing nature of the workplace, such as a growing service industry sector and warehouse distribution networks. Still, this framing of the working class remains tied to class-based theorizing with not as much discussion devoted the role of race and gender within capitalism. What needs to be addressed is the construction of the white working class itself.

Just as it is simplistic to assume that racism's origins lie within the white working class (Myerson, 2017), it is also simplistic to assume that one's membership in the white working class precludes one from being fully racist or somehow minimizes the impacts of one's racism. Asserting that the working class didn't invent racism is not the same thing as exonerating them from their racist actions. While racism does not originate in the white working class, it continues to play a prominent role in white workers' conceptions of themselves as a class:

> Class, for Marx, is neither simply monolithic nor static. Under capitalist economic laws of motion, the working class in particular is constantly decomposed and reconstituted due to changes in the forces of production... class-consciousness does not follow automatically or inevitably from the fact of class position. (Hill, Sanders, & Hankin, 2002, p. 173)

If we want to understand why the white working class seems to persistently identify with the capitalist class or other whites versus forming bonds of solidarity with minorities as part of a larger class consciousness, we have to understand the history of capitalism's construction through race and gender (McClaren & Farahmandpur, 2002). Capitalism's very formation is tied to colonialism, the emergence of the global slave trade and the corresponding racial categorizations needed to harness labor. This makes racism far more than a simple ruling class "strategy to divide the working class," as many leftists unfortunately conclude in a form of touch-and-go, neat and tidy analysis. This rationale is deployed to skirt around the difficulties with confronting racism in activist contexts, especially when encountering racism of the white working class. This is a form of "competitive virtue signaling, a game that does little more than build the personal brands of those playing it" and "it does not provide an adequate account of the phenomenon it seeks to explain" (Maison, 2017, para. 27).

This section analyzes three components of the construction of capitalism through race and gender. First, a dialectical historical overview of the creation of the white working class is presented, with a focus on Martinot's (2000) analysis. A discussion of color-blind racism follows, including how it operates ideologically in both conservative and left discourse. The section concludes with an examination of the functions of white rural geographies, in particular, Appalachia.

Historical Overview

The notion that racism is a key strategy of control used by the capitalist class to maintain divisions among workers is quite common on the left. However, this explanation is radically insufficient for understanding what has led to the persistence, even over hundreds of years, of racism, albeit it taking various forms (Stanley, 2018; Martinot, 2000). In examining the landscape of labor throughout history, we have to face the fact that segregation and exclusion have been the *norm*, not the exception. This is because "whiteness and white supremacy did not evolve out of race relations, but were themselves the sociopolitical relations that brought race into existence" (p. 50). While important to study, the few counter-examples of working-class solidarity are not enough to justify ignoring this fact. In other words, there are only so many times that the left can point to Bacon's Rebellion before the tactic wears kind of thin.

Historical understanding from a dialectical materialist framework is an essential component of beginning to dismantle the mythology around the authentic working class, including simplistic leftist readings of labor. What we see today in the working-class are "byproducts of centuries, shaped by deep-rooted systems of production and their social debris" (Stanley, 2018, p. 40). We have to start with the origins of capitalism itself in order to understand how race was an integral aspect of its formation. This enables us to see that race is simultaneously both durable but also constantly under threat (Piascik, 2018). While race as a construct has been around since the 1600s, it has to be continuously monitored and resurrected in different forms order to keep the focus off of capitalism so that the working class will not unite.

Martinot (2000) examines the emergence of capitalism through the use of colonization, involving genocide of native populations and chattel slavery:

> In the colonies and the nation that emerged from them, whiteness (and from it, race) is the form that domination took. Within a structure of corporate social control, racism and white supremacy were not invented to "divide and rule" the working class, within an existing class structure, but to serve as the primary mode of organizing the structure of labor itself. Racism is the very name of the process whereby a class structure itself was produced. (p. 51)

The process of colonization involved providing low cost or free land to settlers in exchange for their agreement to police native populations, or what DeVega (2018) characterizes as an "intergenerational welfare payment to White America" (para. 3). Without over 400 years of seized resources from native populations and enforced labor of slavery, capitalism would have never been able to "pull itself up by its bootstraps" so to speak.

The plantation system itself created the foundation for the corporate state, with the capitalist class able to secure allegiance of white workers by using race as a means of identity, i.e. "not-black" (Martinot, 2000). This created the illusion of "white solidarity and the integration of labor relations into the white confraternal society" (McLaren & Farahmandpur, 2002, p. 54). Even as the slave economy was declining, this white solidarity was transferred into the industrial workplace where white workers saw themselves as "productive" compared to slave labor which they were competing against:

> This ideology derived from the Jacksonian valorization of the "producing class" of workers and artisans. It affirmed the dignity and honor of work, and opposed slavery as demeaning to labor—but only within a white orientation. Ideologically, it equated black workers, both free and slave, with slavery and

servility. It thus became part of the rationale for advocating the exclusion of all African-Americans from the new territories, on the claim that their mere presence would degrade the honor of white labor. All in all, white workers opposed slavery to exclude black people, and opposed black people to exclude slavery. (Martinot, 2000, p. 44)

As Martinot (2000) notes, these exclusions were not so much about *dividing* the working class as they were about *defining* the working class as white. White workers envisioned themselves as upwardly mobile, embracing middle-class aspirations while "consigning nonwhite labor, through exclusion, to permanent proletarianization" (p. 45). Martinot provides the example of craft unions in the North, who initially supported abolition because they saw slave owners as depressing wages, but then excluded freed slaves from joining their unions after the Civil War. The Black worker then became their enemy, not the capitalist class itself. This "free labor" ideology was one of the key hallmarks of populism in the 1800s and continues today (DeVega, 2018; Piascik, 2018). The extension of suffrage to women only strengthened white working-class identity more so than disrupted it, as "white segregationist women capitalized on their roles in social welfare institutions, public education, partisan politics, and popular culture to shape the Jim Crow Order" (McRae, 2018, p. 4).

The impact of this history continues to manifest itself in how race and gender operates within the working class today. For Martinot (2000), race was not simply a divisive tactic, it was part of the very construction of the white working class and has impacted how that group of workers sees its needs as oppositional to minority workers, thus preventing organizing:

Because white workers in the United States have a different relation to black workers...and because the primary relation between white workers and capital is not mainly across the means of production but through a social administrative hierarchy...the idea of working-class struggle aimed at the overthrow of class society has never made sense to the white working class in the United States, whose resistance to class exploitation rarely attempted to undermine profitability or contested its legitimacy...this no doubt goes a long way in explaining why, for instance, the United States labor movement does not call for solidarity with Mexican workers against NAFTA, but remains in solidarity with the U.S. business/corporate order even as it protests unfair labor practices. (McLaren & Farahmandpur, 2002, p. 55)

Part of maintaining alliances within the white working class involves a reluctance to correct racist behavior and actions in order to not offend friends, family, or co-workers (Waldman, 2018). Even when white women join activist efforts, they often limit their demands to equal opportunity, "or what is legitimate for men and capitalists," thus leaving race and class intact, especially if they are middle-class (Bonilla-Silva, 2018, p. 179). Despite these historical limitations, there are some possibilities for creating openings that could lead to and have successfully led to working-class solidarity. One is the proximity of working-class whites to minorities compared to more prosperous middle-class whites (DiAngelo, 2006). Bonilla-Silva (2018) found that working-class white women regularly interact and are more open to forming alliances with people of color compared to middle-class white women. The final section of this chapter will assert that fully acknowledging the diversity of the working class is one way to disrupt the racist historical narrative.

Thier's (2018) analysis of the right-wing Israeli working class is instructive in understanding the contemporary dynamics of race and labor. Israel presents a challenge to socialists, who often support the Israeli working class as the best hope for the Middle East and a single state solution that accommodates everyone. To conceptualize this requires overlooking the role of the left, such as the United Workers Party, in carrying out the apartheid colonial-settler state, using tactics like forced removal and ethnic cleansing of Palestinians. As Thier explains, "the commitment of a laboring class to colonization can only be expected when it is offered a stake in the settlement, an incentive to sacrifice and to struggle against the indigenous population" (p. 118). Even when organizing does happen among the most oppressed of the Israeli population today, the goal is not to extend rights to all workers, but to demand *what they feel they are owed* in an era of neoliberal decline. Thus, "the denial of one's freedom is the precondition of the other's livelihood" (p. 128).

It is obvious that while the white working-class still retains a degree of privilege compared to working-class minorities, they share more in common with each other economically speaking. Yet, throughout history, working-class whites, with few exceptions, have retained racist and xenophobic viewpoints which has hindered activism, particularly within union organizing (Martinot, 2000). DeVega (2018) notes a collective forgetting of the large, violent strike actions at the turn of the 20th century, where countless white workers were injured and killed, in favor of vague promises of reclaiming their share of the American Dream. For Bonilla-Silva (2018), racism has served to create an allegiance within capitalism that is detrimental to organizing:

> It has been white male workers who have historically supported the racial order…whether in periods of economic security or insecurity, white masculinity has provided white men with economic and noneconomic benefits…the white male bond thus has prevented working-class white men from joining progressive racial movements in masse. (p. 156)

Colorblind Racism

Bonilla-Silva's (2018) concept of colorblind racism is useful for understanding how race functions within discourse surrounding the authentic white worker. The term "color-blind" refers to the common statement, "I don't see color, I see a person," which also taps into the hyper-individualism that has long been a part of the American landscape (DiAngelo, 2006). Colorblind racism's staying power can be attributed to its deep connections with anti-dialectical and ahistorical thinking that help sustain its ideology. These beliefs are woven into conceptualizations of the authentic white working class who, as the narrative goes, works hard, abides by the rules, and is self-reliant. Those who are not able to be successful—and many of those are minorities—must have inherent flaws in their character that need to be addressed, but just not anything at a structural level.

While Jim Crow era racism was more overt and in the open, today's colorblind racism is more insidious and difficult to confront because nothing, apparently, counts as racism anymore. This creates many contradictions between what whites say they support and their actions. For example, even though national annual surveys might show a steady increase in the percentage of whites who affirm civil rights concepts like equality of the races and integration, they "object in practice to almost all of the policies that have been developed to make these goals a reality" (Bonilla-Silva, 2018, p. 142). Or, whites might explain aspects of racism as an individual matter, such as blacks "self-segregating" rather than there being structural factors that lead to residential segregation. As Bonilla-Silva notes, "negotiating the seemingly contradictory views that "race does not matter" but, at the same time, that "race matters" a little bit for minorities and a lot for whites in the form of reverse discrimination is not an easy task" (p. 84).

Much of the backlash and resentment discourse emerging from the "forgotten white worker" falls within a color-blind frame. Notions of minorities as illegitimate recipients of welfare, or displaying negative cultural attributes while white workers—who have done everything right—are ignored, are regular features of this discourse. The most potent of these is the concept of "reverse racism," which is applied to any policy or law that might be taken to redress inequality, like affirmative action (DeVega, 2016). As Bonilla-Silva (2018) notes, "because whites believe discrimination is a thing of the past, minorities' protestations about being racially profiled, experiencing discrimination in the housing and labor markets, and being discriminated against in restaurants, stores, and other social settings are interpreted as "excuses" (p. 142). Myths of bootstrapism are other manifestations of color-blind racism that are difficult to dislodge, because the ability to be judged by characteristics other than skin color is a privilege reserved for whites (Waldman, 2018).

Colorblind racism is what allows Trump supporters to flat-out deny that the Muslim travel ban or calling Haiti a "shithole country" are racist actions, because they can point to other factors that might lead to those actions (concerns about national security or Haiti's poverty) (Walters, 2017). Another aspect of colorblind racism is the notion that if white people don't *intend* to be racist, then their actions are not racist. Instead, the problem is one of minorities "seeing race" in everything and overreacting, not racism itself, as DiAngelo (2006) explains:

We then spend great energy explaining to people of color why our behavior is not racism at all. This invalidates their perspectives while enabling us to deny responsibility for making the effort to understand enough about racism to see our behavior's impact in both the immediate interaction and the broader, historical context. (p. 55)

The segregated structure of society only further segments whites from having to confront issues of race to the point where its very mention tends to bring up defensiveness and denial (Waldman, 2018). DiAngelo (2006) points out the challenges that the white working class in particular has in acknowledging racism when they themselves experience classism or other oppressions, such as being identified as disabled or being gay or lesbian: "It is often very difficult for Whites who have not been validated for the oppression they experience elsewhere to keep their attention on a form of oppression from which they benefit" (p. 56).

Colorblind racism is also bound up in conceptualizations of the white middle class, like home ownership and its connections with property values and school districts. These have been used as ways to maintain the structure of segregation within a post-civil-rights-era context:

> Their material security bound up in the value of their real-estate assets, suburban white people had powerful incentives to keep their neighborhoods white. Just by their very proximity, black people would make their neighborhoods less desirable to future white home-buyers, thereby depreciating the value of the location. Location being the first rule of real estate, suburban homeowners nurtured racist attitudes, while deluding themselves that they weren't excluding black people for reasons beyond their pocketbooks. (Myerson, 2017, para. 7)

The anti-bussing movement of the 1970s, which was led by white women, vehemently denied being racially motivated, instead pointing to concepts like the right of parents to choose where to send their children to school (McRae, 2018). This is similar to the "school choice" movement today where supporters use civil rights language to bolster what are essentially racist policies.

The left also manifests problematic aspects of colorblind racism (and sexism) by their insistence that social problems be attributed to class and not to matters of identity. Theweleit (2010a) identifies "the patriarchal man of the left" who declares that "in the class struggle there may be both men and women, but only one sex, that of the wage earner" (p. 167). Even if leftists support racial justice, by them insisting on a class-only emphasis, it creates an unintentional alliance "between those who wish to combine emphases on race and class and those who would rather see race off the agenda altogether" (Roediger, 2017, p. 16).

Colorblind racism also sustains the illusion that everyone can benefit from class-based policies without having to directly confront racism. Roediger (2017) takes on the flawed notion that Democrats have been so overwhelmingly focused on minority and women's rights that they have completely ignored the white working class, noting that it is often "racial justice" that has been set aside "in the service of lamentably vague class talk" (p. 18). The authentic white working-class meme also glosses over the vibrant and multi-racial coalitions that have been a necessary part of activism surrounding major legislation.

Strategic Use of White Rurality

A powerful manifestation of colorblind racism and its culmination in the construction of the authentic working class is the strategic use of white rurality. While the discourse around industrial "small town America" can also be utilized by conservative and liberal politicians and journalists, white rural spaces are essential touchpoints for minimizing issues of race through superficially highlighting class. As Maison (2017) explains, "contemporary privilege theory ostensibly seeks to center and defer to the agency of people of color, but it consistently brings the focus of attention back to the thoughts, motivations, and actions of white people" (para. 26). Unfortunately, the left plays a major role in this process by repeating the same uncritical line of, "all of the working class suffers under capitalism" without a more nuanced discussion of how specifically capital uses race to construct itself. Invoking white rural spaces is a way to steer the conversation away from a wider range of capitalism's victims, which only serves to support conservative discourse even if that isn't the intent.

White rural spaces are part of an overall urban/rural dichotomy which is used to delegitimize certain types of work while valorizing others, along with determining which geographic areas are treated with more sociological sympathy (Shenk, 2017; Jones, 2017). For example, leading up to the 2016 election, it is no coincidence that just as multi-racial activism was forming around racism and policing, out came a barrage of news stories about the forgotten white working class in rust belt and rural towns. Catte (2018) sees the recent spotlight on Appalachia, its decline of coal mining, and opioid addiction as part of this effort:

> Whenever the nation turns its attention to issues of race that is when a big rediscovery of Appalachia happens. Because Appalachia is often thought of as a white space, some use it to argue we've been paying attention to the wrong problems, like police violence. (p. 72)

For Catte, Appalachia therefore functions as a "counterpoint" or "whataboutism" in order to minimize the impacts of racism in poor and minority communities, particularly large urban centers like Chicago, a discursive target of Trump during the first few months of his administration.

A. Nichols (2017) views the utilization of white rural spaces by prominent liberals and conservatives as a form of an ongoing "atonement" for class privilege, a process that pre-dates Trump. In bad economic situations, poor whites in particular and authoritarian populism in general is responded to with a form of quasi-sympathy, reinforcing its legitimacy. The "white trash voter" is a key figure in the tenuous quest to use class to not talk about class in a meaningful way:

Scapegoat, prophet, moron, rogue—the poor white is a shapeshifter. He changes forms as the needs of his beholders change. When liberals need to blame a class for Donald Trump's presidency, the poor white will do; never mind that two-thirds of all Trump supporters made $50,000 or more a year. When conservatives need to cast liberals as aloof elitists. they appoint themselves the poor white's defenders—until their ideology is threatened, and then it is time to take out the trash. (Jones, 2017, para. 1)

One author who has managed to cash in on the fragile positioning of white rurality is venture capitalist J.D. Vance (2016), and his bestselling book, *Hillbilly Elegy*. Vance is successful precisely because he is all things to all people: liberals appreciate his folksy retelling of his "making it out of poverty" narrative while conservatives are grateful for his recycling of the bootstrapping and personal accountability messaging aimed at poor whites (Isenberg, 2018; Jones, 2016; Solod, 2017). The book manages to avoid any sort of larger social context other than descriptive markers of poverty that set the scenes for various retellings involving a cast of colorful characters, which are tied to conclusions the reader is supposed to draw about poor whites. Vance is able to achieve this because he declares at the start of his book that he does not intend to apply any kind of academic inquiry, which "ostensibly liberates him from the burden of analyzing the loaded, culturally constructed word 'hillbilly'" (Isenberg, 2018, p. 16).

Class narratives about escaping poverty reflect a specific form of literary capitalism where the problem is never the economic system itself, but a variety of "cultural" deficiencies, such as families not delaying gratification, or rampant laziness. These narratives can have a variety of settings but the audience is typically those looking to exonerate capitalism, including justifying eroding the social safety net (Rader, 2017). Maison (2017) and Rader (2017) note how Vance's "making it" out of his white trash background is presented as evidence of a deeper failing on the part of rural whites he left behind. Indeed, Vance has made appearances with Charles Murray and relies on the conclusions of culture-of-poverty authors like Richard Bell and Thomas Ford (Stanley, 2018). Their ideas are reflected in Vance's writing:

For Vance, class is not a matter of political-economic structures but cultural identity, something close to a racial category in itself. In his view, the poor Scots-Irish Americans he grew up with aren't held back by the bleak economic prospects confronting them, but by a Lamarckian moral degeneracy transmitted from one generation of hillbillies to the next. (Maison, 2017, para. 16)

When socio-historical problems, such the kind in rural spaces, are summarized as a result of "mono-casual bad behavior," problems become hyper-individualized, "somewhat mystic, laying beyond the analytical, the material, and the historic" (Stanley, 2018, p. 41). This is indicative of an additional function of white rural spaces—that of discouraging activist solidarity or any sort of confrontation with the capitalist class (unless they are liberal) and replacing these with looking to the past as a solution to social crises. Jones (2016) relates how Vance extends his cultural argument to a gendered longing for a past when men were more religious and masculine, viewing secularism as one of the main contributors to drug use and economic collapse:

> This failure to embed his family's failings within any larger social context reflects Vance's need to celebrate individual agency at all costs. For Vance, "hillbilly" is a term of endearment, a state of mind, a group moniker, a source of chaos and anger, but it is more often than not disconnected from real economic conditions that shaped his family's class identity. The "hillbilly" that he invokes is both a composite of his memories and a literary device. (Isenberg, 2018, p. 18)

Luckily, there are critical responses to Vance in the form of deliberately asserting the dialectical, materialist history of regions like Appalachia. Stanley (2018) takes on the shallow analysis of culture-of-poverty proponents by directly connecting historical factors to the present:

> Appalachians aren't poorer than other Americans because they're lazy or uneducated; they're poorer because of a history of nonarable land, extractive capitalism, exploitable labor, and environmental destruction. Black Americans aren't poorer because of a lack of self-responsibility or a profusion of saggy pants; they're poorer because of four hundred years of enslavement, Jim Crow, and systemic racism. Native Americans aren't poorer because of drug use or alcoholism; they're poorer because of a past that includes policies of extermination, subjugation, removal, and apartheid. And women aren't poorer because they prefer low paid or domestic work; they're poorer because of a pervasive patriarchy that is undergirded by capitalism and exacerbated by economic inequality. There is no "regressive culture." They've simply been robbed. (p. 52)

The history of Appalachia involves a complex interplay of different factors, beginning with the colonization of the US and displacement of native Americans from that region to capitalist extraction of mineral resources like coal and its environmental impacts. The mining industry is essentially a secondary form of colonization, with the seizure of resources and exploitation of workers being committed by citizens of the US rather than outside of the country (Catte, 2018). Isenberg (2018) traces the development of extraction industries and subsistence economies seen in West Virginia today and applies a more complex analysis which includes gender and race along with the impact of law. In 1891, Dillon's Rule was upheld by the Supreme Court which allowed those living in a community to be considered tenants who could be evicted at whim. All mine owners had to do was to bribe politicians to minimize resistance from communities.

Another legal tactic was to assign mineral rights to coal that lay below ground. The inevitable poverty that resulted made it easy for "fixers" to swoop in and seize land from those who couldn't pay their taxes. It was only a matter of time until mountain families who had subsisted off of the land were forced into coal mining camps and their exploitative system of company stores which kept them locked in. It should also be noted that more prosperous miners participated in the exploitation of poor newcomers (Isenberg, 2018).

Tourism is an additional aspect of rural white geographies. Shenk's (2017) inquiry into the historical shaping of rural identity within Wisconsin includes the politics of resentment and its development over time. This involves both a sense of rural identity, such as what it means to come from a small community alongside "distributive injustice" or "thinking that people in rural communities do not get their fair share of power, resources, or respect" (para. 5). Many rural Wisconsinites see the state as having only two geographic areas: (1) Milwaukee/Madison and (2) the rest of Wisconsin. This contributes to a lingering perception that rural areas pay more taxes to support the cities with affluent liberals and the minority populations they defend at the expense of authentic rural Americans (when urban revenue overwhelmingly goes to support rural areas). Because tourism is a major aspect of rural states like Wisconsin, the presence of more affluent outsiders in small towns only contributes to these perceptions, where "they see the construction of expensive vacation homes and watch as their property taxes go up" (para. 7).

A major challenge for white rural spaces is going to be their pressing through the accumulated history and racism in order to reject the capitalist messaging of resentment. Forsetti (2016) recounts his experiences growing up and living in a rural town for 24 years, including witnessing economic decline and infrastructure erosion. Yet people he grew up with never attributed these things to capitalism, but to liberals, immigration, welfare, and minorities. Refuting the misconception that rural Americans are another species, Forsetti points out that "the problem isn't that I don't understand these people. The problem is that they don't understand themselves, the reasons for their anger/frustrations, and don't seem to care to know why" (para. 2). Forsetti ties this resistance to dialectical understanding to a fundamentalist mindset and hostility toward those seen as outsiders. This is encapsulated in their notions of authenticity, self-reliance, and insistence on solving problems from within, often making them vulnerable to closed-loop messaging from Fox News, which reflects their existing assumptions.

DIVERSITY OF THE WORKING CLASS

One of the major challenges to building a strong, militant working class is the insistence that white industrial workers are a de-facto stand-in for all of labor, and that it is unnecessary or even divisive to address the working class as a diverse entity. The mass media has devoted endless resources to sustaining this "performance of authenticity" where those who occupy this specific segment of the working class receive attention way in excess of their actual numbers (Bouie, 2017). This "authentic worker" proposition is based on fundamentally flawed understandings of today's global working class, as Winant (2017) asserts:

> Whatever program will appeal to the entity known as the "white working class" will not appeal to "minority groups," who are joined together in this analysis with "moderate voters in the suburbs." ...The American working class is, after all, less white than the rest of American society, and, by all survey evidence, has more left-wing political views—by dint of its composition by race and gender, as well as its class experiences. (para. 8)

There are exclusionary aspects of framing class as the default white male worker, where "a small-town white American narrative is being treated as though it's about all of us or all of us who count" (Solnit, n.d., para. 8). Often, the working class of small towns are described as undergoing extreme changes, as if immigrants themselves or those who live in large cities have not also experienced massive upheavals under neoliberalism.

The working class today needs to be reconceptualized in terms of several factors including "feminization, racial diversification, and increasing precarity: care work, immigrant work, low-wage work, and the gig economy" (Winant, 2017, para. 12). Additionally, issues of police brutality and mass incarceration, rising housing costs, unavailable child care, lack of access to post-secondary education, and privatized health care hit specific segments of the working class especially hard. Unfortunately, assumptions that the authentic working class is white and male easily lead to authoritarian populist assumptions that "all of us who are not like them are menaces and intrusions who need to be cleared out of the way" (Solnit, n.d., para.6). A corollary to the authentic working class is the fetishization of the "middle class" that is often referred to in liberal discourse. This serves to further reduce the possibilities of organizing as a diverse working class (Myerson, 2017).

This section first presents some demographic considerations that decenter notions of the authentic working class away from white male industrial workers. Next, divisions that persist between traditional jobs and other sectors like retail and service are explored. Important reconfigurations of the US workforce such as gendered and racialized concentrations of labor are addressed. The section concludes with important implications for activism and the need to acknowledge a working class that is the largest and most vibrant it has ever been.

Demographics

A quick look at the demographics of the US working class illustrates the diversity of this group and further problematizes the authentic working-class meme. While the percentage of white non-Hispanics is likely to experience a 20% drop by 2050 (from 73%), other racial and ethnic group numbers will steadily rise (Bonilla-Silva, 2018, p. 156). Latinx and Asians alone are going to double their numbers less than 40 years from now (p. 156). The fastest growing segment of the working class are immigrants, making up 2/3 of the Service Employees International Union, also the most rapidly growing union of 1.8 million members (Chacon, 2017, p. 39). Even areas less friendly to unions, such as the South and Midwest, boast membership in the United Food and Commercial Workers Union, of which half of their 250,000 members are Latino immigrants (p. 39). This reflects the overall global trend of internationalizing labor, with over 230 million people migrating to other countries (p. 40). In the US alone, 42 million residents were born elsewhere (p. 40). To put population changes into perspective, the population of immigrants in New York City alone dwarfs the population total in Kansas or any other rural state (Solnit, n.d., para. 8).

This increasing diversity of the working class also translates into intensification of economic impacts particular to race and gender. For example, many working-class people are younger minorities who live and work in urban areas where finding affordable housing is difficult, especially if they have part-time or temporary work with few benefits (Jaffe, 2017). Additionally, despite women making up over four out of every ten wage earners in the US, they take home much lower wages, often working in sectors with the least protections (Windham, 2017, p. 10; Penny, 2011). Kelly (2002) notes that women's participation in waged labor continues to increase at the same moment as dramatic cuts in social services are happening, putting more of a burden on women to make ends meet while also handling domestic labor. This reveals a longstanding reliance on the unpaid labor of women as a form of reproduction under capitalism:

> These contradictions include the conflict between the need to develop the forces of production, including the paid labor of women, with the private reproduction of labor power, including fulfilling the functions once carried out by the welfare state; the conflict between women's childbearing capacity and the role as wage laborer; and the potential conflict between the tendency to remove tasks of domestic labor such as cooking, laundering, sewing, education and health care into the profit-making sector, thus drawing more women into the workforce. (p. 230)

Persistent Divisions

At the same time that women make up a majority of the population and just under half of the working class, they occupy the less prestigious jobs, regardless of level. Globally, less than 23% of legislative offices are held by women, with just over 18% as government ministers (Rothkopf, 2017, para. 8). As of January 2017, just 10 women were heads of state and 9 as head of government (para. 8). Across all job sectors, women hold fewer than one fifth of senior-level positions (para. 8). Despite women making up nearly half of the working class as well as a significant number of single heads of households, the perception remains that their wages are supplementary and not essential (Kelly, 2002).

This is a holdover from the earlier separation of the spheres for men and women during the onset of the industrial revolution in the late 1700s as capitalism solidified its cultural and social shifts from rural to urban centers of production (Penny, 2011). Women's work, particularly in the middle classes, was relegated to the unpaid domestic sphere, centered on reproduction of the workforce. Fewer women are financially able to exclusively provide unpaid labor within the home. Yet, this lingering gendered notion of labor has partly led to the workforce divide between what is considered authentic working class (male, industrial and mining sector workers) and the rest of labor that is seen as outside the prevue of labor policy, such as public employees, retail, and service industry work which often happen to be heavily feminized (Jaffe, 2017).

One of the challenges involved with tracking today's working class is that entities such as the Bureau of Labor Statistics (BLS) often perpetuate the divide between "traditional" and part-time or contingent work by minimizing the prevalence of the latter in order to "prioritize" the loss of factory jobs (Rasmus, 2018a). For example, gig work like Uber, Lyft, or AirBNB are not counted in BLS surveys. Temporary work is only counted if it is tied to a temp agency when employers often directly hire temps. BLS surveys are also administered in the spring, which leaves out holiday retail hires. Likewise, retail workers tend to get overlooked in employment discourse because of assumptions that these jobs are "unskilled" or a stepping stone on the way to more lucrative work (Jaffe, 2017). Terms like "service jobs" are also a misnomer because the rapid consolidation within the health care industry, for example, has transformed this sector into major value-producing concentrations of workers (Moody, 2018).

Geography also plays a role in associations of employment with race and gender. Retail, public sector, and service work tends to cluster within diverse large cities and suburban areas with the bulk of industrial and mining jobs located in rural and key swing voting areas, which are predominantly white (Bouie, 2017; Moody, 2018). Political factors such as the Electoral College and partisan gerrymandering add to the overall devaluation of the non-industrial workforce and reinforces notions of the authentic working class:

> Heavy manufacturing, industrial, and extraction work is overwhelmingly white and male. What's more, it's tied to a particular image of the standalone (and often unionized) worker who can provide for his family on one income. Americans have historically had an almost romantic attachment to the hard-hat worker, usually white, in a way that we don't to any other profession. (Bouie, 2017, para. 9)

Even the media hype around Trump's stunt of claiming to protect jobs at Indianapolis' Carrier plant overlooked the fact that women made up nearly half of its workforce (Jaffe, 2017, para. 7).

Reconfigurations

In terms of sheer numbers, less than 10% of Americans are employed in the manufacturing sector, with 150th of 1% working in coal mining (A. Nichols, 2017, para. 7). As Solnit (n.d.) points out, more people in the US are employed by museums than in the entire coal industry. By contrast, excluding farm work, 71% of the workforce are employed in the service sector, with nursing and caretaking the fastest growing segments (para. 7). These jobs are occupied in great numbers by minority females. Three fourths of those who teach in public schools are women, making public sector work another intersectional location that also happens to be unionized (Catte, 2018). Then there is the uncounted sector of reproductive labor in the US, performed by mostly women, who "should in theory be owed for their unpaid caring and domestic work [that] runs into some six times the national defense budget" (Penny, 2011, p. 50).

Retail work, a sector which accounts for half of consumer spending, comprises 10% of total employment in the US (Bouie, 2017, para. 2; Jaffe, 2017, para. 5). This work occurs in a variety of location scope and size from small businesses and malls to big box stores like Walmart, and an even wider range of goods. Retail labor is also highly gendered and racialized work, with a workforce that is 60% female and 40% of those are minorities (Bouie, 2017, para. 8). The median hourly wage for retail salespeople is less than $9.50 and 90% of cashiers make below $13.30 an hour (Jaffe, 2017, para. 14). Additional problems associated with the retail sector include high turnover, withheld wages, discrimination and few promotion opportunities. This is evidenced by women making up nearly 60% of supervisor positions, but only 18% of upper-management (Jaffe, 2017, para. 13).

Slaughter (2017) addresses the vulnerabilities that women and minorities face in retail and service industry work. The restaurant industry itself has the largest number of sexual harassment claims filed, with one out of every ten employees indicating they or a coworker have experienced harassment on the job (p. 11). Women who do agricultural labor are often at the mercy of crew bosses who hold their paychecks hostage as are women who work late at night in janitorial positions. Female hotel workers are often targeted for sexual harassment and assault by male guests who assume that "if there's a woman in the bedroom she must be available" (p. 11). The factors of isolation and immigration status only exacerbate these situations.

Moody's (2018) scholarship tracks the growth of the logistics center or warehouse as a major point of production, and increasingly resembling a factory. Rather than just storing products, warehouses involve e-commerce, transport and organization of goods, and custom assembly (Abrams & Gebeloff, 2017). Warehousing has also transformed local geographies into intermodal hubs where a mixture of blue- and white-collar workers commute from various locations within a wide radius. Moody (2018) sees this profound shift in production as a key opportunity for labor organizing since former factory workforces have been re-concentrated in the form of the logistics center:

What we're looking at today doesn't include all of what we think of as the working class of the 1930s or '40s or '50s. Yet it is a working class. It is employed by capital. It is subjected to the rule of capital at the workplace, and it has power. Yet these workers aren't unionized for the most part. (p. 55)

Customer fulfillment centers like Amazon are located in urban areas of 250,000 people or more and are considered part of the retail landscape. Following the pattern of decreased employment in rural areas, only 13% of e-commerce jobs are located in those places (Abrams & Gebeloff, 2017, para. 6).

Activism

Often the messaging around labor organizing is highly pessimistic, with a focus on declining membership, the growth of business unionism, and passage of right-to-work legislation (Moody, 2018). While having a sober assessment is important, it is also critical to acknowledge that the working class and job sectors are far more diverse than often presented, with unions themselves "vastly more diverse in race, gender, and occupation than the overwhelmingly male, anti-immigrant, and craft-oriented unions of the early 20th century" (Sustar, 2018, p. 28). This has revived the potential for widening class consciousness through labor, essential in order for the working class to move from forming a class "in itself" to becoming a class "for itself," as Winant (2017) outlines:

It was not prior to struggle, but through struggle, that the workers established that English society was organized along class lines, and that they, a class, were a real group who held things in common, not least their enemies. The existence of the working class was in this sense the product of the working-class movement, not the other way around. (para. 16)

It is important to understand that while identity politics have always been a part of social activism, things have dramatically changed in terms of said identities breaking away from the default settings of white and male. Walters (2017) explains how this has profoundly altered the conversation around activist movements, law and policy:

When we say "women's rights are human rights," we implode the assumption of an unmarked maleness that cannot be named. Further, today's identity politics—drawing from the collective self-making of both civil rights organizing and feminist consciousness-raising—insists on its own definitions and mores. As distinct from interest groups as *objects* to be targeted, the social movements formed in and through identity politics do not signify a cordoned-off minority to be addressed. Rather, they assert a fundamental challenge to both white male hegemony and the relentless process of marking and unmarking that has allowed "identity" to be only located in those who have been actively denied citizenship and subjectivity. (para. 7)

As part of the overall changing landscape of the working class and unions, we are seeing exciting and unexpected developments in rank-and-file organizing, including, more recently, a wave of teachers' strikes in red, right-to-work states that primarily went for Trump (Blanchard, 2018). This is starting to overturn a long-standing tradition of top-down business unionism that features a hierarchical structure that discourages participation and retains patriarchal privilege, both in terms of organization and discourse (Theweleit, 2010a). Women and minorities are also heading many of rank-and-file efforts such as the Women's March on Washington, Fight for Fifteen, National Domestic Workers Alliance and Restaurant Opportunity Centers (Windham, 2017). Currently, three of the biggest US unions have female presidents, with women projected to represent a majority of union membership in less than 5 years (p. 10). Windham sees a historical thread between working class feminist organizing in the 1970s, legal challenges to sexual harassment in the 1980s, and today's rank-and-file approach.

Intersectional organizing is another reflection of an increasingly diverse working class where "white women and racial minorities increasingly share similar class conditions in the workplace as well as social debasement" (Bonilla-Silva, 2018, p. 156). This is reflected in current movements like #MeToo, created and organized by black women with white allies, and the later #TimesUp. Union organizer Priscilla Murolo, in an interview with Piascik (2018) points out how grass-roots, intersectional movements for causes like a living wage, tenants' rights, healthcare, and the environment, have often translated into larger support for union struggles. Intersectionality can also be deployed in rapid fashion, as when Trump declared a travel ban for Muslims and protests immediately followed at airports with people from all walks of life joining in efforts to show support for victims of the ban (Chacon, 2017; Kellner, 2017).

Immigrants are often at the center of intersectional activism and as Bacon (2018) points out, "many immigrants bring organizing skills and working-class political consciousness with them, depending on where they come from" (p. 34). The example of the Justice for Janitors action in Los Angeles, where Central American immigrant janitors suffered police brutality but eventually secured a contract, illustrates the power of "workers on the bottom with not much to lose" (p. 34). Another example includes Alianza Nacional de Campesinas, an organization of 700,000 farmworker women in the US. After #TimesUp was created in reaction to Harvey Weinstein's decades-long sexual harassment in Hollywood, the farmworkers' association wrote a letter in support "expressing their sorrow and outrage over the horror stories, and sharing a few of their own from the fields" (Sen, 2018, para. 6). Several actresses, including America Ferrera, replied to the letter and created a legal defense fund.

One of the more remarkable instances of labor activism includes the recent wave of red state teachers' strikes, beginning in 2017, in reaction to deep and ongoing cuts impacting education and other sectors (Blanchard, 2018). The Facebook page West Virginia Public Employees United was key to building cross-county activism centered around issues like insurance costs. It is important to note that the Facebook page creators were teachers with a more radical orientation, including some who openly identify as socialists. The fact they were able to initiate momentum in a state with low union membership and strong right-to-work laws is remarkable, but also due to their understanding the importance of opening meetings and the Facebook group to "every public education worker regardless of what union they were in or whether they were even in a union or not" (p. 14).

Early rumblings of resistance began in 2018 with teachers in West Virginia organizing a "sick out" for one day, using their sick days in large groups and causing schools to close. Actions built on each other with community and parent support, culminating in a strike and large protests. In the end, teachers scored a major victory, not only a 5% raise and insurance increases, but stopping new charter schools. Blanchard (2018) recounts one of the highlights of the strike, when "Governor Jim Justice came out into the crowd and said, "We have a deal, y'all can go home now." The crowd responded by chanting, "We'll believe you when you put it in writing, we're not leaving till you sign it" (p. 15). The success of West Virginia soon spread to other locations, with over 30,000 public education employees gathering at the state capitol in North Carolina and one million students walking out, "making it possibly the single largest work stoppage in state history" (p. 21). Most importantly, what the teachers' strikes illustrated was that through participation in collective action centered on sound, intersectional politics, even Trump supporters started to gain class consciousness and began to reject right-wing populism.

Blanchard (2018) then turns her analysis to what went wrong with the Oklahoma teachers' strike, the most critical factor being unfamiliarity with rank-and-file organizing like town halls, or in-person mobilization. While Oklahoma teachers had massive support from parents and the community (72% indicated support for the strike) they were not able to translate this into anything as significant as in West Virginia, partly because some superintendents kept schools open during the strike (p. 17). The inability to draw on rank-and-file mobilization had immediate impacts:

> They felt their collective strength; but without a democratic union or bases of organization at the school and district level, they were unable to keep the walkout going after the Oklahoma Educational Association leadership struck a deal with the politicians based on promised funding, not real legislation. (p. 17)

Both the Oklahoma and Kentucky teachers' strikes were also hampered by not taking advantage of key intersectional moments that could have increased support and enhanced community connections. Blanchard (2018) provides the example of HB 169, or the *Youth Incarceration Bill*, passed during the strike planning. Kentucky teachers should have made the fight against youth incarceration a key part of their organizing platform but many viewed the issue as unconnected to school funding. This is part of an overall blind spot that remains within union organizing, which Blanchard targets in her summary of red state teacher activism:

A final common challenge in all the battles was how to confront not only the economic dimensions of the crisis in the schools, but also the social ones, especially the education system's institutional sexism and racism. In some cases, the economic and social were mistakenly counterposed, instead of combined. For the movement to go forward, teachers will have to develop an intersectional approach to the class struggle that recognizes the gender and racial dimensions of the education crisis and raises specific reforms to redress them. (p. 13)

Another example of potential problems that can emerge within activist groups is the gilets jaunes, or Yellow Vest protest movement in France. The movement originated with rural motorists protesting the rising cost of fuel, but soon grew into an undefined range of economic issues (Daguerre, 2019). While on the surface the movement emphasizes the right to protest, worker solidarity and equality, authoritarian populist elements have become more prominent, such as anti-immigrant sentiment, demonstrators carrying anti-Semitic signs that connect Macron with the Rothschild family and surrounding Alain Finkielkrat, a French intellectual, while yelling anti-Jewish insults in public (McAuley, 2019). The current nature of the movement seems to be universally anti-establishment and rejects political parties and leaders, but as history has shown as recently as 2016, this is usually ripe fodder for right wing elements to gain a foothold. Most disturbingly, those involved in the movement see any attempt to call out racism as part of a larger plot by the government to dismantle the movement (McCauley, 2019).

Widening our understanding of who constitutes the working class is essential. Beyond understanding demographics, this necessitates that we respect what the working class contributes to activism and to the wider world. In her extensive work with union organizing, Priscilla Murolo has found the diversity of the working class to be a major strength, especially since people engage with activism for different reasons:

Life has taught me that working people are multi-dimensional. They care about many things in addition to work and unions, and they bring multiple concerns and aspirations to any movement they get involved with. For some women, for example, getting active in a union can be a way of getting out from under the thumb of your husband as well as getting a fair shake at work. (Piascik, 2018, p. 24)

At the same time, "workers' struggles alone will not be sufficient to unite the working classes" (Daher, 2017, p. 109). In addition to addressing issues of class, activists, including in unions, have to openly support rights and protections for women, minorities and LGBTQ people. Hill, Sanders and Hankin (2002) echo this need to understand the diversity of the working class in order for the working class as a whole to develop class consciousness:

This form of class consciousness must recognize practically and theoretically the heterogeneous nature of the working class, as well as its common experience—of being in exploited wage labor. In particular, it must address the problematic relationship between class, gender, race, religion, sexuality, disability, and other aspects of subjectivity, and seek to build solidarity on the basis of respect and toleration for difference rather than for its obliteration. (p. 174)

CONCLUSION

The valorization of the white worker is *not* about recovering a lost voice. It comes *with* the exclusion of non-white, heterosexual, rural, Christian males. It isn't about "please recognize us," it's about "get the hell out of my country so we can be real Americans again." It would be one thing if these calls for the recognition of the white worker were about focusing on how capitalism harms working class whites, but *this* is not *that*. For leftists to continue to push the simplistic thinking behind "the forgotten white worker" is to assist in capitalism's use of racism and sexism to perpetuate itself, thereby making it all the more difficult to overcome. It is insulting to those dedicated to socialist organizing to insist on waving away racism and sexism as "divisive tools of the capitalist class" rather than digging deep into one's analysis to confront the historical construction of class through these means.

It is hoped that by deliberately decentering the white male industrial worker as this chapter does, we can create the space needed for an inclusive working class and alternatives to tired narratives that overlook how "the American dream is being used to rationalize a national nightmare" (Szalavitz, 2017, para. 3). To attempt to resurrect the American dream is to willfully ignore demographic reality, which is that white people make up an ever-decreasing part of the working class and no longer have the ability to bar women, minorities, and LGBTQI people when it comes to employment and education to the same degree as before. As Resnikoff (2017) asserts, "to stop "leaving behind" white workers would mean to reify America's caste system so they can regain those privileges. The white nationalists of the "alt-right" understand this and make it explicit. On the white left, it remains subtext" (para. 56).

From a materialist feminist viewpoint, because women—especially minority women—make up a significant portion of the working class, it is no coincidence they are the ones constantly called upon to be civil, to reach out, to nurture, and to forgive those who oppress them while hiding behind their mantra of being the forgotten-yet-authentic-working-class. As Solnit (n.d.) reminds us, "It is this population we are constantly asked to pay more attention to and forgive even when they hate us or seek to harm us" (para. 4). We see this in the media's consistent dismissal of the reactions of women who had enough sense to vote against Trump in favor of a vague populism (Solod, 2017). Mason's (2016) outrage is apt:

Those who tell you the left has to somehow "reconnect" with people whose minds are full of white supremacy and misogyny must finish the sentence, by what means? By throwing our black brothers and sisters under a bus? Eighty years ago, the poets and miners of the International Brigades did not march into battle saying: "Mind you, the fascists have got a point." (para. 17)

Rather than being an impediment to class consciousness, as center-left journalists assert, issues of identity are at the heart of economic policy and have been throughout history. Writers like Mark Lilla, who posit that identity is divisive are usually those who are most shielded by the impacts of identity and are able to make their assessments from a position of massive privilege (Young, 2016). If one examines major social movements in the US, they all involve aspects of identity integrated into solidarity, as Walters (2017) astutely points out:

> Let's be clear: most social change and political activism happens in and through identity politics—whether it is the righteous rage of Black Lives Matter, the fight for Indian autonomy and water rights at Standing Rock, the immigrant rights movement, or indeed the recent Women's March in DC and around the world…the truth is this: feminist organizing (and, yes, by women in the name of women) made this happen, brought millions together around the world in a collective roar of resistance to (among other things) patriarchal power, racism and xenophobia, homophobia, economic inequality. A women's march rallied the masses. Deal with it. (para. 15)

We can either recognize evolving forms of organizing and solidary or we can continue to insist on reviving exclusionary concepts such as color-blind class analysis. Whatever leftists choose to acknowledge or act upon, things are moving forward, and some are going to be left behind because of their unwillingness to share power (Solnit, n.d.). This means that workers' stories are not only going to be about white male workers, but about everyone (Thorton, 2016). The trajectory of the working class is happening in real time and it is not an artifact of the past. In the words of Priscilla Murolo,

> The labor movement may be down, but it's never down for the count. Every day for more than 400 years, working people have been devising new ways to defend themselves against indignity, depravation, and injustice. When one line of defense fails, another takes its place, and since collective strategies are invariably the most effective for the most people, the arc bends in that direction. (Piascik, 2018, p. 28)

CHAPTER 4

BERNIE BREAKDOWN

Challenges Facing the Left in the Wake of the Sanders Campaign

INTRODUCTION

On April 30, 2015, Senator and self-proclaimed Democratic socialist Bernie Sanders announced his candidacy for president, presenting, for a brief moment, a disruption of both the right-wing populism of Donald Trump and mainstream liberalism of Hillary Clinton. Part of the power of the Sanders campaign was the strategic decision of organizers to engage with the electoral system *within* the Democratic Party, instead of the traditional insurgent third-party route. As Trudell (2016) described, Sanders was unique in his bringing democratic socialist ideas that had long been marginalized since the post-Great Depression era and making them part of mainstream political demands. While there remains debate on the left of the utility or futility of working within the Democratic Party (Crane, 2018; Selfa, 2008) or if democratic socialism is radical enough or not, millions of people who were previously disengaged from socialist ideas or electoral participation began to more vocally support concepts like national health care, free college tuition, and a living wage.

It is important to situate Sanders' campaign against the larger backdrop of growing activism since the 2008 financial crisis and what it represented: "the concentration of wealth in the hands of a tiny number of billionaires, the increasing class polarization of US society and the rapacious destruction of people's lives and environments" (Trudell, 2016, para. 5). Movements such as Occupy Wall Street, and later mass mobilizations for immigrant rights, Black Lives Matter, and labor actions created conditions ripe for alternative possibilities. For Rehmann (2016), "the so-called political middle has been shrinking considerably. It has lost hegemonic traction" (p. 4). This also creates tensions within the left on how to most effectively organize— via structured political parties or through more anarchist forms (Lynd & Grubacic, 2008).

A second important background against which the 2016 presidential election took place was a further entrenchment of white supremacist and aggressive right-wing populism within the Republican Party itself. Building on the success of the corporate-funded Tea Party movement, Trump pushed conservative rhetoric farther to the right, essentially dismantling the already shaky ideological structures the Republicans have continually used to sustain the false consciousness of their voting base. Any of the prior lines of thinking such as free market economics, family values, personal responsibility, law and order, and patriotism have been torn to shreds by the conduct of Trump and his associates, including evangelical voters who have made it clear there is nothing Trump can do that would erode their support (Burton, 2018b). It is apparent by now that not only are Republicans incapable of controlling Trump and his base, they simply have no desire to do so (Trudell, 2016).

The third critical aspect that must be considered when examining the Sanders' campaign is the role of social media and analytics in elections, as Chadwick & Stromer-Galley (2016) outline:

> By the analytics turn we mean the increased use by campaign elites of experimental data science methods to interrogate large-scale aggregations of behavioral information from public voter records and digital media environments, with the aim of organizing and mobilizing key segments of the electorate to vote and to publicly and privately share their decision with others. Still in its early stages, the analytics turn is currently most advanced in the United States. (p. 2)

One could argue that Russia was ahead of this analytic turn with their skilled deployment of targeted bots and fake profiles in key swing states, as is just starting to come to light. In of many examples, Facebook's economic model is based on the use of hyper-tailored, targeted advertising, which explains much in the way of their reluctance to address the problem of monitoring post content (Halpern, 2019).

So, while Trump may represent a disruption of "business as usual" for his supporters, his presidency has not produced any viable solutions other than further concentrating wealth into the hands of a few. Rehmann (2016) views the Trump presidency as representative of a hegemonic crisis, where prior ideologies are no longer sufficient to keep the working and middle classes under control. Citing Gramsci's (1971) "the old is dying and the new cannot be born" (p. 556), Rehmann (2016) notes that the ruling class can only serve as placeholders to citizens who are experiencing a paralyzing form of skepticism. The problem is that contrary to the beliefs of some on the left, economic crisis alone does not ensure change, but only sets up a situation where different paths could be taken, including fascism or socialism:

> What we face, rather, is an interregnum, an open and unstable situation in which hearts and minds are up for grabs. In this situation, there is not only danger but also opportunity: the chance to build a new left. (Fraser, 2017, para.10)

This chapter is organized into four sections that examine lessons learned from the Sanders' campaign and how it presents an opportunity for a socialist feminist analysis of leftist organizing as a whole during our current hegemonic crisis. After an overview of key aspects of the Sanders' campaign, the sections to be discussed include stridency without substance, party problems, dualistic thinking, and colorblind class analysis.

THE SANDERS CAMPAIGN: LESSONS LEARNED

One of the more remarkable aspects of Sanders' insurgent run for president was his success compared to past attempts by higher profile progressive Democrats or third-party candidates such as Dennis Kucinich, Ralph Nader, or Jesse Jackson. As Gallagher (2016) points out, Eugene V. Debs was the last candidate from an existing leftist political party to reach 6% of the national vote in 1912 (para. 22). Awareness of this history was also a likely factor compelling Sanders to run as a Democrat versus the usual failed third-party route. Trudell (2016) expressed the mixture of trepidation and support on the left at the time:

> On the one hand...his candidature therefore risks trapping the aspirations of the social movements within the Democratic Party machine, and the party has a long history of co-opting the energy and hopes of social movements...On the other hand, however, at this stage Sanders' campaign, precisely because it is taking place within the Democratic Party, is bringing the external crisis home to the institution and exposing the rifts and weaknesses in the Democrats' electoral base. (para. 6)

Sanders' run also reflected a major shift in the population's political attitudes, stemming from the 2008 financial crisis and the Occupy movement. His platform included universal health care, free college tuition, regulating Wall Street and progressive taxation, which put in firmly in the category of outsider (Kellner, 2017; Warner et al., 2017). His candidacy captured not only the discontent of leftist voters, but 86% of Democrats and 61% of independents who agreed that "money and wealth should be distributed among a larger percentage of the people" (Gallagher, 2016, para. 8). Those who were already inclined to vote for an openly socialist candidate included nearly 60% of Democrats and 70% under age 30 (Gallagher, 2016, para. 18; Myerson, p. 27). In Iowa, for example, 43% of likely Democratic caucus voters described themselves as socialist along with 39% of Democrats in South Carolina (Myerson, 2016, p. 30). The notion that leftist ideas appealed to just Marxists was out the window.

A hallmark of Sanders' campaign was his activation of younger voters, including those not previously attracted to politics. He was the only presidential candidate to have a net positive rating among younger voters hovering at around 54% (Meyerson, 2016, p. 30). As an example of the duality of age and support, Sanders attracted 71% of voters under 30 (including young black voters), while Clinton captured the same percentage with those over 64 (p. 27). In Michigan's primary, Sanders gained an unimaginable 81% of the under-30 vote, leading to his unexpected win (Trudell, 2016, para. 3). Primary wins like this only increased the funding momentum and dispelled myths that people would never accept a socialist presidential candidate beyond the state of Vermont:

> The fact that Bernie Sanders actually told people what he really thought, specifically that he called himself a socialist, was long considered a

limiting factor in his career. Yet it was clearly the widespread perception of his genuineness that thrust him to the fore in the presidential race…if you wondered why Bernie Sanders was saying the things he said on the campaign trail, there was a simple answer: It was because he believed them to be true, and had in most cases believed them to be true for some time…Likewise, the no-frippery, let's-get-to-the-issues style that might border on the gruff also seemed to work surprisingly well in the presidential arena this time around. (Gallagher, 2016, para. 12)

Meyerson (2016) also notes how Sanders' base of support was different from past progressive Democratic presidential candidates like Howard Dean or Eugene McCarthy who appealed to a more upper-class white liberal voter. Sanders' no-nonsense discourse could appeal to both younger voters and older, blue collar ones.

Another major factor leading to Sanders' success was his ability to mobilize social media organizing from the ground up, far exceeding Obama's 2008 ground game. Within a matter of days, supporters created state-level Facebook pages, Twitter accounts and sub-Reddits, encouraging friends to join both online and in-person events. Spending more money on online organizing than other candidates, Sanders relied on the expertise of groups such as Revolution Messaging who had prior experience working with Obama's 2008 campaign, combining the role of digital and finance management director (Chadwick & Stromer-Galley, 2016). Sanders' popularity was represented by his incredible fundraising abilities, breaking prior Democratic Party numbers (including Obama's) from a large swath of individual, small-donation contributors whose average donation was $27.00, many contributing as little as one dollar (Chadwick & Stromer-Galley, 2016, para. 1; Trudell, 2016, para. 3).

This momentum and organizing helped propel Sanders to primary victories in nine states, including more conservative ones like Oklahoma and Nebraska (Trudell, 2016). Rallies drew incredible crowds—including 25,000 in Boston which exceeded Obama's primary rally attendance of 10,000—as well as small towns where 25–33% of their populations attended meetings (para. 10). Rehmann (2016) captures this sense of potential:

In this regard, the Sanders campaign's achievements were extraordinary. It expressed and articulated what I just characterized as the second layer of people's common sense, the moral outrage against an economic system that produces an increasing income and wealth polarity between the 1% and the 99%. This is the message that Sanders was hammering home to his audience, regardless of the concrete questions he was asked by the anchors and journalists of the corporate media. And by doing so, he was actually attacking neoliberal capitalism at the "weakest link in the imperialist chain," to use a famous expression of Lenin in a different context. (p. 7)

It is also important to point out that contrary to media efforts to draw a simplistic parallel between Sanders and Trump, Sanders utilized a positive, progressive populism versus Trump's appeal to racism, sexism, and nationalism (Kellner, 2017).

In the end, however, Hillary Clinton secured the Democratic nomination and eventually won 48.5% of the popular vote in the general election, the Electoral College rendering this total irrelevant for the second time in 16 years. It is worth investigating why, when presented with a more progressive vision of populism that Sanders represented, "only Trump's reactionary populism survived" (Fraser, 2017, para. 8). The Sanders' campaign presents us with an opportunity to critically examine the mobilization of his supporters, and some of the weaknesses they reveal within leftist organizing as a whole. These include 1) stridency without substance within leftist groups; 2) rejection of party structures; 3) the narrowness of dualistic thinking and 4) colorblind class analysis. Each of these will be examined in turn.

Stridency without Substance

Social media is now an integral part of leftist organizing and the interactive platforms that Facebook and Twitter provide have magnified the intensity of discourse and distribution within leftist spaces. A particular form of this discourse can best be labeled "stridency without substance," referring to the overall aggressive and unyielding tone that talks big but ultimately offers nothing to people interested in building a socialist future. Stridency without substance sums up a left that immediately and defensively derides anything hinting at incrementalism or mainstream popularity while valorizing hyper-masculinized authoritarian figures such as Joseph Stalin.

Priding themselves on "never settling," they ignore the realities of our current political system and offer nothing to address the concerns of those most vulnerable in society other than promising the glorious instability and excitement of revolution as the solution to everything, as if things would magically fall into place if the current system were suddenly dismantled. Rehmann (2016) characterizes it as, "a hyper-revolutionary but also empty discourse without any consideration of the hegemonic constellations on the ground and the subjects that are supposed to carry through the proclaimed revolution" (pp. 5–6).

The first characteristic of this discourse is its domineering and patronizing tone— often gendered—as Morris (2010) recounts looking back on past email exchanges:

> I am shocked at the number of e-mails from men I organized with that were abusive in tone and content, how easily they would talk down to others for minor mistakes. I am more surprised at my meek, diplomatic responses—like an abuse survivor—as I attempted to placate compañeros who saw nothing wrong with yelling at their partners, friends, and other organizers. There were men like this in various organizations I worked with. (para. 14)

Morris connects her experiences to those of famous leftist women such as Angela Davis and Roxanne Dunbar who also put up with harassment and abuse from high-profile men in their groups.

A quick perusal of the comments sections of Marxist and socialist Facebook pages such as Grouchy Socialists or Marxist Memes yields endless examples of defensive attacking language even when legitimate questions are posed about aspects of socialism. This same kind of posting discourse was rampant on Bernie Sanders' social media outlets. While one can argue that aggressive discourse is a feature of social media overall (see: Rösner & Krämer, 2016; Daniels, 2009), the fact that it is occurring in so-called leftist spaces is especially ironic. West (2017) speculates that the attraction of the online "dirtbag left" persona offers psychological benefits to its adherents, even as it alienates others genuinely interested in Marxist and socialist alternatives:

> You can be good without ever seeming uncool in front of your buddies, you can be an advocate for social justice without ever considering there might be social forces beyond your ken, you can be a crusader for positive change without ever killing anyone's buzz, you can be a progressive hero without ever taking identity politics seriously. It's an ambitious contortion, and one that affords straight white men a luxurious degree of stasis. (para. 13)

Part of the defensiveness of this discourse has to do with two closely held and massively contradictory beliefs within these groups: 1) we need to build a mass movement in order for socialism to become a reality and 2) we can't ever be mainstream or "normie." Arnove (2018) points out how Marx was adamant that socialism required "an immense majority" acting in the majority's interest in order to overcome capitalism: "those self-identified Marxists who had built, or those who continue to build, sects, cults of personality, and even gulags in the name of Karl Marx, don't understand the first thing about Marxists" (p. 83). Indeed, if earlier movements had avoided becoming mainstream, things like the 8-hour workday, voting rights, reproductive rights, and public health regulations would never have existed (Sen, 2018).

A second feature of stridency without substance connected to the idea of not going mainstream is "never settling." Never settling means compiling endless lists of reasons why a particular leftist approach, policy, or candidate for office doesn't go far enough and discussion is therefore shut down, usually by demeaning the person who shared the information (Leonard, 2017). This practice severely limits the range of options for building social movements, prompting Weida (2017) to observe, "whichever Conservative coined "not going to settle" deserves the prize of hamstringing the left" (para. 31). As one example, Democratic Representative and Civil Rights Movement participant John Lewis was attacked on social media for being a sell-out for not remembering Bernie Sanders being part of a crowd of 250,000 at the March on Washington back in 1963 (Leonard, 2017).

In discussing the upcoming presidential election in 2020, McEwan (2017b) notes how Kamala Harris and Elizabeth Warren were originally put forward "to routinely make the lists of Women We'd Vote for Who Aren't Hillary Clinton to Prove We're Not Misogynists" but who are now currently branded as "insufficiently progressive" (para. 2). Even Sanders himself was critiqued for not being leftist enough, despite his distinctive policy views compared to more centrist candidates (Rehmann, 2016). When proposed policies such as work requirements for Medicaid are routinely floated by Republicans as legitimate solutions, to immediately dismiss Sanders as *only* a progressive Democrat seem pretty shortsighted.

The third characteristic of stridency without substance is the insistence that revolution by itself will be the catalyst to lasting change, or that things have to get really bad before people will be moved to act. Wolcott (2017) levels a devastating reminder about the limits of this line of thinking:

> The left's romance with revolution has always been a reality-blinder, this thermodynamic belief that things need to get bad beyond the breaking point so that people will take the vape pens out of their mouths, rise up, and storm the Bastille. But the history of non-democracies and authoritarian personality cults shows that things can stay bad and get worse for a long time, leaving unhealable wounds. (para. 4)

One of the most disturbing aspects of the revolution at all costs way of thinking is the total dismissal of the most vulnerable in society, such as the poor, those with different abilities, older people, minorities, and children who do not have the resources to withstand backlash from authoritarian and right-wing regimes should moves toward revolution be made (McEwan, 2017b). When called out on their cynicism, or challenged for their vocal refusal to participate in mainstream politics by voting against the most lethal candidates, they "wash their hands of their complicity and say, 'don't blame me, I voted for (fringe minor party candidate),'" followed by a hefty helping of complaining about how messed up the world is and how people are too complacent (Leonard, 2017, para. 11).

Exchanges, whether on social media or in person, become a matter of competing and one-upping to see who has the most radial rhetoric (Rehmann, 2016). Lost in the contest is any kind of deep examination of the privileges involved in making these kinds of recommendations, as McEwan (2017b) outlines:

> Marginalized people, especially those who live in states with legislatures governed by a Republican majority, are thrown into constant chaos by abortion restrictions, "religious liberty" bills, "trans bathroom" bills, housing and employment discrimination, voter disenfranchisement, and all the other political tug-of-war we are obliged to navigate, in addition to social oppression and a ceaseless onslaught of microaggressions that can leave us reeling. (paras. 20–21)

These kinds of concerns are misread by some on the left as marginalized voters being overly dependent on the Democratic Party, in thrall to bourgeois thinking, settling for less, or not wanting change instead of viewing them as legitimate concerns and potential areas to build socialist coalitions around. The political situation in many parts of the US are such that, "the Democratic Party—the establishment—is the only well-funded institution prepared to hold the line against conservative oppression" (para. 29). While there is much analysis of Hillary Clinton's failures by leftist outlets, perhaps a similar type of analysis should be done of Sanders and his inability to instill confidence in minority voters to support him, in light of this situation (Starr, 2017). It should go without saying that if a basic set of democratic socialist policies fail to gain support, revolutionary politics *won't*, at least the way they are currently presented.

Ultimately, stridency without substance represents a nihilistic form of purity, an "everything is corrupt" cynicism that works against the very changes its proponents advocate:

> [the belief that] there is no usefulness in trying to change or reform existing systems, leaves very little—if any—room for good people to make mistakes in judgement, ruthlessly purges people for being imperfect, and mandates that the current society must be completely burned down and destroyed by a massive revolt of the people to allow the ideologically pure to gain control and build a utopia for all to prosper. Hence the term nihilistic purity. (Leonard, 2017, para. 13)

Whenever a significant form of protest occurs, as with Black Lives Matter or #MeToo, instead of looking to build on those actions, they are accused of being "symbolic" and not "real change" (Sen, 2018, para. 9). But as Sen points out, symbols can be a start and if the left cannot work from them, momentum has no hope of occurring.

Party Problems

The contentious relationship with traditional US political parties operating within a very entrenched two-party system has created a problem for the left in terms of how to build a workers' party and what to do in the interim of developing the type of mass support needed to compete electorally, versus simply serving as an unintentional assistant to either the Democrats or Republicans winning every two to four years. For the left, current options include not voting, voting for Democratic candidates, or voting for third party or write-in candidates, all of which have their respective negatives. Another core issue to confront is the rejection of the notion of organizing by party itself, most recently expressed within the Occupy Wall Street movement that began after the 2008 economic collapse. Since the Sanders campaign emerged to a great degree from Occupy (Gallagher, 2016), it is important to examine the problematics associated with party organizing and hostility toward party structures among the left.

Before examining party problematics, it is critical to address two interrelated features of contemporary approaches to participation within parties. The first is the impact of social media in terms of how people engage with parties:

> In some cases, parties are renewing themselves from the outside in. Citizens are breathing new life into the party form, remaking parties in their own changed participatory image, and doing so via digital means. The overall outcome might prove more positive for democratic engagement and the decentralization of political power than has often been assumed. (Chadwick & Stromer-Galley, 2016, p. 4)

Certainly, one could argue that the recent campaign and victory of 29-year-old Representative Alexandria Ocascio-Cortez has served this purpose. Her ability to maneuver social media has reached younger voters and others not previously engaged with the Democratic Party (Wagner, 2019). It has now become increasingly possible for more insurgent candidates to run and win within party structures precisely because of these changes in the landscape of campaigning (Warner et al., 2017).

The second feature is the tendency of people to frame parties as another aspect of personalized choice within the capitalist market as a form of expression and authenticity: "This party-as-movement mentality can easily accommodate populist appeals and angry protest—on both the right and the left" (Chadwick & Stromer-Galley, 2016, p. 8). Both of these features interact to impact each other—the more that people view parties as authentic means of expressing what's in their hearts and minds, the more that parties begin to market themselves to niche groups of voters. This can lead to the idea that voting represents one's identity and values, rather than a distinct set of political platforms that may or may not directly impact you as much as other people. Voting becomes viewed as a matter of personal choice or endorsement, not contributing to larger consequences, such as rejecting a candidate because they aren't leftist enough on an issue when the candidate might support things like health care or education far better than a right wing one. The phrase "vote your conscience" reflects this type of thinking.

At the same time, political parties have had to contend with a wave of participation of people formerly uninvolved with the political process. As Brenner and Fraser (2017) point out, populism has become a global phenomenon which has shaped the demands people are placing on political parties:

> Although they differ in ideology and goals, these electoral mutinies share a common target: all are rejections of corporate globalization, neoliberalism, and the political establishments that have promoted them. In every case, voters are saying "No!" to the lethal combination of austerity, free trade, predatory debt, and precarious, ill-paid work that characterize financialized capitalism today. (p. 130)

Many of those participating in the 2016 primaries were not familiar with the function of political parties and quickly became impatient with their formal procedures

(Rehmann, 2016). Within the right wing, much of this anger had already been carefully propelled into a corporate-funded Tea Party movement, which led directly to Trump's primary win. A key difference in outcome was that the Republican Party was more adept at rapidly accommodating itself to right-wing populism as compared to the Democratic Party being shaped by more leftist candidates, though considerable progress has been made within the House of Representatives after the 2018 midterm elections.

Within the midst of these dramatic changes comes the temptation to view the primary process as diametrically opposed to street action, as if the two operate separately and at counter purposes (Brennan & Fraser, 2017). Certainly, the Democrats have a long history of derailing social movements (Selfa, 2012) but at the same time they have been shown to respond to pressure from social movements. Rehmann (2016) reminds us that "the fundamental question for any serious transformation of the system is how to effectively connect social movements to the struggles within the institutions of civil society, including the domain of political representation" (p. 6). Yet a key problem is that people who become involved with candidates through rallies or even caucus nominating systems tend to be those with the most available means, time, or motivation to participate. Warner et al. (2017) note that one tenth of those surveyed nationally had attended a rally or speech with only six percent having ever gone to an organized protest (p. 6). This can often create a vulnerability where those participating in the political process are the most partisan and less likely to shape policies for optimal movement building, including having patience with political parties.

Ansara's (2016) essay on the eve of the 2016 election offers a poignant perspective regarding political participation as he recalls an important choice that he and his friends made in 1968. At that time, he had decided to sit out the election, because he thought that both Humphrey and Nixon would continue the war in Vietnam and that there was no difference between the two. He asserts that this cynical decision was made at a time when he and his colleagues had never experienced what right wing governments in the United States could do and were operating within a system where the worst it had been was well within the spectrum of centrist liberal policies.

Not anticipating what could happen and how much worse it could get represented for him a "great failure of the political and moral imagination" (Ansara, 2016, p. 24). He reflected that while their framing of Humphrey as a centrist democrat might have been correct, "our failure was not in our assessment of Humphrey but in our failure to understand Nixon and what was at stake" (p. 24). The consequences of Nixon winning went far beyond the 1968 election:

> Our refusal to participate started a process of making our movement profoundly irrelevant. We allowed Richard Nixon to come to power. We allowed a right-wing counter-reformation to hold power and warp American politics for most of the next four decades. Within our movement, we allowed militancy to replace strategy. (p. 24)

Dualistic Thinking

The United States has a firmly entrenched and overarching two-party system that shows no sign of stopping (Feist, 2019; Selfa, 2012). This is a major contributor to leftists making the decision to vote for the Democratic candidate often by default, in order to prevent the Republican candidate from winning. Even in cases where a third party provides a platform more in line with leftist policies, that candidate has no hopes of winning, their greatest impact usually ending up splitting the vote and enabling the Republican to win. Not voting will accomplish the same thing and has shown no signs of budging political party platforms. Indeed, instead of operating as a means to apply pressure, lower turnout continually favors Republicans (McElwee & McAuliffe, 2018). Nevertheless, many on the left minimize or refuse to acknowledge this reality, citing the flaws of "lesser of two evil voting" (see: Bachtell, 2017; Crane, 2018; Sanders, 2018).

This refusal to address the two-party dilemma other than the repeated and nebulous suggestion of building a workers' party and not voting until that happens has led to a form of dualistic thinking within leftist communities that a candidate is *either* socialist or fascist/neoliberal. Related to this is the practice of detailed critiques of Democratic candidates for not adhering to a specific list of characteristics deemed "leftist enough" (the social media term is *purity trolling*) and somehow never finding a viable candidate to support. Nagel (2017) provides a compelling analysis of the role of social media in supporting the rise of purity discourse on the left. Notions of prioritizing adherence to a specific identity and branding that become amplified on social media have hit a crisis point now that social media participation has become more ubiquitous with a wider range of demographic groups:

> The value of the currency of virtue that those who had made their social media cultural capital was in danger of being suddenly devalued. As a result, I believe, a culture of purging had to take place, largely targeting those in competition for this precious currency. Thus, the attacks increasingly focused on other liberals and leftists often with seemingly pristine progressive credentials, instead of those who engaged in any actual racism, sexism, or homophobia. (p. 77)

Discourse emerging within Sanders' social media groups often took on the tone of "leftist" being defined in exclusionary terms: if you didn't support Sanders, you weren't a leftist (McEwan, 2017b). Another problematic aspect of dualist thinking is the notion that liberals are automatically on the side of fascism and must be opposed to the same degree as one would fascists. This can lead to a ready acceptance of oppressive regimes or groups because they might be opposed to US imperialism or assuming solidarity with Trump supporters because they misread them as allies in the fight against global capitalism. These issues are addressed in the two sections below, "Not Leftist Enough" and Misplaced Solidarity

"Not leftist enough." A key aspect of socialist solidarity is advancing a distinct and clearly articulated platform, such as the one stated by the Freedom Socialist Party, a socialist feminist organization. This platform includes universal human rights, reproductive freedom, environmental protection, and health care within the framework of seeking to abolish capitalism (Freedom Socialist Party Platform, n.d.). Part of establishing clarity and solidarity around this type of platform involves decisions about which political candidates to support or reject, based on that platform. Yet Roediger (2017) examines problematic aspects of an uncritical notion of solidarity on the left that can lead to "impossible expectations leaving us coming up forever short of an unexamined ideal" (p. 161).

One unfortunate outcome of dualist thinking is overlooking the possible alliances that could be made with liberals, who are often relegated to the "not leftist" category, or as McEwan (2017b) states, "you're either a supporter of "big money elites," or you're a "Sanders Democrat" and thus a leftist" (para. 9). This viewpoint is highly short-sighted and overly simplistic. For example, just over half of Hillary Clinton supporters reported a favorable view of socialism, indicating that "the Sanders campaign didn't create a new American left so much as revel it" (Meyerson, 2016, p. 30).

Indeed, Quam and Ryshina-Pankova's (2016) analysis concluded that the linguistic strategies utilized by Clinton and Sanders in political speeches had more in common than either one did with Trump's speeches. Rather than being a new political development, Meyerson (2016) notes how the Sanders campaign is an indication of how the Democratic Party has been slowing its rightward momentum compared to the past couple of decades. Hillary Clinton herself advanced ideas such as subsidized child care, increased critiques of NAFTA and the Trans-Pacific Partnership, supported raising the minimum wage and expanding Social Security and workers' rights.

While critique of any candidate is important and should be encouraged on the left, there seems to be an uncritical either/or thinking, evidenced by the typical rundown on blogs and social media of how a Democratic candidate fails to be leftist enough:

> Since she "lost" to Donald Trump, the most die-hard Sandernistas have developed a complete loathing of anyone who represents the "Democratic establishment" like Corey Booker and Kristen Gillibrand. With yesterday's hit piece in *Mic*, we're now seeing it happen to the Democrats' brightest rising star, California Senator Kamala Harris. (Fassler, 2017, para. 1)

The recent attacks from the left on Elizabeth Warren are one example, legitimizing the right-wing fixation about her offering DNA testing evidence to establish Native American heritage (Ward, 2018). Beto O'Rourke received the usual *Common Dreams* purity treatment, as if leftists should be somehow shocked that he has the same centrist tendencies as just about any other liberal politician currently serving in a capitalist government (Solomon, 2018). Based on the discourse of social media coverage, some leftists appear to have somehow missed the fact that we live in a capitalist society where the political institutions are going to reflect that reality.

McEwan (2017b) notes how a special sort of scrutiny seems to be reserved for female and minority candidates, contradicting the notion that the opposition is solely because of their neoliberalism. During the election, it often became difficult to distinguish between the anti-Clinton rhetoric on pro-Sanders and pro-Trump pages, reflecting a decades-long anti-Clinton messaging machine (Kellner, 2017; Weida, 2017). This was against the backdrop of Trump already receiving an unprecedented amount of attention from the media with few hard questions asked about things like his racist language or fraudulent business practices while maintaining a rolling, super-detailed critique of Clinton's actions, real and imagined. Kellner (2017) outlines how

> for weeks Trump had been droning on about Clinton's "criminal scheme" and "criminal conduct," which was given substance by Comey's letter, a barrage of rumors by Giuliani and the trump campaign that criminal indictments were going to be levelled against Clinton. (p. 31)

Sanders supporters inadvertently strengthened these right-wing tactics by spreading the same narrative and conspiracy theories, albeit utilizing leftist terminology. It became more about being anti-Clinton than pro-Sanders.

Though Sanders received far less media coverage than Trump or Clinton, Quam and Ryshina-Pankova (2016) point out how Sanders' masculinist rhetoric and style of speaking assisted with his relatively positive media treatment despite his openly democratic socialist platform. In some ways, this has contributed to the persistent yet naive notion that Sanders could have beaten Trump, since the press was favorable to him during the primaries. A quick review of the Swiftboat Veterans for Truth attack on 2006 Democratic candidate John Kerry provides an important lesson in how the right wing will select the most dominant attribute of a candidate (in that case, Kerry's military record) to target (Rosenbaum, 2017). It is foolish to think that the right wing wouldn't have launched an immediate barrage against socialism had Sanders won the primary.

Weida's (2017) critique of Sanders supporters adds an important perspective for default dualistic thinking on the left. A common misconception Weida addresses is that Clinton was a default "lesser of two evils" choice for voters, when many women and minorities adopted her as their candidate precisely because of her perceived record supporting policies like child care, workplace discrimination and reproductive rights. Related to this is the notion is the Clinton supporters were misinformed, "thinking with their ovaries" or didn't know any better because they didn't back Sanders in the primaries. Weida quotes black females who voted for Clinton in both the primaries and the general election, who were turned off by Sanders and his male supporters:

> I feel like it [criticism of her support of Clinton] is extremely unfair and that he is a divisive figure on the left. He used us and his fans have harassed, stalked,

and doxed me. Bernie allows this. An old white man who ignores the identity of anyone not white and male is not the future. (para. 28)

While some on the left might immediately respond by citing several examples of Clinton's centrism, it is critical for them to also reflect on why "the only "Bern" Clinton voters have felt is the one that comes from being harassed online by an army of Bernie bros they say are infected with rabid conspiracy theories" (para. 26). Maybe instead of sympathetically listening to Trump supporters, we should consider extending the same courtesy to liberals.

Misplaced solidarity. Rehmann (2017) presents three possible outcomes of the current crisis of neoliberalism and how these outcomes are adopted into popular thought. One possibility is to turn toward right-wing populism, authoritarianism and scapegoating of minority groups, immigrants, and the public sector. A second option is a growing awareness of economic and social inequality, even by formerly centrist people, with blame placed on the financial sector and the wealthy. The third potential outcome is a movement toward a rejection of capitalism itself, viewing it as ultimately unsustainable and a barrier to meaningful change. For Rehmann, the third option "still remains mostly latent, blocked from consciousness by fear of being ostracized as radical lunacy, and by the lack of an appealing democratic-socialist alternative" (p. 5). This essentially leaves the first two options of commonsense thinking as immediate challenges, and leftists are deluding themselves if they think they can somehow work within the first option of trying to connect with oppressive regimes or reactionary groups.

In the absence of a strong, organized left, it is easy for right-wing options to present themselves under the veneer of liberatory possibilities. A. Smith (2017) provides the example of those on the left who support Putin and Assad because they supposedly serve as checks on US imperialism, justifying this "reactionary position with the preposterous claim that Putin's Russia and Assad's brutal dictatorship are an anti-imperialist alliance standing up to Washington's alleged policy of regime change in Syria" (p. 57). Associated with this stance is the ready acceptance of unsubstantiated conspiracies, such as the 9/11 Truther movement or the deep state, conspiracies heavily promoted by the right wing. (DiMaggio, 2017). Pomerantsev and Weiss (2014) explain further, presenting the role of *RT America*, a pay TV channel designed to carry a pro-Putin message:

> I see how parts of the left are pulled into watching the American RT because it confirms their view of the world that the reality around them is rigged. RT doesn't try to introduce a new vision; it's enough to sow doubt and eat away at the fabric of a reality-based conversation...While RT helps feed the American left, religious conservatives are seduced by Putin's anti-LGBT stance and libertarians like Rand Paul by the idea of a common enemy—the US government. A further level of pressure is added by business lobbies who oppose sanctions against the Kremlin. (Pomerantsev & Weiss, 2014, p. 28)

Draitser (2017) notes how this is part of a larger rightist strategy of making inroads into the left and connecting it to the far right, creating a curious outcome where progressives will insist on detailed evidence regarding what the US media reports, while taking at face value what Russian media says. Dennis Kucinich, a former progressive Democratic candidate for president, congratulated Trump after he was inaugurated and regularly promotes deep state conspiracies as in one Tweet where he asserted, "#WakeUpAmerica, enough of the BS re #Russia stealing election =CIA& State Dept propaganda to legitimize hostilities" (Wolcott, 2017, para. 6).

The creation of left-right alliances also applies to Brexit, where "European right-nationalists are seduced by the anti-EU message; members of the far-left are brought in by tales of fighting US hegemony" (Pomerantsev & Weiss, 2014, p. 19). Other examples of the left-right alliance include George Galloway's support of Saddam Hussein, and Russia's funding of anti-fracking groups which appeals to leftists but is done to keep Europe financially connected to Russian energy supply lines (Pomerantsev & Weiss, 2014). It is also interesting to note how most of the opposition to US imperialism seems to be heavily tilted in favor of Trump, as with Julian Assange's highly selective and expertly timed Wikileaks release of documents associated with Hillary Clinton (Kellner, 2017; Freedland, 2016). Of course, the fact that Putin's regime as well as Trump and the GOP regularly attack leftist groups and causes remains conveniently overlooked (Kellner, 2017).

In short, when presented with the more obvious problematic support for oppressive historical and contemporary figures or movements, the left is going to have to come up with a more compelling rationale than, "well the US does/did [insert oppressive thing] too." This type of whataboutism needs to hit the dustbin of history, fast. As A. Smith (2017) observes, "the emerging new Left must instead base itself on principled opposition to all imperialisms" (p. 57). At the same time, leftist groups often correctly point to interference by the right as a reason why their vision hasn't come to pass in various global contexts (Chretien, 2018). However, the hard truth is that if a movement cannot withstand the problem of a repressive, well-funded, organized and powerful right-wing, then a Marxist future will not happen.

On a smaller scale, there have been recent proposals on the left to reach out to the right wing (Davidson, 2017; Renton, 2019). Davidson (2017) outlines rationale as:

the claim that working-class demands or actions which might appear reactionary actually contain a rational core which renders them defensible by the left: in relation to migration this is sometimes expressed as the need for socialists to pay heed to the "genuine concerns" of the working class, as if the sincerity of the belief rendered it valid. (p. 67)

DiMaggio (2017) provides the example of Green Party members proposing a "brown-red alliance" with white nationalist groups and Trump supporters. The rationale is that the experience of being working class and exploited should be the common focus of organizing, with less emphasis placed on issues such as racism and sexism. An excellent historical analysis of similar attempts at reactionary and revolutionary alliances is provided by ARoamingVagabond (2018), illustrating that unfortunately, this is not a new concept. Ultimately, of course, "one can't realistically "work with" right-wing nationalists one minute, then claim common cause with minority groups that are the targets of reactionary fascists" (DiMaggio, 2017, para. 12).

Colorblind Class Analysis

One of the more problematic outcomes of the Sanders campaign was the insistence of his supporters on framing class apart from its associations with race, gender, and sexuality, particularly as a strategic form of outreach to white voters. Roediger (2017) sees the retreat from race as a disturbing development within liberal and left circles to the point where even the mention of race is discouraged in favor of advocating for "universal programs" (p. 35). As Walters (2017) outlines,

> for these critics, identity politics are issues "we" (women, blacks, queers, etc.) spend too much time on, issues that ostensibly push away that white male voter (who doesn't have an "identity" presumably). Under the cover of this so-called concern, critics can attack abortion rights, gay rights, civil rights. As long as these rights are the property of certain identities, they can be denied as distractions by many on the Left and as narrow "special rights" by most conservatives. (para. 10)

While Sanders himself has a long record of supporting civil rights causes and cannot remotely be considered a racist, there was a reluctance within his campaign and supporters to confront "what it means that a large segment of the US population… is motivated primarily by white nationalism and an anxiety over the fast-changing demographics of the country" (Matthews, 2016, para. 29). What Sanders could have done was to more clearly articulate issues of class with race, gender, and sexuality; in other words, a more accurate depiction of how capitalism operates (Fletcher, 2016; Roediger, 2017).

A key moment in the Sanders campaign happened in the summer of 2015 when Black Lives Matter activists Marissa Johnson and Mara Willaford interrupted his rally in Seattle to ask pointed questions about the candidate's policies toward African Americans (Johnson, 2016; Warner et al., 2017). Sanders' eventual response was to meet with representatives of BLM and other groups to listen to their concerns (McMorris-Santo, 2016). However, Sanders supporters, in particular younger white males, had an immediate and defensive reaction on social media, posting memes reminding blacks in particular of Sanders' record on civil rights, outraged that Sanders was challenged and not Clinton. Johnson (2016) recounts her experience:

> I'll be honest and say that I was not prepared for this backlash. Though our action ended up being a great reveal of the racism in progressive spaces, I myself was unaware of the depths of this underlying white supremacy. I did not expect to have water bottles thrown at me by "socialists"—nor for progressives

to call for my being tased by a police department that is still under federal consent decree. (para. 7)

Additionally, Roediger (2017) discusses the reaction among the left to an opinion piece by Ta-Nehshi Coates, that challenged Sanders' position on reparations. Sanders argued that reparations were not only impossible to implement, but were divisive compared to his proposal of a higher minimum wage or free college tuition. Coats was critiquing the ability of these colorblind reforms alone to fully address racism because of a refusal to confront the history of white supremacy, not attacking democratic socialism as Roediger explains:

Coates also stressed the absence of strong support for affirmative action in Sanders' program, underlining that the grand universalist strategy deployed by some socialists, and not only the controversial specifics of reparations, was at issue. There was not a hint that the article opposed socialism itself. (p. 13)

Roediger observed that in response to the opinion piece, Coats was labeled bourgeois, attacked for his awards from the "establishment," and implications that he was a class traitor using fashionable identity politics instead of focusing on class. An extreme example came from political scientist Adolph Reed Jr., who accused Coats of being an agent of the US government or working for Clinton, even though Coats was, ironically enough, a Sanders supporter at the time.

The inevitable outcome to the colorblind universalist approach was Sanders' immense defeat on Super Tuesday and Clinton's securing of more than 85% of the black female vote across most of the states (Starr, 2017, para. 12). Starr reads these results as Sanders making assumptions that a universalist set of social programs would automatically attract black voters. One example she presents included an activist recounting her experiences with Sanders' reluctance to connect environmental issues with race:

That was a perfect opportunity to display empathy for the specific plight of black mothers who have to raise children in unsafe areas plagued by environmental racism. But, in typical Sanders fashion, he got defensive and refused to take on her challenge that he lacks a racial analysis. (para. 16)

Sanders' statement shows a typical progressive attempt to steer the conversation toward a colorblind analysis: "What I just indicated in my view is that when you have...you and I may have disagreements because it's not just black, it is Latino; there are areas of America, in poor rural areas, where it's white" (Starr, 2017, para. 17). Additional statements about supporting Trump so long as he stands up to corporations further illustrates the problematic aspects of universalist approaches (Walters, 2017).

Vanderbeck's (2006) analysis of race within Vermont politics is instructive in placing Sanders along a continuum of white progressive candidates. As he notes, "Vermont has been imagined as one of the last remaining spaces of authentic Yankee whiteness while more recently becoming an imagined homeland for particular brands of white liberal politics and social practice in the United States" (p. 641). This type of authenticity was a major feature of the 2004 primary run of Howard Dean, another veteran Vermont politician who made social class a centerpiece of his messaging. A strategy of the white liberal progressive in this vein is to set himself apart from other white politicians, such as southern conservatives. This stance is seen by supporters as sufficient enough to demonstrate opposition to racism and sexism and therefore calls for more direct addressing of women and minority issues are seen as "divisive." Waldman (2018) sees this tendency within white progressive circles as a "self-serving approach to ongoing anti-racism efforts" (para. 4).

Unfortunately, the resistance among many on the left to examining race, gender, and sexuality as specific instances of capitalist oppression has been an ongoing problem (Roediger, 2017). Essentially, this line of thinking postulates that a focus on issues of identity is a threat to the solidarity needed to confront capitalism because everyone remains in their own identity camp focused on micro-local concerns (Resnikoff, 2017). Race, gender, and sexuality are swept under the rug, so to speak, with a blanket statement along the lines of, "once capitalism is gone, racism and sexism will disappear" or "it goes without saying that women and minority rights are important but getting rid of capitalism will take care of all that." What women, minorities and LGBTQI people are supposed to do in the interim remains magically unaddressed, other than a re-emphasis of the central importance of class.

Part of the dismissal of identity within socialist circles has originated in neoliberalism's successful coopting of the language of diversity. Fraser (2017) explains:

Identifying "progress" with meritocracy instead of equality, these terms equated "emancipation" with the rise of a small elite of "talented" women, minorities, and gays in the winner-takes-all corporate hierarchy instead of with the latter's abolition. These liberal-individualist understandings of "progress" gradually replaced the more expansive, anti-hierarchical, egalitarian, class-sensitive, anti-capitalist understandings of emancipation that had flourished in the 1960s and 1970s. As the New Left waned, its structural critique of capitalist society faded, and the country's characteristic liberal-individualist mindset reasserted itself, imperceptibly shrinking the aspirations of "progressives" and self-proclaimed leftists. (para. 5)

Roediger (2017) sees the left's rejection of identity as a grave mistake. Just because corporate America has adopted practices such as diversity training and implemented anti-sexual-harassment policies does not automatically make diverse organizing oppositional to class analysis.

Meyerson (2016) acknowledges that the enthusiasm of Sanders supporters lies in Sanders' ability to clearly name economic inequality as the core defining driver of oppression, a message that is attractive to younger, less financially secure white voters who also reject Trump's authoritarian populism. However, Meyerson attributes this support to something more, a colorblind notion of class:

> Fundamentally, he [Sanders] is saying that the Democratic Party needs to pivot back to class politics, to add a renewed focus on economic inequality to the party's emphasis on the inequities of race, ethnicity, gender, and sexual orientation that has largely defined it since the presidency of Lyndon Johnson. (p. 28)

It is one thing to critique the Democratic Party for abandoning strong class analysis after the rise of neoliberalism, but it is another thing altogether to assert that *white voters* have somehow been ignored simply because Democrats have made inclusion a part of its outreach. This type of zero-sum thinking is a major analytical flaw, mainly assuming that identity issues are somehow separate from and not an integral part of capitalism.

Related to this is the "alt-left" edgy tone of the discourse of Sanders supporters which tended to alienate those not young, white, and male (Fassler, 2017). Resnikoff (2017) demonstrates how easily colorblind alt-left discourse can be coopted by right-wing groups by discussing Kilpatrick's (2016) highly flawed *Jacobin* piece where he declared, "when racism can be blamed, capitalism can be exonerated" (para. 33). Not long after, the essay and that quote in particular was approvingly cited by American Renaissance, a white supremacist website seeking to recruit socialists who only focus on economics and "have little respect for theories about white privilege or authoritarian personalities" (Resnikoff, 2017, para. 60). The fact that one's supposedly socialist discourse is that easily adopted by white supremacists should give one major pause.

Another issue that Sanders campaign and supporters failed to confront was their profound misunderstanding about the black vote, encapsulated by their insistence that the Democratic National Committee (DNC) somehow stole the primary victory from Sanders. To buy into this line of thinking means overlooking that Clinton won the popular primary vote by over 3 million, and a key segment of that vote came from women and minorities (Leonard, 2017; Walters, 2017). Additionally, more than ¾ of black voters voted for Clinton in the primary as opposed to less than ¼ for Sanders (Starr, 2017, para. 11; Leonard, 2017, para. 8). Starr (2017) attributes this to Sanders' targeting of younger voters while overlooking the South, a key source of the black vote. Reflecting on Sanders supporters, Leonard (2017) doesn't hold back:

> Most Black voters were justifiably insulted by the methods his campaign used to get their support, were very turned off by his rabid cult of worshippers, and made Sanders pay dearly for it…That really angered his cult, who made it clear that if Sanders didn't get the nomination then fuck civil rights, fuck gender equality, fuck all of that—it's all "identity politics" that only the "elites" care about and they don't matter anyway; only the "economic anxiety" of "real working-class Americans" matters (read: white males easily baited

by racist and sexist dog whistles) and the Democrats have to get with the program and win them over in order to start their "progressive revolution." (para. 8)

Even though Sanders made economics the centerpiece of his campaign, it was shortsighted to assume that economic programs alone would win over white voters and end racism. As Matthews (2016) points out, while strong social welfare programs are important, they are no guarantee that racism and sexism will end. A form of welfare chauvinism exists where white voters find it acceptable to support programs, so long as minorities and immigrants are prevented from participating. Until the left recognizes this, merely suggesting student loan forgiveness or national health care without any connection to race and gender is doomed to failure:

> Any solution has to begin with a correct diagnosis of the problem. If Trump's supporters are not, in fact, motivated by economic marginalization, then even full Bernie Sanders-style social democracy is not going to prevent a Trump recurrence. Nor are GOP-style tax cuts, and liberal pundits aggressively signaling virtue to each other by writing ad nauseam about the need to empathize with the Trump Voter aren't doing anyone any good. (Matthews, 2016, para. 33)

Ultimately, the left is going to have to more clearly articulate what exactly is meant by a "universal" class analysis, or concepts like "solidarity," especially since notions of the common good are irrevocably linked to race, gender and sexuality (Roediger, 2017; Walters, 2017). If winning over Trump supporters means removing any mention of race or gender in order to make socialism seem more palatable, then one has to wonder whose interests are being served in the process and if that socialist vision is really prepared to meet everyone's needs. Rehmann (2016) sums it up best:

> The Sanders campaign obviously did not have enough time to overcome the difficulty that any focus on class is still perceived as a white issue, as if poor blacks and women were not part of the working class. The question of how to overcome the fragmentation of social movements by a coherent unity, with and through manifold differences and contradictions, remains a difficult and urgent task for the left in general. (p. 8)

CONCLUSION

There is no doubt that the campaign of Bernie Sanders made a major impact in activating formerly disengaged voters while re-introducing democratic socialist concepts to a wide range of people, including those who might consider themselves centrist. It was no longer strange to talk about socialism and Marxism. The grassroots energy and excitement surrounding the well-attended campaign rallies and on social media was something not seen in a long time. People were looking forward to supporting Sanders for his platform and clearly articulated views rather than just to prevent Trump from winning.

At the same time, discourse within the Sanders campaign and supporters on social media revealed some problematic aspects that have emerged within the left. Based on the reluctance—some would say hostility—toward including issues that have the most direct impact on women and minorities, one has to wonder if the default setting for "economic issues" remains white and male? The irony is that if the goal is to defeat capitalism, the *worst* thing for the left to do is to use colorblind class analysis. This only entrenches capitalism because the key ways that it functions through the use of race and gender are never confronted.

Further, it is not possible to have a movement both strong enough to defeat capitalism and white supremacy/misogyny at the same time. To confront these aspects of fascism and right-wing populism *requires* using discourse about race and gender to dismantle racism and sexism. Why some leftists persist in using colorblind class analysis remains a mystery. It is time to draw the line and give racism and sexism the boot rather than tolerating and accommodating them so as not to upset coalitions with Trump supporters. For once we need to prioritize those who are most impacted by racism, sexism, and homophobia versus sacrificing them "for the good of the cause." While it is understandable that the working class often holds contradictory beliefs in these areas, there should be zero tolerance for racism and misogyny in all aspects of leftist organizing.

Ultimately, the Sanders campaign represents a missed opportunity. By failing to connect women and minority issues to class analysis in an effort to win more conservative white males, they lost the momentum to build a stronger movement. Yet, the 2018 midterms were a testament to the power of clearly articulated economic issues tied to race, gender, and sexuality, albeit within left-liberal bounds. Rather than turning away white voters, it is important to notice how successful candidates such as Alexandria Ocascio-Cortez, Rashida Tlaib and Deb Haaland widened electoral participation. Illinois Representative Lauren Underwood, an African-American nurse, ran for and won in a majority white suburban/rural district, her direct message about health care attracting voters and giving them something to hope for. By focusing on diverse voters rather than avoiding the issues so as not to upset conservative ones, a possible template for moving forward has presented itself.

CHAPTER 5

WELL, ACTUALLY

Cyber Sexism and Racism within Online Settings and the Enabling Discourse of E-Libertarianism

INTRODUCTION

Since its inception, the Internet has been hailed as a great equalizer, promoter of progress and democracy with unlimited potential and reach. What propels this mythology is the concept of the Internet as a neutral site, where identity is irrelevant other than the persona one chooses to create and share. Social life on the Internet is presented as an idealized, random collection of atomized individuals who happen to come together to interact over shared interests, with collectivity stopping there. Of course, this mythology has always been attractive to a certain segment of the population, who has always been able to utilize the Internet and shape society as they wished:

> Straight white men, often considered the default Internet user, see the Internet as a neutral tool because it conforms so exactly to their expectations, everyone else had to make adjustments and look for loopholes in order to use the Internet in the way they wanted. (Poland, 2016, p. 213)

Indeed, for the women and minorities who are constantly harassed on the Internet, they are met with the dismissive (if not hostile) attitude that this is the price to pay for having the nerve to disrupt the "wide, open cyberspaces" that they are violating because of their unwillingness to no longer let racism, sexism, and homophobia go unnoticed. This can take the form of name calling, threats, and a blurring of online and offline stalking and violence.

Far from being a neutral, idealized space, what the Internet reveals is "a story of how the deepest prejudices in a society can take purchase in new settings due to technology" which has been in the process of "transforming not only online spaces but real lives and potentially even the trajectory of our politics" for some time now (Beauchamp, 2019, para. 9). Though presented as hip, progressive, and current, the very foundation of the tech industry itself is misogynistic, with women occupying less than 30% of jobs at major tech firms such as Apple, Google, and Microsoft (Jotanovic, 2018, p. 32). Among leadership jobs, women hold only 10% of higher-level positions and these are virtually nonexistent for non-white women (p. 32). Lee

(2017) captures the experiences of being female in the tech industry, not unlike the experience of being a woman who interacts online:

> To be a woman in tech is to know the thrill of participating in one of the most transformative revolutions humankind has known, to experience the crystalline satisfaction of finding an elegant solution to an algorithmic challenge, to want to throw the monitor out the window in frustration with a bug and, later, to do a happy dance in a chair while finally fixing it. To be a woman in tech is also to always and forever be faced with skepticism that I do and feel all those things authentically enough to truly belong. There is always a jury, and it's always still out. (para. 13)

Added to this, conservative discourse on social media has experienced many structural changes since the late 1990s, the most important being its global organizing and reach. Daniels (2009) identifies this as the formation of a "translocal white identity" where whiteness is privileged over national origin as a point of connection (p. 68). This is paired with more anarchistic organizational structures that are no longer one-way or top-down in terms of communication as was the case in the pre-digital era. The sheer reach of social media via its sharing features has transformed disinformation into a major weapon, turning "the right-wing media system into an internally coherent, relatively insulated knowledge community, reinforcing the shared worldview of readers and shielding them from journalism that challenges it" (Benkler et al., 2017, para. 4). Here, outright lies are not even needed, just enough of an insertion of doubt and let sharing accomplish the rest.

The irony is that underneath the innovative, subversive trappings of hacker culture and trolling, the philosophy underlying all right-wing movements on the Internet is profoundly traditionalist and retrograde (Nagel, 2017; Penny, 2017b). Discourse surrounding feminism and its contribution to the decline of the West is a common sight in comments, blogs, and websites. As Burton (2018a) notes, the Internet provides a powerful forum for cultivating right-wing political beliefs, first by promoting the mythic, where "the world has an inherently meaningful and exciting structure" (para. 20). This is then paired with participation and the immediacy of response, which represents the power of "belonging to a cohesive group with the thrill of cultural transgression" (para. 23). This combination of rigidity and transgression is highly alluring, making things like racism, sexism, homophobia and violence something refreshing and different when presented in online contexts, where "to be a traditionalist is, increasingly, to be countercultural" (para. 21).

While Facebook has formally banned white supremacist and separatist groups from its site as of March 27, 2019, and Twitter taking similar measures, this has made barely a dent into hostile discourse in cyberspace as a whole. This chapter first outlines the philosophy of e-libertarianism, which is foundational to the formation and distribution of discourse on the internet, in particular, harassment of women and minorities. Next, an overview of the persona of the troll and functions of trolling are presented as a major aspect of this discourse, using the countercultural frame. Cyber organizing is then addressed, highlighting some key aspects of right-wing content distribution and translocal white identity underlying alliance-building. This culminates in a discussion of the misogyny inherent within the online manosphere, consisting of groups such as men's rights activists, new atheists, incels, and pick up artists.

E-LIBERTARIANISM

The ideological foundation of the Internet can best be conceptualized as *e-libertarianism*. A fusion of the tenets of traditional libertarianism with online settings, e-libertarianism asserts that the Internet is a self-governing, neutral location with equal access to all that should not be interfered with by regulations of any kind. This is reflected in Barlow's (1996) widely distributed acerbic and patronizing white male missive, *A Declaration of the Independence of Cyberspace* where he states that the Internet is a different space, apart from society:

> You claim there are problems among us that you need to solve. You use this claim as an excuse to invade our precincts. Many of these problems don't exist. Where there are real conflicts, where there are wrongs, we will identify them and address them by our means. We are forming our own Social Contract. This governance will arise according to the conditions of our world, not yours. Our world is different. (para. 5)

At the same time, e-libertarians aggressively support the notion of the invisible hand of the free market, self-interest, and monetizing the Internet, not seeing the glaring contradiction between these concepts and their claims that the Internet is a naturally evolving, neutral space or that it promotes equality for all. As Daniels (2009) explains,

> those who share this perspective envision the internet as a sort of unregulated marketplace usually only found in economics textbooks…the cyberlibertarian view of the internet is one rooted in a particular American geography imbued with a frontier ethos, tied to both a free-market analysis of the internet and a very recent (mis)reading of the first amendment as an absolute protection of all speech. (p. 181)

E-libertarianism asserts four claims that drive its discourse and structures: (1) First Amendment Absolutism; (2) the Internet is neutral; (3) the Internet isn't real, and (4) harassment is the price of admission. These claims are interrelated and serve to reinforce an overall hands-off ideology that provides the climate for right wing populism and fascism online.

First Amendment Absolutism

A key tenet of e-libertarianism is that unrestricted free speech, or First Amendment absolutism, is the optimal policy to govern the Internet. Any attempt to regulate speech is viewed as an anti-democratic transgression that is evidence of government overreach that always seems to lurk around the corner. Citing "slippery slope" logic, proponents of free speech on the Internet assert that if something racist is banned or moderated, the floodgates to repression will open where an increasing amount of ideas will be banned. It is important to note that e-libertarians never invoke the more likely *reverse* scenario of the slippery slope argument: that allowing unrestricted white supremacist or misogynistic speech will result in normalization of such speech and an increase in racist/sexist discourse and violence. For this reason, Daniels (2009) posits that the e-libertarian conceptualization of the First Amendment "is an interpretation born out of a white racial frame, rooted in colonialism, and stands at odds with the wider democratic global community" (p. 162). It is also a concept that is hegemonically embedded within cyberculture; you'll only realize its presence when you attempt to challenge aspects of it online.

Free speech as envisioned by e-libertarians is hyper-individualized and devoid of social context (Daniels, 2009). This frames all speech as initially equal in value, with the "marketplace of ideas" ultimately the decider of which speech is more popular. If a white supremacist website that openly advocates violence happens to get more views than a scholarly site discussing immigration research, then those opposed to such sites need to compete more effectively with their own ideas rather than monitoring them. This stance assumes that the Internet is an open space with no political or market influences or things like human-designed search algorithms. Poland (2016) sees an immediate problem with false equivalency of speech:

By relying on an ethos that insists all conversation is valuable and must be treated as an individual discussion and never regarded as part of an overall pattern and by accepting that there is an implied burden of proof that women, specifically, are required to meet when sharing stories about their own lives, cybersexists endeavor to capture and waste women's time and attention. (p. 171)

False equivalency combined with social context also end up creating severe disadvantages for members of minority groups, overlooking the deliberate use of the Internet as a global means to cultivate white supremacy (Daniels, 2009).

In particular, free speech is used as a way to justify the harassment of women and minorities online. If someone challenges misogynistic, homophobic, or racist ideas via a social media platform, all e-libertarians have to do is reframe these arguments as assaults on free speech rather than a critical interrogation of the status quo (Daniels, 2009; Poland, 2016). This then places a target on the backs of the original poster who will likely be cyber-mobbed or doxed, with personal contact information publicly posted. A side benefit to this is that the content of the original post is now hijacked in the service of e-libertarianism. It is pretty apparent that when it comes to free speech proponents on the Internet, "what they all share is not a general commitment to intellectual free exchange but a specific political hostility to "multiculturalism" and all that it entails" (Ferrell, 2018, para. 12). Or, as Penny (2017a) observes about Internet speech, "it was about making it OK to say racist, sexist, transphobic, and xenophobic things, about tolerating the public expression of those views right up to the point where it becomes financially unwise to do so" (para. 9).

Of course, the irony is that First Amendment absolutists fail to grasp the first corollary to free speech: if you have the right to speak, then others have the right to respond to your speech. As Poland (2016) points out, "sexists assume that free speech also includes the ability to be free from criticism or social repercussions" (p. 44). At the same time, free speech proponents demand that their perspectives be heard and responded to, even if this means women and minorities would have to devote hours of their time responding to circular arguments providing evidence that never seem to satisfy the e-libertarian looking for a "debate." The second corollary to free speech—that one can opt out of listening to your speech—is therefore conveniently ignored. This was evident in right wing cyber-celebrity Ben Shapiro's demand that NY Representative Alexandria Ocascio-Cortez accept $10,000 to debate him, an offer she turned down, comparing it to the practice of catcalling where women have to respond to the catcaller or they are a "bitch" by default (Foderaro, 2018).

Olson's (2014) content analysis of child pornography boards on the hosting site 8chan is an example of free speech fundamentalism taken to an extreme when it comes to the hands-off philosophy of site moderators. Noting that the presence of photos and videos of underage girls is often defended as "free expression" or equivalent to photos that parents take of their children, Olson aims his critique at the lack of site moderation in the name of free speech:

> The content on these boards persist because while it is often very illegal the posters and moderators and owners of 8chan are well aware that resources for these cases are limited, and the situation is fraught with legal and jurisdictional issues. So long as they remain out of the realm of hardcore pornography they can, and do, fly just beyond the effort of federal investigators who spend their limited resources pursuing producers or trading groups for more extreme material. (para. 32)

Poland (2016) points out that rather than ostracizing child pornographers, other 8chan boards defended the site owner, hailed the bravery of the "artistic" photographers for pushing the boundaries of art, and accused opponents of suppressing free speech. Even though child pornography of the type hosted on 8chan is absolutely illegal, the lack of moderation is openly exploited by users to promote violence and misogyny.

More contrite e-libertarians will often agree that some things they see are unacceptable, but protest that there is nothing they can do about content because there is too much of it to oversee and therefore it is not practical to intervene (Olson, 2014; Poland, 2016). More dedicated proponents assert that free speech needs to be prioritized as the very first thing to protect; those who are victimized by harassing speech are secondary concerns. Illing (2017b) points out how similar arguments were once used in support of spam—now highly regulated—during the early years of the Internet, where business owners prioritized their right to advertise as they saw fit and besides, they claimed, it wasn't "hurting anyone":

> But there was an obvious problem: It was ruining everything for everyone else. You don't even have to get into this free speech bullshit. Was this platform created with the intent that neo-Nazis would harass and ruin people's lives? If not, then you need to fucking do something about it, and that's ultimately how spam got dealt with. This is impeding the intended function of this platform. This is taking up space. It is ruining this thing that we've built, so we need to actually do something about it. Now anti-spam stuff is a $1 billion industry. I don't see how that is not the exact same thing going on here, except way more harmful for the people that are on the receiving end of it. (para. 45–46)

The Internet Is Neutral

Closely related to First Amendment absolutism is the notion that the Internet is a neutral space with equal access rendering markers of identity irrelevant. This is a form of "techno-mysticism" where technology is portrayed as free from race, gender, or class (Daniels, 2009). Much of this belief is wrapped up with the creation of the Internet, accounts of which have begun to take on the discursive structures of legends or myths. In these retellings, the Internet was a vast open realm of possibility where freedom ruled...until women and minorities began to hijack these spaces:

> This was part of a broader trend within male-dominated geeky online subcultures whereby women are viewed as a threat to the edginess of the subculture, instead seen as a force for bringing the moral and behavioral constraints and the inauthenticity of the mainstream platforms into the subcultural realm. (Nagel, 2017, p. 112)

West (2017) sees the patronizing terms *Social Justice Warrior (SJW)* and *political correctness* as manifestations of associating women and minorities with regulatory limitations on behavior, in other words, "killing the mood." Further, these terms are meant as a way to diminish the concerns of women and minorities as frivolous (Nagel, 2017; Poland, 2016).

This neutrality-protected hostility toward women and minorities within these segments of tech and geek cultures has a long history, stretching into the 1970s and 1980s. Auerbach (2017) traces the philosophical beliefs of right-wing science fiction writers such as Jerry Pournelle, Larry Niven, David Drake, and Janet Morris who advocated a vision of techno-futurism combined with nativist beliefs. Many of the white characters in their books enact rugged individualism against a backdrop of alien invasion. The views of these authors were adopted by Republicans like Newt Gingrich, who in the early 80s asserted the need for technology in the service of capitalism. Technology was also meant to replace the liberal concept of social services, "leaving only the limits of a free people's ingenuity, daring, and courage" (para. 23). Tor Books, a science fiction publishing house, even published Gingrich's first book, also co-written by Drake and Morris. The intertwining of geek culture with conservativism was now solidified.

Neutrality also minimizes the sexist and racist face of the tech industry as a whole, because it points to the existing demographic composition of the workforce and justifies it by making bogus claims such as women not being interested in science or math-related fields. This was the message of "Google Bro" James Damore, who asserted in a widely shared manifesto that women were biologically less capable of handling stressful jobs like tech work (Rothkopf, 2017). The manifesto itself was written in a matter-of-fact scientific-sounding tone, a common tactic that draws on the neutrality myth. Those who understandably reacted negatively to the manifesto were accused of becoming too emotional and bringing politics into the issue. Despite this, Google itself was forced to acknowledge that only 20% of those currently employed in tech jobs were women and the Labor Department reported an extreme level of discrimination at the company (para. 7).

As Poland (2016) outlines, rather than emerging naturally, technology has been situated "in the domain of cigender white men of a certain class and education level" where the "privileges and oppressions that exist necessarily shaped the outcome" (p. 205). For example, in the early days of computer development and programming, women and minorities played a more significant role, because it was less expensive to hire them. Only when profit increased did we start to see an association between tech work and men, particularly in the US. These associations have remained, with survey studies showing men being linked to concepts of "science" and "work" with women to "family" and "arts" (Jotanovic, 2018). Rothkopf (2017) connects the dismissive attitudes of Google Bro and elements of geek culture to a larger problem of misogyny:

No problem has caused more damage to more people in the course of human history than the subjugation of women, who make up about half of the world's population. From the millions of girls and women who still die yearly because they are seen as unworthy of equal medical care as males, to millions who lead less-fulfilling lives because they are denied opportunities by male-dominated societies, the suffering involved is not open to debate. (para. 5)

Neutrality provides a way to minimize misogyny by "degendering the problem and gendering the blame" as the status quo is upheld while women are simultaneously targeted as the cause of problems online (Poland, 2016, p. 52). At the same time that women and minorities are portrayed as "invading" or "taking up too much space" online, it is men, with few exceptions (and usually those are carefully monitored spaces), who occupy the bulk of online commenting and content creation. Women who seek to interact online have to continually grapple with being reduced to sexual terms in a supposedly "neutral" online world:

Of course, it's gendered. It's sexualizing me for the purpose of making me uncomfortable, of reminding my audience and colleagues and detractors that I'm a sex thing first and a human being thing second. That my ideas are secondary to my body. (West, 2016, p. 117)

Ultimately, neutrality is another e-libertarian fiction because rather than being a choice, oppression is directly tied to group membership. As Richards (2017) explains, "most of the time individuals have no choice as to which groups they belong to, and have no agency to leave" (para. 13). Further, it is clear that "social structures are not built on individual experiences" but are sustained collectively, with some having far more capacity to function freely than others (para. 13). The claim that the Internet is just responding to what the public wants overlooks how the tech industry itself has influenced discourse and regulatory structures. It also gives social media sites "credible deniability" that it isn't responsible for the content, just the algorithms (Siegel, 2017). Further, we cannot overlook that people don't search the Internet in order to correct flawed information; "rather, they ask the electronic oracle to confirm them in their ignorance" (T. Nichols, 2017, p. 112). Neutrality, therefore, needs to be actively confronted. If the tech industry is indeed innovative like is claimed, "it needs to start creating for the world that is" (Jotanovic, 2018, p. 33).

The Internet Isn't Real

Paired with the neutrality of the Internet is the assumption that things said or done online do not carry the same repercussions as done in person. However, the worlds of online and face to face spaces have been blurred for some time, especially when it comes to racist and violent actions such as the New Zealand mosque shooting and accompanying YouTube live manifesto that originated on 8chan. It is increasingly common to see news stories of people being fired or resigning for racist or sexist Facebook or Twitter posts and states have begun to enact laws covering cyberharassment and other crimes. Yet the idea persists that online events are somehow less threatening or serious and that such legal actions are overblown:

The argument that the Internet is not real and therefore cannot be harmful is deeply rooted in the mindset attributed to the years of the early Internet, when there was an assumption of unfettered freedom to do or say anything, because there weren't many people around to hear it. The audience was mostly composed of other white men (or people presumed to be other white men) who were more likely to cosign stereotypes than challenge them. (Poland, 2016, p. 90)

Indeed, this is supported by Barlow's (n.d.) manifesto declaration that, "legal concepts of property, expression, identity, movement, and context do not apply to us. They are based on matter, and there is no matter here" (para. 9).

Asserting the "less real" status of the Internet serves several purposes. A key one is that it provides an important out for those who make harmful statements, either by people dismissing these actions as "trolling," or by shielding the racist or sexist poster from criticism (Poland, 2016). They can simply claim that "it wasn't them," just some joke they posted online that they didn't mean. This rationale is enabled by the feature of anonymity, which is "used as a shield between an individual's real beliefs and their real identity" (p. 23). K. Burns (2017) notes the practice of response YouTube videos that are created to suppress feminist perspectives online. These videos often feature threats, doxing, and violent language but the creators of the videos "claim that their content does not itself constitute harassment" (para. 10). At the same time, the video creators, adhering to an e-libertarian ethos, do nothing about the escalating violence in the video's comments left by viewers. Usually they claim their free speech rights are of primary importance.

Contrary to the idea that harassment is less real when conducted on the Internet, it can often be *more* threatening because the victim has less of a chance of discovering the identity of the stalkers and confronting them (Poland, 2016). These harassers also benefit from the convenience of social media platforms and their instant sharing features under anonymous cover to create cyber-mobbing situations and to extend the harassment in terms of length of time and audience reach. Combined with the reluctance and resistance of site owners to moderate content, online harassment becomes an entrenched practice meant to suppress the voices critical of racism, sexism and homophobia. West (2016) recounts her experiences with online harassment, illustrating that far from being less real, it encompasses the physical:

> Flooding in through every possible channel, it moves and changes my body. It puts me on the phone with the FBI, it gives me tension headaches and anxiety attacks; it alters my day-to-day behavior (Am I safe? Is that guy staring at me? Is he a troll?); it alienates my friends; it steals time from my family. The goal is to traumatize me, erode my mental health, force me to quit my job. (p. 111)

Harassment Is the Price of Admission

Even when, in the face of overwhelming evidence of online harassment, e-libertarians reluctantly acknowledge that such practices do exist, they usually move to their final line of defense: that such harassment is the price we have to pay in order to have a free society. This argument is stunningly similar to ones used to justify access to military grade firearms in the US and makes it clear that the freedom is considered of more worth than the victims. Put bluntly, the freedom of white men to have their idealized Internet must be subsidized at all costs by women and minorities:

> Through cybersexist harassment, men attempt to recreate the offline conversational patterns they already dominate, enabling them to continue controlling online spaces as well. Sexist harassment is intended to intimidate

women, silence their voices, or force them to conform to men's chosen conversational norms for a specific space. (Poland, 2016, p. 99)

The belief that women and minorities must tolerate abuse and harassment is baked into the e-libertarian ethos. When confronting this attitude, West (2016) found that, "the best they could give me was a sympathetic brow-knit and a shrug. The Internet's a cesspool. That's just the Internet. We all get rude comments. Can't make an Internet without getting a little Internet on your Internet" (p. 113). Women and minorities are continually lectured by e-libertarian males that the Internet is a public forum, its privatization and monetization are conveniently overlooked. In some cases, harassers and those who enable them attempt to point out how those in the US have nothing to complain about compared to citizens of other countries who experience "real" abuse (Poland, 2016). In actuality, those least likely to be harassed are the very ones getting to set the parameters for what is or is not an acceptable response.

Mostly in reaction to the increased unapologetic presence of women and minorities in online settings, harassment is a form of backlash so pervasive as to approach the ordinary. This is especially the case within the gaming community, as Illing (2017b) recounts:

Back when I was a teenager running around in game circles, this was the first thing. If anybody found out you were a girl, they'd be like, "Tits or get the fuck out." That was the joke. You had to show your tits or get out. There's always been this "you don't belong here" attitude. The same thing happens for a lot of people who are Jewish or people who are not white. That stuff's been going on for a long time. (para. 30)

Those who track online harassment have found that close to 75% of people reporting abusive situations were women, with 50% of them having no prior association with their harassers (Poland, 2016, p. 93). Nearly three fourths of adults on the Internet have witnessed harassment with 40% having it happen to themselves—a majority of those belonging to marginalized groups (K. Burns, 2017, para. 2).

Online harassment takes several forms, ranging in intensity from unsolicited mocking comments and trolling to threatening speech, cyber-mobbing and stalking. Typically, most interactions with online misogynists "involve an assessment of women's physical appeal according to narrow standards" along with "displays of power and dominance in traditionally patriarchal ways" (Poland, 2016, p. 41). This continues to escalate, as other posters are quickly rallied in large numbers to harass the target (Nagel, 2017). Within moderated spaces, the ones who get removed tend to be because of posting spam or unrelated content, not for calling women and minorities snowflakes, children, social justice warriors or slurs related to their identity group (Szoldra, 2016).

In the Gamergate harassment campaign, women in the tech industry and those who supported them had their addresses publicly posted, fake pornographic photos of them distributed, were threatened with rape or death, or the police sent to their house on a false report (Hatewatch Staff, 2018; Illing, 2017b). These tactics were first practiced by 4chan users targeting black women via stereotypes about the black family, with the #EndFathersDay hashtag (Poland, 2016). The origins of Gamergate itself was a personal vendetta against a game designer by her ex-boyfriend:

> It picked up steam when someone floated a rumor that I had slept with somebody for positive reviews of my game, even though the person in question had never reviewed my game and worked for a site that I had already written for and I would have needed a time machine to make this possible, but none of that ever really seemed to matter. It didn't matter that the review never existed. People ran with it and used it as a convenient smoke screen to say that they cared about ethics in games journalism. (Illing, 2017b, para. 12–13)

This illustrates that when called out on their harassing behavior, men will then revert to the classic tactic of portraying themselves as victims, usually within the framework of being a brave martyr in the cause of free speech, or turning an issue of misogyny into "ethics in journalism" (McEwan, 2017a). Or, they will accuse feminists who respond to their harassment of also posting angry content, attempting to create a false equivalency between the two acts (Penny, 2017b).

Several factors serve to perpetuate online harassment within an e-libertarian ethos. The first is the sheer accessibility of the Internet and social media sites with very low entry checkpoints. This means that even if a harasser is blocked, they can easily register under a new account and name (Poland, 2016). Second is the ability of social media sites to work off of tacit approval from the public at large concerning stereotypes, more recently aimed at immigrants and Muslims (Daniels, 2009; Poland, 2016). Because these groups are already marginalized in the mainstream media, online abuse is viewed as partly justified. A third factor is the "cyberhate divide" in the US where white supremacist and other hate groups are able to post abusive content compared to other nations that have stricter hate speech laws (Daniels, 2009, p. 176). Abusers realize that harassment will be tolerated and overlooked within US hosted sites. All of this creates a climate where "misogyny is explicitly, visibly incentivized and rewarded. You can watch it self-perpetuate in front of your eyes" (West, 2016, p. 210).

Even though there has been an increase in awareness of online harassment and legal measures enacted, traditional responses to online harassment have been ineffective. This is due to the e-libertarian preference for steering solutions toward keyword-based filtering software which is both inefficient and runs the risk of blocking legitimate sites while leaving cloaked websites unaffected (Daniels, 2009). Individual attempts to block harassers might initially help, but not for long, as Poland (2016) provides in her example of the inadequacy of Twitter's block system:

> While going directly to their profile page will inform individuals if they have been blocked, searching for their target's tweets by username or clicking

on responses from other users who are not blocked both enable harassers to continue seeing and interacting with tweets from someone who has blocked them. A link to a tweet posted by another user also allows someone who has been blocked to see the content and even provides the option to retweet, favorite, or reply to that tweet, although retweeting and favoring will bring a pop-up notice that the action cannot be completed...blocking someone on Twitter does not prevent them from continuing to tweet at a target—it just prevents the target from seeing it. (pp. 166–167)

Another ineffective measure is to classify all online harassment as cyberbullying, which diminishes the centrality of gender or race in the majority of instances (Poland, 2016). Cyberbullying makes harassment about the pathology of the individual rather than larger societal issues of racism, misogyny, and homophobia. The common mantra of "don't feed the trolls" also fails to work in the cases where harassers simply escalate their attacks when they perceive that they are not being acknowledged to their liking. When victims of cyber-harassment talk about their experiences, they are often questioned about not going to the police; again, the neutrality-based assumption is that the justice system treats everyone the same. When harassment goes unreported (mostly due to the sheer unresponsiveness or extreme burdens of proof required by the legal system), this only confirms to harassers that what they are doing is not wrong (Poland, 2016).

In one instance, a man who assumed that his female friends' accounts of online harassment were exaggerated decided to pose as a woman on a dating app. He lasted just over two hours:

Guys would become hostile when I told them I wasn't interested in sex, or guys that had started normal and nice quickly turned the conversation into something explicitly sexual in nature. Seemingly nice dudes in quite esteemed careers asking to hook up in 24 hours and sending them naked pics of myself despite multiple times telling them that I didn't want to. (Rose, 2014, para. 8)

The fact that the man had to experience online harassment for himself in order to acknowledge that such abuse occurs regularly rather than trusting the accounts of thousands of women is telling in and of itself. He had to see for himself what other women have always known: that "the expectation that women online should be present only to serve as fodder for heterosexual male fantasies is common" and that sexual objectification is a form of silencing women (Poland, 2016, p. 39).

Ultimately, it is unrealistic to expect women and minorities to "get off the Internet" if they can't handle harassment. Setting aside the human rights violations of harassment and cordoning off space for exclusive white male use, the notion of "like it or leave it" denies the integrated online and offline spaces that we now occupy. Women and minorities depend on social media for their academic work, business presence, networking, communication with family and friends, and, yes, sheer entertainment (Poland, 2016). The "solution" of leaving also assumes that harassment will cease once the victim logs off, which is not the case. Abuse can easily continue on social media, blogs, videos, and websites as many have testified (Illing, 2017b; Nagel, 2017; West, 2016). What needs to happen is an absolute militant repudiation of the assumption that white men are entitled to harass women and minorities and that the Internet is by default a patriarchal, racist space that requires abuse as a condition of entry.

FORMS AND FUNCTIONS OF TROLLING

A major component of right-wing online interaction involves the cultivation of the persona of the troll. Trolling itself is a complex social activity that is profoundly underestimated and as a result, the practice has pretty much forced itself upon all but the most tightly moderated online spaces. For the purposes of this chapter, *trolling* refers to a set of retrograde discursive practices embedded in a specific philosophy of disruption for its own sake and often with the aim to halt meaningful discourse, particularly among women and minorities:

> By giving women more opportunities to speak, to participate in the public conversation with lower barriers to entry, the Internet also provided more opportunity for people to insert themselves as arbiters, contrarians, devil's advocates, disruptors, and silencers…the movement against smart women is largely led by (primarily although not exclusively) white men whose interactions with us are not evidently abusive, but are insistently disrespectful, condescending, patronizing, and hallmarked by pervasive wrongness about basic facts. (McEwan, 2017a, para. 10–11)

Certainly not all trolling is designed to be political, as is commonly seen with random, snarky, unrelated comments that appear in otherwise innocuous discussions of movies or TV shows. The trolling discussed here is overtly political, done in bad faith, and reflects authoritarian populist and fascist ideologies.

One problem preventing the effective confronting of trolling is the persistent stereotype of trolls as exclusively basement-dwelling thirteen-year-olds—an easy assumption to make based on the intellectual content level of garden variety troll commentary. Trolling has also become a ubiquitous term used to apply to any type of disruptive practice which diminishes its impact on women and minorities (Poland, 2016). In the studies done of those who adopt a trolling persona, it turns out very few are directly linked to traditional conservative organizations, preferring more loosely organized anarchic structures (Daniels, 2009; Poland, 2019; Roose, 2019). Instead of focusing on issues like taxes or trade, trolls tend to comment on free speech and anti-feminism, which are often gateway topics into white supremacy. In one interview study, a participant expressed feeling like he was in an exclusive club after discovering conservative YouTube videos that embraced a trolling aesthetic: "When I found this stuff, I felt like I was chasing uncomfortable truths…I felt like it was giving me power and respect and authority" (Roose, 2019, para. 36).

Cheng's (2017) content analysis of CNN site comments found that 25% of posts that are flagged for abusive language are posted by those who have no prior record of such. This indicates that such disruptive posts are made by regular users, not just those outside societal norms as is often thought. Additionally, "a user's propensity to troll rises and falls in parallel with known population level mood shifts throughout the day...suggesting that negative mood from bad events linger" (p. 1). Much of this is dependent on the number of posts about a topic and how those are ordered. Negative mood can also spread to others, increasing the likelihood that someone can adopt a trolling persona, even if they hadn't done so in the past. Trolling can also occur across all age demographics, so it is common to have 40–60-year-old men leaving disruptive comments. Of course, the biggest troll of all is Trump, "asocial and apparently devoid of empathy, unable to grasp or articulate much beyond a sound-bite or Twitter blast, with attacks and invective his distinctive mode of social interaction" (Kellner, 2017, p. xvi).

This section first addresses the inversion of countercultural philosophy behind trolling, which flourishes in an e-libertarian environment. Next, an examination of the tactics used by trolls illustrates the varied means at their disposal to derail meaningful interaction. Finally, a brief overview of the larger functions that trolling serves connects this practice to the larger efforts by authoritarian populists and fascists to erode pluralism, democracy and activism.

Philosophy

An outgrowth of the e-libertarianism which sustains it, trolling encompasses a philosophical worldview that is best described as countercultural inversion: the taking of what are essentially conservative ideas and transforming those into cutting-edge acts of rebellion and transgression (Marantz, 2017; Nagel, 2017; Penny, 2017b). This is done using the tenets of disruption for its own sake; discursive, dehumanizing, winner-take-all modes of communication; and use of humor in bad faith to keep one's self at arm's length from accountability. Essentially, trolling takes the anarchic ideology of the alt-right as a whole and enacts it through a specific aesthetic performance:

> The idea of the inherent value of aesthetic qualities that have dominated in Western pop culture since the 60s, like transgression, subversion and counterculture, have turned out to be the defining features of an online far right that finds itself full of old bigotries of the far right but liberated from any Christian moral constraints by its Nietzschean anti-moralism. It feels full of righteous contempt for anything mainstream, conformist, basic. (Nagel, 2017, pp. 115–116)

Essentially, the alt-right has carried forward this "allure of the transgressive" aspect of media culture and adapted it for its own use because they have witnessed the success of the social movements of the 1960s as compared to less-inspiring attempts to implement traditional values (Penny, 2017b).

Countercultural inversion requires maintaining a constant tension between what are essentially repackaged repressive concepts and unrestrained secular society (Nagel, 2017). This juxtaposition has a long history, including libertarianism's ability to provide an outlet for rebellion for white, conservative middle-class teenagers who "get to argue with their peers about social justice while rebelling against their parents by advocating cannabis legislation" (Gulliver-Needham, 2019, para. 10). As Burton (2018a) points out, rebellious traditionalists have always figured prominently in right-wing groups. An example of countercultural inversion is Jordan Peterson, who presents his 19th century worldviews packaged as daring, cutting-edge beliefs. He also utilizes the trope of the brave truth-teller who goes against the norm, all in the hopes of "owning the libs" and keeping feminists in line. As Burton (2018a) notes, "to follow Peterson is thus to be able to participate in the thrill of being transgressive without, well, having to do anything particularly transgressive" (para. 43).

Trolling also reflects the insistent need to be perceived as anti-establishment as possible, constantly upping the ante, but still within the boundaries of upholding right-wing ideology. Combined with this ideology is the absolute insistence on no restrictions, any challenge to such risks being labeled as "anti-fun" (Penny, 2011). As Nagle (2017a) explains,

> It is a career disaster now to signal your left-behind cluelessness as a basic bitch, a normie, or a member of the corrupt media mainstream in any way. Instead, we see online the emergence of a new kind of anti-establishment sensibility expressing itself in the kind of DIY culture of memes and user-generated content that cyberutopian true believers have evangelized about for many years but had not imagined taking on this particular political form. (pp. 2–3)

It doesn't matter how absurd this content becomes, because ultimately trolls are about amusing themselves, or as Sartre (1976) says concerning anti-Semites, "they have the right to play" and you don't (p. 13). Discourse is fodder for their aim to "discredit the seriousness of their interlocutors" and to "intimidate and disconcert" (p. 13).

Trolling is a deindividuated blood sport where the goal is absolute domination of online discourse in the absence of self-reflection (Marantz, 2017; Poland, 2016). In order to sustain a winner-take-all discourse, trolls have to dehumanize their targets and, in some cases, each other. Discursive tactics include insults, continual pointing out of flaws, gaslighting, or pretending to not understand what could possibly be offensive about what they are saying. Escalation and endurance are the characteristics of winners (Poland, 2016). In describing the posting style of their white supremacist son, Mike Enoch's parents noted, "he strikes me as someone without a core, who only knows how to oppose and who chooses his positions based on what will be most upsetting to people around him" (Marantz, 2017, para. 24). Yet it isn't enough to utilize abusive language or humor in bad faith; trolls have to place their own intentions and subjectivity above all else, asserting that "they should get to dictate not only the content of their statements, but the emotional reactions those statements get" (Poland, 2016, p. 31). At no time to victims have the right to the validity of their own experiences or interpretations unless they mirror the troll's.

For trolls, imperviousness is the starting point, not acting on the strength of one's positions—everything begins from the choice to remain unmovable (Sartre, 1976). At the same time that trolls practice discursive dominance by cultivating the persona of a rugged yet carefree beacon of truth, they tend to launch into a massive campaign of outrage if they perceive that they have been insulted or treated unfairly. A double-standard of discourse becomes readily apparent:

> A fundamental tenet of far-right pro-trolling is that it's only other people's feelings that are frivolous. Their own feelings, by contrast, including the capacity to feel shame when they're held accountable for their actions, are so momentous that infringing them is tantamount to censure, practically fascism in and of itself. (Penny, 2017a, para. 32)

It becomes clear, then, that the freedom to harass and abuse others in an online setting without consequence is the real goal, not simply seeking attention as is naively assumed (Poland, 2016). Nagel (2017) sees this as consistent with de Sade's dominance-centered transgressive beliefs; also similar to how the Nazis adopted Nietzsche "to excuse and rationalize an utter dehumanization of women and ethnic minorities" only now this is happening in online settings (p. 38).

Tactics

Trolls utilize several discursive tactics in order to enact their philosophical beliefs, which culminates in derailing a discussion. Derailment itself is an elaborate style of interrupting by inserting one's self into an online conversation and then assuming the role of arbiter of what is or isn't an acceptable level of relevance, emotion, or evidence. Trolls do this in order to move the conversation to patriarchal topics and interaction patterns they are more comfortable with, "to challenge the participants' understanding of their own conversation" while trying to "refocus women's attention on another topic or even on the derailer himself" (Poland, 2016, p. 36). One thing all of these tactics have in common is the basic tenet that they are entitled to the time and energy of women and minorities, ignoring the free association component of free speech. The conversational strategies used by women have no effect on reducing trolling, with verbal harassment often continuing despite their attempts to adapt.

Mansplaining and *whitesplaining* are framing tactics trolls use to present themselves as more of an expert on being a woman or a minority than those who actually occupy those identities (Poland, 2016). This serves to reinforce a "not all men" or "not all white people" form of derailment, along with situating minorities and women as too "biased" to have an objective view of issues related to their identity. As with other trolling tactics, there is a certain predictive quality they give to online interactions—you can see it coming:

> When women discuss the specific, gendered forms of harassment and abuse often experienced in online spaces, we can safely assume that a straight white man will appear within a matter of minutes to remind us that everyone gets harassed online and that we're just being overly dramatic about it. (p. 68)

Contrarianism is a way of engaging combatively with an audience so they become bogged down replying to one's devil's advocate style responses. At the same time, well-meaning replies back will never meet the satisfaction of those using contrarian tactics, which are deliberately designed to divert feminists and anti-racists. Circular logic is a crucial aspect of contrarian discourse:

> When Muslims try to resist oppression using legal means, Islamophobes claim this is "lawfare"—an attempt to subvert the judicial system. When Islamophobes are called out for their bigotry, they claim that the left, which they paint as "in" on the conspiracy, uses "political correctness" to silence them. (Sunshine, 2017, para. 8)

Some trolls elect to maintain a detached, smug style of interacting, usually paired with academic sounding racist, sexist, or homophobic statements (Marantz, 2017). The idea behind this tactic is to remain calm, letting the victims of such statements become "triggered" so they can be declared too sensitive or emotional. Then the next tactic of tone policing can be unleashed, asserting that one's point is immediately rendered invalid if they cannot remain calm and scientific (Poland, 2016). A related approach involves gaslighting, where trolls will assert that what they just said was a joke or simple irony (Marantz, 2017). This serves to create a disorienting effect, where minorities and women might start to question the veracity of their own experiences in an attempt to be open-minded.

In some cases, trolls turn on each other, which isn't surprising considering the climate of sniping and backbiting they create. This can be likened to Theweleit's (2010b) description of the Nazi criminals at Nuremburg when they were seized with the sudden need to chat up journalists, attempting to throw each other under the bus:

> Each depicts the rest (himself excepted) as a collection of reprobates whom he would gladly have restrained had he been able (which he regrettably was not)…it became standard procedure for the accused voluntarily to express their distance from other Nazis, fellow defendants included; at the same time, almost all of them held fast to what they called the "idea" of Nazism. In so doing, they re-established their own sense of coherence; while others could be presented as deranged and incompetent, they themselves could be seen to have remained good Nazis. (p. 340)

The most prominent example of troll backbiting includes Milo Yiannopoulos, who was ousted from the Conservative Political Action Conference after his comments about pedophilia. Not long after, he lashed out at fans and other right-wing figures for their lack of support (Link, 2018). When white-nationalist Mike Enoch was outed by anti-fascist activists as having a Jewish wife, commenters immediately attacked him by insisting he get a divorce or making statements like "I can't believe all you fags still support this Jew fucker" (Marantz, 2017, para. 8).

Of course, when the more elaborate troll tactics fail to make a dent, the reliable standbys of misogyny and racism will always do. These include the interconnected strategies of shaming, intimidating and discrediting; invoking identity markers to undermine one's contributions to a discussion and slurs and insults about one's appearance—for women, usually the words "fat," "bitch" or "slut" (Sobieraj, 2017). When trolls find themselves having to admit defeat, one of two things will happen so they can swiftly exit stage right: 1) a grudging acknowledgment paired with a dismissal of importance of the topic they just spent hours debating or 2) declaring that their opinions are just as valid as facts, often paired with a sexist or racist slur (McEwan, 2017a; Sartre, 1976). A troll will usually insist that it is then time to "move on" to other, more pressing matters, as if they are the final arbiter of a topic's overall significance, in a conversation they were not asked to be a part of in the first place.

Functions

Trolling serves several key functions for right wing populist and fascist movements, not the least of which is convincing people that being present online isn't worth it. Technological platforms operated by those with an e-libertarian ethos already enable harassment to flourish. The more that people leave sites because they become frustrated with the constant distraction and harassment of trolls means that right-wing perspectives get the most hearing and the illusion of support. As Poland (2016) notes,

> writers avoid engaging in discussion in the comments on their own pieces because the immediate and overwhelming toxicity has a tendency to render such conversation pointless and unpleasant, especially on topics to things like gender or race, or even certain areas of science. (pp. 183–184)

Further, the advice to not feed the trolls is highly naïve because it assumes that trolling is an aberration rather than an integral aspect of online aesthetic performance and organizing on the right. This advice also reinforces the message that women and minorities' experiences should not be acknowledged while the problem gets pushed under the rug.

Another function of trolling is to normalize racism, sexism, and homophobia under the guise of irony, humor, and deadpan "it's just the facts" discourse. Carter (2018) and Ferrell (2018) note how classical liberalism plays a similar role for those who want to "dress up" their racism to make it appear more respectable and academic. Such websites and celebrities like Jordan Petersen "are good at presenting racism in a 'we're just being reasonable/this is what the science says, why are you acting so upset?' type of way" (Hatewatch Staff, 2018, para. 22). Proud Boys founder Gavin McInnes commonly employs the "just joking" rhetorical out, claiming that those offended either don't have a sense of humor or are attempting to impose censorship. Of course, these "jokes" contain racist, sexist, homophobic, ableist, and other aggressive discourse:

> By constantly reinforcing stereotypes, he sends the subliminal message that there are fundamental things that are different and essential about each of these groups—and that the best group, and the one most in danger, is none other than white men. (Coutts, 2017, para. 52)

Finally, trolling is used as a means of destabilizing democracy by recruiting online participants to far-right ideologies, as will be explored further under the Cyber Organizing section of this chapter. As Hatewatch (2018) explains,

> many of those who were eventually radicalized by 4chan came there relatively innocently. One user said memes led them to 4chan in the mid-2000s, but they eventually found their way to overtly racist/pol/after Obama was elected for a second term. Others noted they "ironically" looked at/pol/, or they were led there by the more absurdist "random" board,/b/. One wrote that their friend, who they specified was not right-wing, told them to "surf/pol/for fun." "Humor is a powerful drug," explained a poster who came for the political discussions but "stayed for the racist memes. (para. 34)

Trump himself regularly utilizes Twitter as a way of subverting the values of dialogue, deliberation, and notions of compromise and consensus (Kellner, 2017).

Ultimately, as Farrell (2018) points out, "dark web intellectuals, like Donald Trump supporters and the online alt-right, have experienced a sharp decline in their relative status over time" which is contributing to the escalation of their rhetoric in the face of growing diversity on the Internet (para. 5). Right-wing satire and trolling also fail in comparison to pointed leftist humor because it "punches down" on those most vulnerable rather than critiquing power. Satire also requires a sense of the absurd for it to work, and it is often too hard to distinguish between satire and directly stated right-wing views (Nagel, 2017). Despite these vulnerabilities, it is extremely important to maintain a vigilance about trolling. While the "standard online shtick for politically serious members of the alt-right has been to flirt with Nazism but then to laugh at anyone who took these gestures at face value," the culmination of such tactics resulted in the murder of Heather Heyer during the Charlottesville alt-right demonstration (Nagel, 2017).

CYBER ORGANIZING

Coined by white nationalist Richard Spencer, the term *alt-right*—short for alternative right—refers to a loosely composed rightist movement of those opposed to what they consider to be mainstream conservatives, in addition to liberals and leftists (Alt Right: A Primer, 2019; Sedillo, 2017). The term came into common parlance within the mass media during the 2016 election and in the aftermath of the 2017 Unite the Right rally in Charlottesville, Virginia. Hatewatch Staff (2018) categorizes the alt right as an umbrella "motley movement" representing subcultures and ideologies such as libertarians, long-term white supremacist groups, the alt lite (a milder version of the alt right), atheist/skeptics, men's rights activists and conspiracy theorists, with a few mainstream conservatives thrown in for opportunistic reasons. It is important to note that the term alt-left is also a creation of the alt-right and is an attempt to sustain the narrative of false equivalency (Sedillo, 2017).

Though the alt-right is often classified as being diverse, nearly all of its more prominent Internet figures are middle-to-upper-middle class white males with college degrees who work in professional fields like the tech industry (Wilkinson, 2017). However, in some cases, the right wing and racist internet celebrities are themselves members of the very groups they target (Bernstein, 2017). Examples include Milo Yiannopoulos who is gay and married to a black man, Tomi Lahren, a woman who combines white supremacy and anti-feminist rhetoric, and anti-Semite Mike Enoch (Michael Peinovich), who is married to a Jewish woman. These contradictions are utilized strategically and are marshalled to defeat charges of racism, sexism, or homophobia. It also allows a strange positioning where you one can ladder privilege by statements like, "I'm gay but I don't want our borders overrun by Mexicans" or "pride festival was great until the trash from the South Side showed up."

Followers of the alt-right themselves often skew younger, though the movement's popularity is growing among older men who are bridging the divide between the aging talk radio audience and younger males on the Internet (Coutts, 2017; Kimmel, 2017; Penny, 2017a). Coutts (2017) found that within the alt right Proud Boys men's rights group, the profiles that were verified included some with violent criminal records, with several having served in the military and police. The age differences between the adult alt right celebrities, their mannerisms, and the more youthful image of the Internet segment create a situation where the media often treats the alt right as underage teenage boys. This is in stark comparison to how black and Latino young men are portrayed, as Penny (2017a) points out:

> It is vital that we talk about who gets to be treated like a child, and what that means. All of the people on Yiannopoulos' tour are over 18 and legally responsible for their actions. They are also young, terribly young, young in a way that only privileged young men really get to be young in America, where your race, sex, and class determine whether and if you ever get to be a stupid kid, or a kid at all. Mike Brown was also 18, the same age as the Yiannopoulos posse, when he was killed by police in Ferguson, Missouri, in 2014; newspaper reports described him as an adult, and insisted that the teenager was "no angel," as if that justified what was done to him. Tamir Rice was just 12 years old when he was shot and killed in Cleveland for playing with a toy gun. (para.19)

This section addresses cyber-organizing among the alt-right by first examining the structural features of the Internet and social media which create the climate that enables its success. Next, principles of alt-right organizing are presented followed by common recruitment gateways to escalating extremist views. Finally, an overview of the manosphere serves as a case analysis of the central role of misogyny within alt-right online spaces.

Climate

There are numerous structural features of the Internet and social media in interaction with key ideologies that create the optimal climate for right-wing organizing. This is not just a matter of technology alone:

> If technology were the most important driver towards a "post-truth" world, we would expect to see symmetric patterns on the left and the right. Instead, different internal political dynamics in the right and the left led to different patterns in the reception and use of the technology by each wing. While Facebook and Twitter certainly enabled right-wing media to circumvent the gatekeeping power of traditional media, the pattern was not symmetric. (Benkler et al., 2017, para. 8)

Rather than reality following the common narrative of "both sides do it," the right-wing has by far been able to more successfully take advantage of social media's design features and for-profit operation. Benkler et al. note that while disinformation is nothing new nor the exclusive property of the Right, the fusion of attacks on the mainstream media with Trump's Twitter persona and discourse is distinct.

First and foremost, cyber organizing in the US has been legally facilitated by Section 230 of the *Communications Decency Act* (1996) which does not hold Internet service providers liable for most content posted. This has created a situation where site hosts simply declare themselves as content middlemen or domain name service providers, absolving themselves of responsibility. This, along with the Internet being composed of autonomous private networks creates the ideal climate for globally mobilizing the far-right in a rapid manner (Bode, 2018; Peterson, 2017). For example, Cloudfare is a content delivery network that shields white supremacist sites like DailyStormer.com from denial of service attacks (Peterson, 2017). As a result of the Internet's uniquely sheltered conditions, most hate websites are based in the US (Daniels, 2009).

Search engines themselves, along with search features within sites like YouTube, rather than naturally evolving technologies, are structured around algorithms, which can have unintended—or some argue, intended—results:

> The YouTube algorithm, which determines what will auto play after one video has finished and places recommended videos in the sidebar, also plays a role in coaxing viewers into the deeper depths of the alt-right by presenting them with

ever more extreme content...YouTube promotes material that tend to keep people on their site longer, and those videos often happen to be among the more extreme content on the site. (Hatewatch Staff, 2018, para. 51)

K. Burns (2017) explains how the ease of video creation combined with an algorithm that prioritizes prolific content, views, and comments fosters the rapid growth of alt-right ideas. Essentially, "gaming the very closely held secret of the YouTube algorithm became a de facto path to Internet stardom" (para. 14). At the same time, students researching topics for a class history project are more likely to see first page results of the likes of best-selling author Bill O'Reilly than academics who specialize in the period (T. Nichols, 2017).

Interactive features are designed to increase time spent on social media sites, which derive their profit from advertising revenue. More extreme content results in more interaction in the form of comments and views; as Nimen (2019) puts simply, "haters are the most voracious clickers" (para. 17). The Frontline documentary series, *The Facebook Dilemma* (2018) provides an in-depth examination of the origins and functions of the social media site. Both parts of the series demonstrate how the structural features of Facebook—especially its economic model—enabled it to be immediately coopted by global reactionary and far-right interests. The also reveals why no significant actions have been taken or are likely to be taken against racism, sexism, and homophobia on the site or other profit-dependent social media sites in the near future (Burns, K., 2017; Illing, 2017b; Nimen, 2019; Ryan, 2016).

Social media sites like Facebook collect countless data points that users leave through their interactions on the site. This feature has been readily exploited globally by the alt-right to conduct "media-based psych-ops campaigns," ranging from the 2016 US election to Brexit as well as the earlier cooptation of the Arab Spring movement (Facebook Dilemma, 2018; Niman, 2019). The mass-creation of fake profiles on Twitter and Facebook, known as *sockpuppets* (human-created fake profiles) and *bots* (computer-generated fake profiles) have engineered conditions where entities like the "unofficial Twitter Group of Tennessee Republicans" have ten times the membership as the real Republican Party of Tennessee (Niman, 2019, para. 7). Humans then interact with these fake profiles, spreading their content as if it were generated by a specific person. One St. Petersburg-created sockpuppet, Jenna Abrams, was regularly quoted by the New York Times and The Washington Post among other outlets (para. 8).

Botnets then take ideological outsourcing the next level by essentially creating a mass following that doesn't even require the mobilization of large numbers of real people:

They can almost instantly propel any tweet or post into mega-virality by robotically seeding a seemingly organic viral orgy of reposting—enough to trick social media site algorithms into seeing the messages as naturally trending, and thus, make them actually trend into millions of news and social feeds. (Nimen, 2019, para. 10).

Nimen provides a particularly disturbing example of ProPublica's outing of a bot that resulted in a replacement bot's Tweet which instantly mustered a bot army numbering 60,000—thus generating more readers than the original ProPublica exposé. Only a few social media users are needed to share a story versus networks of thousands.

Taking advantage of this, the Breitbart/Yiannopoulos/Mercer connection illustrates the big money and interrelated networks of tech industry males who work together to manufacture online social movements. Buzzfeed traces these connections in a detailed piece (Bernstein, 2017) that uses email chains to show how the alt-right creates the current Internet culture and climate that is hostile to women and minorities:

> It was a brilliant audience expansion machine, financed by billionaires, designed to draw in people disgusted by some combination of identity politics, Muslim and Hispanic immigration, and the idea of Hillary Clinton or Barack Obama in the White House. And if expanding that audience meant involving white nationalists and neo-Nazis, their participation could always be laundered to hide their contributions. (para. 164)

The most disturbing aspect of the alt-right is how its content is regularly spread on a global scale by prominent conservative politicians positioning it as legitimate news and as inspiration for laws and policies (Bevins, 2018; Bernstein, 2017; Coutts, 2017). Trump's 2016 political team including Steve Bannon, Roger Stone and Stephen Miller maintain ties to white supremacist organizations via spreading content from sites like Breitbart or groups such as the Proud Boys. As Ryan (2016) points out, the Trump team had no need to present original ideas because "they didn't need to confirm or deny anything, they simply gave Trump's army their megaphone" (para. 8).

This also highlights the enabling role of the mainstream media in creating the climate for alt-right organizing. Despite doing some investigative pieces on the Trump administration, for the most part, the alt-right, using Breitbart and its satellite support sites set the agenda leading up to the 2016 election, particularly around the issues of immigration and coverage of Hillary Clinton (Benkler et al., 2017). Likewise, supposedly progressive sites such as *Jacobin* and journalist Glenn Greenwald "exert a powerful reality-distortion field online and foster factionalism on the lib-left" (Wolcott, 2017, para. 3). This includes Tulsi Gabbard who met with Trump after he was elected, along with Mickey Kraus who was once a progressive journalist and now supports Trump's border wall.

Finally, it cannot be overlooked that alt-right ideas are personally lucrative, or, as Malik (2018) notes, "the Dark Web is not a black hole, it is a career ladder" (para. 16). The fact that many alt-right celebrities are able to make a living out of speaking fees, publishing books and online content provides a form of justification of the soundness of their ideas when challenged (Penny, 2018). K. Burns (2017) found that "there's a lot of money in anti-feminism," as in the case of once-progressive Laci

Green who achieved more followers once she joined the alt-right (para. 13). Mike Enoch, founder of the Right Stuff website, has a link for making donations while others offer video subscriptions (Marantz, 2017).

It should be clear by now that with the ease of access and speed of social media, the alt-right can no longer be ignored in the hopes that it will lose popularity on its own. No longer confined to print media, social media has created the conditions where anyone who can log on can immediately find authoritarian populist and fascist content, often disguised and promoted by mainstream media outlets as legitimate (Nimen, 2019). This has created a virtual community in the form of the alt-right, where members (real and bot) can nurture each other's prejudices, conspiracy theories and cement social bonds through

> an inverted epistemology…of ignorance, ironically resulting in whites generally being unable to understand the world that they themselves have made. The epistemology of white supremacy reinforces the white racial frame by allowing whites to retreat from pluralistic civic engagement into a whites-only digital space where they can question the cultural values of tolerance and racial equality unchallenged by anyone outside that frame. (Daniels, 2009, p. 8)

Principles

The primary organizing principle of the alt right is what Daniels (2009) conceptualizes as translocal whiteness, "a form of white identity not tied to a specific region or nation but reimagined as an identity that transcends geography and is linked via a global network" (p. 7). This is reflected in the nearly all-white and mostly male membership of the alt-right and comes across in the majority of their discourse (Coutts, 2017; Torres, 2017; Wilkinson, 2016). Such discourse is either aggressively racist or framed more as topics "up for discussion," such as the intelligence of Black people compared to whites, the eventual forced deportation of non-whites, and the feasibility of genocide. Often this discourse is presented in the form of anti-Islamic and anti-Semitic conspiracy theories (Malik, 2018; Sunshine, 2017). The irony is that globalization—something that authoritarian populists and fascists within the alt-right oppose, is itself utilized to construct this translocal whiteness, which often takes on nationalist characteristics and ideologies.

An example of the ideology of translocal whiteness is encapsulated in the political theory of The Dark Enlightenment (or Neoreaction, NRx), which was promulgated via an online manifesto in 2012 (Hatewatch Staff, 2018). In taking libertarianism to its logical conclusion, "adherents believe that capitalism should be accelerated to the point that corporate powers rule society, allowing natural hierarchies to emerge" (para. 43). Democracy and egalitarianism are viewed as unnatural interferences that are preventing rule by a superior white race. Similar views are advanced by white nationalist and science fiction publisher Vox Day, who asserts that "we must secure the existence of white people and a future for white children," something that can only be done by enforcing a white ethno-state (Auerbach, 2017, para. 38).

A second organizing principle of the alt-right is a rejection of traditional top-down organizational structures such as political parties or activist groups in favor of "loosely organized social networks of supporters rather than members" (Daniels, 2009, p. 49). This is an extension of the e-libertarian and techanarchist ideologies outlined earlier where the alt-right fashions themselves as a vanguard movement that cannot be easily defined or contained. Much of the energy generated through anger is focused on dominating online spaces while setting the agenda for a mainstream media bent on "fair coverage." Ultimately, this creates a dynamic where alt-right discourse might be inflammatory, but on-the-ground political activism is minimal, especially evident when comparing turnout against the Lefts' demonstrations (Nagel, 2017; Poland, 2016). Kimmel (2017) notes how the repressive desublimation among the alt right concerning a rejection of dialectical activism benefits those in power as it fully enables the status quo to continue.

At the same time as structural political organizing strategies are rejected by the alt right, overt authoritarianism is fully celebrated, creating an important contradiction. Figures like Putin, Kim Jong Un, and Bolsonaro are regularly highlighted and connected to the hopes they place into Trump that he will carry on the tradition of male, iron fist rule:

> They're gleeful about some of the harshest policies Trump promised: mass deportations, defunding Planned Parenthood, the wall. They feel like they have scored a victory against feminism and multiculturalism. They're glad that white men are, once again, in control. They were filled with fury at the thought they had been toppled from their rightful place at the top of the social hierarchy; this is vindication. The old order has been defeated; this is their world now. (Wilkinson, 2016, para.11)

Among the alt-right is a growing sense that past right-wing approaches have been too tepid and conventional, requiring more direct policies such as building a border wall and detention centers (Auerbach, 2017; Nagel, 2017). This has created the climate for actual, on-the-ground white supremacist organizations to make their presence known, as in Charlottesville (Nagle, 2017b). Essentially, we are at a moment where the Internet "is now the prime organizing arena for white power groups" and the core of the conservative ideological energy is happening around the alt-right (Kimmel, 2017, p. 238).

This relates to the third organizing principle of the alt-right, which is absolute disruption, but of a regressive form. As Auerbach (2017) explains, the enthusiasm around Trump is more about his ability to destroy the existing system rather than his specific policies or goals: "What Trump does is less important than the fact that he kicks over the table, strengthening America's military state while demolishing bureaucracy and ignoring niceties" (para. 31). Utter destruction is prioritized over any sort of specific vision for society, which in the absence of leftist resistance, creates a dangerous vacuum for fascism. With tribalism serving as the only form of social cohesion, any sort of meaningful solidarity is absent (Torres, 2017).

Related to this is illiberalism, being against anything progressive, and anti-multiculturalism, with Obama and Hillary Clinton often serving as high-status targets (Wolcott, 2017). This was evident in the growth of the alt-right online after Gamergate, which represented a backlash against the online visibility of women, minorities, and the LGBTQI people. As Illing (2017b) explains, "Gamergate was just a big recruitment drive and helped build community, and helped firm up ties between younger online groups and older conservatives who didn't understand how to make things go viral" (para. 36). This backlash against multiculturalism also provided a common organizing ground between the older talk radio type audiences just discovering social media, the online white supremacist groups that had been operating a while, and the younger alt-right.

Kimmel (2017) presents different psychological components of victimhood that compose the angry white male, which supports the alt-right's organizing principles and discourse. These include *ressentiment*, or the "personal sense of self that is defined always in relationship to some perceived injury" in combination with blaming women and minorities who are seen to be the source of injury (p.38). A second powerful rallying component of victimhood is *aggrieved entitlement*, or "the sense that we have had what is rightfully ours taken away from us by them," them being the government which favors undeserving minorities (p. 23). Most importantly, both of these psychological factors work against developing dialectical, collective action against those in power, because they enable manipulation via racism toward the wrong targets. This is primarily because right-wing victimhood is itself marker of privilege denied.

Gateways

The alt-right uses a gateway form of recruiting that slowly acclimates its followers to authoritarian populist and fascist ideologies. Though there are people who directly seek out more overt white supremacist content, it is more common for people to follow a gradual process in forming alt-right identities. A common online pathway to the development of increasingly far-right views is usually one of contrarianism→ libertarianism→social Darwinism→white supremacy:

> Respondents recount a transformation that takes place almost entirely online. Led either by their own curiosity or an algorithm, the content they consumed became increasingly extreme, fostering their radicalization…Their responses reveal a pipeline between the alt-lite and racist "alt-right," with many users explaining that alt-lite figures like Gavin McInnes were the first to introduce them to hardcore, veteran white nationalists. (Hatewatch Staff, 2018, para. 2)

One of the reasons a more gradual pathway to the alt-right exists is that much of the content on more widespread sites tends to traverse the edges of acceptability in order to provide plausible deniability of racism. For example, the common portrayal in the media of white supremacists as ignorant, overweight hillbillies totally overlooks the more sophisticated and social media savvy proponents, such as early digital media adopter David Duke (Daniels, 2009). While Duke's viewpoints are more clearly affiliated with white supremacy, other figures like Breitbart's former employee Yiannopoulos "led the site in a coy dance around the movement's nastier edges, writing stories that minimized the role of neo-Nazis and white nationalists while giving politer voices a fair hearing" (Bernstein, 2017, para. 4).

The ability of figures like Yiannopoulos to simultaneously keep racists at an arm's length while cultivating a large audience that includes white nationalists is critical for building a following. As Bernstein (2017) notes, the very term "alt-right" serves as a distancing strategy, so that proponents can reassure critics that they aren't Nazis, they are just members of the alt-right. This is similar to the strategy of racist sites denying they are racist, but insisting they are white nationalists instead. Figures like Yiannopoulos even have PR teams that often threaten to sue journalists who use white supremacist or racist labels. This delicate dance is essential for smoothing over the pathway to the alt-right:

> TRS and the Daily Stormer both argue that, with the right optics and messaging, they can attract a critical mass of followers to the cause and eventually shift what lies within the respectable terms of political debate. The respondents in these threads show how the current media landscape—replete with podcasts, YouTube channels and blogs that contain tempered bits of white nationalist propaganda under the guise of patriotism, "Western chauvinism," science or hard truths—can aid that agenda, coaxing the "normies" down the path to white nationalism. (Hatewatch Staff, 2018, para. 11)

Pathways to the alt-right are also facilitated by the presence of more extreme groups within supposedly mainstream spaces, or as Steve Bannon notes, "they come in through Gamergate or whatever and then get turned onto politics and Trump" (Ferrell, 2018, para. 23). The white nationalist and misogynist Proud Boys groups regularly feature links and invitations from global neo-Nazi organizations (Coutts, 2017). Different content types can also mix, as in links to Jared Taylor's race realism talks appearing in satirical 4chan posting boards that focus on politically incorrect content (Hatewatch Staff, 2018). It is also important to note that misogyny is ever-present during this pathway and is folded into online commentary. For example, the new atheist movement often posits that religion is associated with the inherent irrationality of women (Gulliver-Needham, 2019; Torres, 2017).

While the radicalization of white males is due to a myriad of sociological factors that aren't directly connected to social media, the immediacy of online content such as YouTube videos is a powerful means of drawing people into the far right, as Roose (2019) notes:

> YouTube has inadvertently created a dangerous on-ramp to extremism by combining two things: a business model that rewards provocative videos with exposure and advertising dollars, and an algorithm that guides users down personalized paths meant to keep them glued to their screens. (para. 10)

Roose goes on to explain how Google, who owns YouTube, has a vested interest in keeping viewers engaged by clicking links. Quoting one design ethicist, "If I'm YouTube and I want you to watch more, I'm always going to steer you toward Crazytown" (para. 11). The practice of binge-watching videos is often cited by those recruited into the alt-right, who look up content based on different interests, from students wanting to win arguments against feminists in their classes, to mothers concerned about their kids' teachers being too liberal (Bernstein, 2017). The comments section of YouTube also provides a reinforcement of alt-right views, creating the sense that there are others who share the same sentiments in large numbers.

Humor is often an important draw into right-wing online spaces where trolling is rewarded and a celebrity status can often attract more followers. The more that humor can be ramped up to approach increasingly forbidden topics, the more that participants can push the boundaries of acceptability, with few challenges (Hatewatch Staff, 2018). Marantz (2017) cites the Opie and Anthony radio show and their "most offensive song contest" (winners included "Baby Raper" and "Stuck in an Oven with Jews") as a major influence on neo-Nazi Mike Enoch. In this context, humor serves as a test of one's endurance—those who do not find the joke funny are the ones who need to grow a thicker skin. Hatewatch Staff (2018) found that alt-right members pointed to humor as a major draw, such as one who appreciated the YouTube series Murdoch Murdoch as "something that doesn't take itself seriously and then you reflect on it all and you realize that funny show you watched is 100% right about everything" (para. 63).

In terms of political philosophies, libertarianism increases the likelihood of one moving to authoritarian populism and fascism, as Gulliver-Needham (2019) asserts:

> Libertarianism is particularly appealing to white middle class men. It seems fairly obvious why; this group is perhaps the most privileged in our society, and sees little reason for a change in the societal order in place. Similarly, the alt-right and all levels of far-right politics hold exactly the same goal…But when the advantages start to erode, that's when they are forced to turn to more reactionary, authoritarian ideologies…Time and time again, libertarians have shown to be willing to abandon what they would claim as their core principles to uphold the societal order, which places them at the top. (para. 5)

Nearly every alt-right celebrity once described themselves as libertarian, including Yiannopoulos, Richard Spencer, and Alex Jones (Hatewatch Staff, 2018; Gulliver-Needham, 2019; Marantz, 2017). Figures like Jim Goad, who started out writing contrarian-style essays about "forgotten white trash" soon moved into alt-right circles. Transformations are typically described in the vein of, "vague dissatisfaction, and desire for social status and sexual success, to full-blown adherence to a cohesive ideology of white supremacy and misogyny" (Wilkinson, 2017, para. 13). Similarly, Marantz (2017) recounts the thoughts of one former libertarian: "Now that he thought about it, he wasn't sure why he should assume that all people were equal. Maybe they weren't. If this was a textbook definition of racism, then so be it— maybe racism was true" (para. 33)

The Manosphere

One of the primary gateways to white supremacist and fascist ideologies is the *manosphere*, an assortment of male-dominated e-locations dedicated to opposing feminism (Beauchamp, 2019; Nagel, 2017; Poland, 2016; Romano, 2016). These groups include men's rights activists (MRAs) and fathers' rights proponents (also affiliated with the anti-abortion movement), pick up artists (PUAs) and the involuntarily celibate (INCELS) and often these labels are used interchangeably when referencing ideologies. In general, INCELs and PUAs tend to be demographically younger, with most under age 30 (Beauchamp, 2019, para. 20). In some cases, women can ally themselves with the manosphere as a means of building an online or even academic following (Poland, 2016).

Though focused on different subsets of patriarchy enforcement and the infighting that subsequently occurs around these issues, the groups are united by misogyny:

> MRAs have decided that feminists are responsible for the harms they have experienced. They have attached their suffering to female advancement and empowerment, and as a result it is impossible for a middle ground to be reached. Following the MRA narrative, the end of feminism is necessary for the end of male suffering. (Richards, 2017, para. 3)

Working in opposition to dialectical feminist analysis, the manosphere remains locked a pattern of decontextualized isolated experiences/anecdotes in order to prevent structural and contextual understanding. This often results in a gross misuse of statistics and demographic information in order to make their points.

The men's rights movement itself was once affiliated with feminism, where proponents asserted that just as patriarchal sex roles limited women's lives, they also harmed men by promoting destructive aspects of macho identity (Beauchamp, 2019; Kimmel, 2017; Nagel, 2017). However, as soon as feminists began to move beyond gender roles to a more structural critique of the actions of men, such as rape and domestic violence, "the men's libbers departed" (Kimmel, 2017, p. 104). This then shifted into the primary talking point of the manosphere: it is women, not men, who hold disproportionate power in society. A corollary to this is that "women are getting too out of hand" in the arenas of reproductive rights, education, the family, and the workplace (Romano, 2016, para. 27). Likewise, nearly every MRA talking point is peppered with nostalgic hostility for a time when women's actions were centered on pleasing men (Beauchamp, 2019; Kimmel, 2017).

The earliest of the manosphere organizations includes the MRA and fathers' rights groups, who got their start offline within the legal system, particularly divorce. Kimmel's (2017) interviews with members of these groups reveal key ideologies and contradictions that are bound up with aggrieved middle-class entitlement and whiteness. For example, though these movements often highlight statistics showing how men are overrepresented in dangerous occupations, MRAs simultaneously oppose efforts of women to break into fields like firefighting, police work, construction, and the military. Likewise, these groups fall silent when it comes to discrimination facing men who are gay, working-class, African-American or Latinx. The fathers' rights movements often highlight aspects of child custody and domestic violence cases that they perceive to be unfair to men, but, as Kimmel notes, they are not interested in

> promoting active, engaged fatherhood; they just want to promote intact marriages and restrict the options for terminating a bad marriage. They like no-divorce laws, covenant marriages, and other policies that restrict women's choices, not promoting engaged fatherhood. (p. 153)

Indeed, Kimmel found through interviewing a custody evaluator that the men involved in divorce cases often overstated their roles in family life and household maintenance, while their children reported that they were typically ignored when it came to child care. Likewise, MRA celebrity Paul Elam abandoned his family twice and has always been financially dependent on women (Nagel, 2017).

Alt-right offshoots of the MRA and fathers' rights groups include the Proud Boys, who make clear their support for Trump and the concept of "Western chauvinism," which connects misogyny to notions of race purity and nationalism (Coutts, 2017). Alt-right Twitter celebrity Roosh echoed the Proud Boys' support for Trump: "I'm in a state of exuberance that we now have a president who rates women on a 1–10 scale in the same way that we do and evaluates women by their appearance and feminine attitude (Nagel, 2017, p. 90). The Proud Boys' YouTube views and Twitter followers' number into the millions (Coutts, 2017, para. 6). In addition to "venerating the housewife," the Proud boys advocate for building a wall to keep out immigrants, free speech fundamentalism, the right to carry military grade weapons and, more oddly, "a loose prohibition on masturbation" (or "no wanks" rule), because sexual acts should only be for producing children (para. 14).

More recent incarnations of the manosphere include PUAs and INCELs, groups focused on sustaining a specific narrative about dating and marriage. Both of these groups have formed in reaction to dramatic social and legal changes emerging from the women's movement:

> Many men who hate women do not have the access to women's bodies that they would have had in an earlier era. The sexual revolution urged women

to seek liberation. The self-esteem movement taught women that they were valuable beyond what convention might dictate. The rise of mainstream feminism gave women certainty and company in these convictions. And the Internet-enabled efficiency of today's sexual marketplace allowed people to find potential sexual partners with a minimum of barriers and restraints. Most American women now grow up understanding that they can and should choose who they want to have sex with. (Tolentino, 2018, para. 5)

As Beauchamp (2019) points out, rather than being an aberration, both of these groups reflect enduring beliefs about women and patriarchy within Western societies that has just happened to collide with social media to make it seem like a new phenomenon.

Though INCELs were once a tongue-in-cheek named social-justice focused support group for people of all genders who had trouble finding someone to date, they have morphed into an affiliation centered on resentment of and entitlement to women's bodies (Beauchamp, 2019). The notion of "involuntary celibacy" has created an elaborate narrative that frames the world as a competition between alpha and beta males, with alpha males (known as "Chads") being the more attractive, wealthy and dominant men who are able to get the most beautiful women (Nagel, 2017). Embracing the less-attractive beta male role, INCELs divide the female population into "Stacys," their name for young, sexy women who reject the "nice guy" betas in favor of the Chads; and "Beckys," more desperate, less attractive lower-status girls. Social media posts abound relating experiences of women rejecting "nice guys" like themselves in favor of attractive men who mistreat them, a practice dubbed "friend zoning."

INCELs describe their process of developing political awareness as inspired through the Matrix movies' concepts of *redpilling* and *blackpilling*. Redpilling consists of recruiting members by casting misogynists and white supremacists as brave truth tellers spreading knowledge that feminists have somehow suppressed (K. Burns, 2017; Nagel, 2017). Typically, this "knowledge" consists of warmed-over eugenics and evolutionary psychology. Those who describe themselves as blackpilled assert they are now fully awake to the idea that there is a sexually stratified class system based on a detailed categorization of physical features, again tied to flawed notions of evolutionary psychology (Beauchamp, 2019). It should be noted that their talking point of the unfairness of appearance-based social stratification does not extend to "the sexual marginalization of trans people, or women who fall outside the boundaries of conventional attractiveness" (Tolentino, 2018, para. 12).

Though spouting the same talking points as INCEL's, PUAs are about cultivating the persona of a promiscuous alpha man out to get revenge on women by sleeping with them and then discarding them. They justify this approach by citing the belief that deep-down women want to be emotionally abused in relationships; in fact, they will respect men the more they are mistreated. Many PUAs describe themselves as former beta males or INCELs, using their experiences to provide hope for betas that there is an alternative avenue for getting what they feel they are entitled to. In some cases, this extends to the colonialist practice of fetishizing Asian women as both more traditional and sexually available. Some PUAs have even created a business out of selling travel guides and video subscriptions that detail how to roam the globe picking up "exotic" women (Marsha, 2018).

As with MRA and fathers' rights groups, INCELs and PUAs hold contradictory positions. For example, both of these groups are united by a desire to have unfettered access to sexually desirable women, so one would assume they would be in full support of legalizing sex work. However, sex workers are continually portrayed as "dirty whores" to be treated accordingly (Tolentino, 2018). Women who work outside the home are feminists out to demasculinize their partners while women who opt to stay home are gold diggers. Despite INCELs and PUAs expecting women to maintain a high level of attractiveness, they regularly critique women who wear makeup or dress up as deliberately misleading men. At the same time, their hostility knows no bounds for any women who is perceived to have "let herself go" by gaining weight or going without makeup. Wilkinson (2016) reveals similar inconsistencies:

> On their forums I've read long, furious manifestos claiming that women are all sluts who "ride the cock carousel" and sleep with a series of "alpha males" until they reach the end of their sexual prime, at which point they seek out a "beta cuck" to settle down with for financial security. I've lurked silently on blogs dedicated to "pick-up artistry" as men argue that uppity, opinionated, feminist women—women like myself—need to be put in their place through "corrective rape." (para. 4)

Nagel (2017) notes a key hypocrisy in this discourse regarding wanting both traditional values but without any sort of restraint or paternalistic sense of duty like one might have seen within Victorian society or the 1950s. Essentially, the manosphere is about wanting the positive features of the sexual revolution (continued access to women) but without women having reproductive rights.

More disturbingly are the currents of fascist violence that run through the manosphere. Romano (2016) sees men emboldened by a dangerous set of contradictory beliefs where they "are encouraged to view women as sexual and/or political targets" that they must dominate, while at the same time asserting that they are not sexist, just "fighting against their own emasculation and sexual repression at the hands of strident feminists" (para. 14). Kimmel's (2017) overview of interview studies with rapists and domestic abusers reveals a common theme of violence not only revenge-filled, but restorative where getting even becomes the solution when they don't get what they are entitled to. In commenting on an account of a domestic abuser, Kimmel notes a key inversion:

> Emile's sense of entitlement leads him to invert cause and effect: she tries to defend herself from his violence, which he interprets as the initiation of violence

and therefore something that he then as to defend himself against. Thus, his escalation is reimagined as self-defense, a defense against emasculation. Entitlement distorts our perceptions, reverses causation, and leads to an ability to justify a "right" that obtains neither in natural nor in civil law. (p. 186)

This is reflected in the manosphere's attitudes toward rape, ranging from it not existing to being over-reported or made up by women as a way to get revenge on men. A common talking point within INCEL communities is that men are driven to rape because they are celibate loners. Tolentino's (2018) critique of the INCEL-friendly proposal that like economic resources, sex should be distributed more equally illustrates the normalization of lines of thinking about rape: "What INCELs want is extremely limited and specific: they want unattractive, uncouth, and unpleasant misogynists to be able to have sex on demand with young, beautiful women. They believe that this is their right" (para. 12). In contrast to the idea that rapists are mostly loners who act out of sexual frustration, Kimmel (2017) notes that instead rapists "have higher levels of consensual sexual activity than other men, are as likely to have significant relationships with women, and are as likely to be fathers as other men" (p. 183).

It is important to note that the lines between the online manosphere and in-person violence have blurred as the INCEL community have openly celebrated murders of women and men at the hands of self-identified INCELs like Eliot Rodgers who killed six people, injuring 14 and the Toronto van ramming attack which killed ten and injured sixteen (Beauchamp, 2019; para. 5; Tolentino, 2018). Both of these attackers were males under the age of 30. Nagle (2017b) poses prescient questions:

What is it about the alt-right that has captured the imagination of so many young people and at least intrigued a great many more? And if it is true that the committed alt-right becomes more isolated but more militant, what will become of all those young people—especially the young men, who have been radicalized by the alt-right's ideas and never convinced otherwise? What will be the real-world consequences of forcing such figures out of their semi-ironic anonymous online fantasyland, and potentially thrusting them into a toxic flirtation with violent offline tactics? (para. 7)

CONCLUSION

Online spaces are a socialist feminist issue that must be addressed. The act of women and minorities spending time repeatedly explaining racism, sexism, and homophobia needs to be reframed as providing free labor, of taking valuable time away from focusing on issues critical to their communities. It is no coincidence that women and minorities are the ones consistently not believed and accused of bias as well as the ones expected to defend themselves while "educating" others. Emanating from e-libertarianism, white men are rarely ordered to provide endless evidence as justification for their assertions, which are taken at face value.

Further, for those who do diligently moderate online spaces, time is lost in wading through harassing comments versus creating content that could engage or inspire (Poland, 2016). Again, women and minorities are typically the ones having to provide the labor needed to police their online spaces 24/7. One response has been to provide page membership screening questions that are difficult to answer for those who are hostile to leftist and social justice beliefs. This has been relatively successful on private Facebook pages and does seem to reduce trolling and harassment. However, it does run the risk of making these spaces harder to locate just doing a general search. Another common suggestion is to reach out and attempt to dialogue with right-wing posters. Again, this suggestion (coming from a position of privilege) overlooks the issue of time and labor and who ends up providing it:

> Angry white male entitlement is the elevator music of our age. Speaking personally, as a feminist-identified person on the internet, my Twitter mentions are full of practically nothing else. I've spent far too much of my one life trying to listen and understand and offer suggestions in good faith, before concluding that it's not actually my job to manage the hurt feelings of men who are prepared to mortgage the entire future of the species to buy back their misplaced pride. It never was. That's not what feminism is about. (Penny, 2018, para. 38)

When a site is taken over by toxicity, the very topics critical for women and minorities are buried in endless negativity. The possibility for real, in-depth online conversation is impeded. It is important that we recognize that this is not coincidental, but intentional and is supported by the structural features of the Internet and social media sites under capitalism. Those interested in important political issues—and, more importantly—those directly impacted by those issues are more likely to steer clear of sites where the right-wing has taken over, viewing them as more trouble than they are worth (Poland, 2016). There is also the risk that the presence of right-wing comments delegitimizes the original content, further marginalizing leftist ideas.

Within the US, it has been clear that section 230 of the *Communications Decency Act* has only served to protect Internet service providers rather than the majority of Internet users. While a list has been compiled of such companies who regularly fail to protect victims, as Poland (2016) concludes, "unless legal or financial penalties can be applied to companies or websites hosting illegal communications, the benefits of such a list seem limited" (p. 240). We need to legally confront the positioning of site owners and hosts as content middlemen and instead hold them financially accountable, by revamping the *Communications Decency Act* (Siegel, 2017). Publicly owned Internet could also introduce some accountability (Bode, 2018). The future of online discourse is only going to get worse, especially as backlash continues, but this is indicative of people starting to set limits, which regressive segments of the Internet do not like:

In absolute terms, dark web intellectuals enjoy far more access to the mainstream than genuine leftists. But in relative terms, they have far lower status than their intellectual forebears of 20 or even 10 years ago. They are not driving the conversation, and sometimes are being driven from it. This loss of relative social status helps explain the anger and resentment…It's hard for erstwhile hegemons to feel happy about their fall. (Ferrell, 2018, para. 16)

One potential turning point includes the growing public awareness of how social media platforms function, particularly the economic model built on advertising and clicks. Rather than reflecting some sort of massive consensus of "the way things are," people are starting to see the artificiality of social media, in combination with growing concerns about private data becoming public as well as election security. The recent revelations of Trump threatening to withhold aid to Ukraine unless they assisted with locating intel on Joe Biden, a 2020 election opponent, only highlights the global scale of the problem, along with casting doubt on the legitimacy of Trump's win in 2016, assisted by big money (domestic and foreign) channeled through social media platforms filled with bots and fake profiles. Indeed, 2020 Democratic presidential candidate Elizabeth Warren brilliantly highlighted how Facebook deliberately aids and abets right-wing disinformation simply because it is profitable. When Facebook refused to remove Republican-sponsored political ads that were blatantly false, she paid for a Facebook ad of her own, which claimed that Mark Zuckerberg supports Trump in the 2020 election (Fung, 2019). The ad included a debriefing about it being false on purpose, to make a larger point about the far-from-neutral practices of the so-called "marketplace of ideas."

CHAPTER 6

ABORTION THROUGH THE LENS OF FETAL PERSONHOOD

Social Meanings and Functions

INTRODUCTION

In the lead-up to the 2016 Republican primaries, Donald Trump asserted that women who seek an abortion "should face some sort of punishment," a comment that was quickly walked back to place the blame on those performing the procedure, once again safely situating the woman as a victim (Diamond, 2016, para. 1; Smith, S., 2017). Since the election, Trump has spoken at "right to life rallies," reinstated the "global gag rule" prohibiting overseas organizations who receive US funding from providing abortions or even basic health information, successfully installed two anti-choice Supreme Court Justices, and, more recently, inspired Mississippi to pass a ban on abortions after 15 weeks (North, 2018; Smith, S., 2017; Redden, 2017). Even Bernie Sanders campaigned for Nebraska's anti-choice mayoral candidate Heath Mello, defending his actions as, "I think you just can't exclude people who disagree with us on one issue" (Detrow, 2017, para. 8). In other words, the assault on the right of women to access abortion services continues apace.

However, it was the 2012 election in the United States that really brought abortion once again to the forefront of social issues, with an intensity of rightist discourse not seen since the early 1980s during the conservative restoration. Fuelled by the Tea Party (the precursor to Trump) and its opposition to the *Affordable Care Act*, politicians and pundits immediately targeted reproductive health services such as contraceptive coverage as a source of their outrage. What made this resurrection of abortion stand out was the lethal language aimed at women as a whole. Everything from dissecting the lives of poor women, to slut shaming, to attempting to define what kind of rape was worthy of sympathy was up for discussion.

Petchesky (2002) connects the presentation of abortion as being ancillary to civil rights to a fragmented political framing in the US regarding women in general:

> One result is a compartmentalization of women's movement work into discrete "issues"—violence, reproductive rights, sexuality, girls and adolescents, women in development (economics, work)—without sufficient attention to the vital points where these intersect. (p. 75)

The public, then, including many leftists, see abortion and contraception as disconnected from the daily lives of the working class because "it's a women's issue." Abortion is presented as an afterthought, as unimportant or a diversionary fringe issue, a bargaining chip for courting conservative voters. Yet far from being a "fringe issue"—as is often presented by the right, center-right, and liberal political spectra in the US—abortion and the larger aim of reproductive freedom is essential for women, who make up a majority of the world's population.

According to Rowland (2004), approximately 60 million women spanning an age range of 15 to their mid-40s live in the US (p. 270). Of that number, 42 million identify as sexually active, not wanting to become pregnant at that particular time:

> Research suggests that a sexually active woman between ages 20 and 45 who wants two children, will spend, on average, almost 5 years of her life trying to become pregnant or postpartum, and more than four times that long trying to avoid pregnancy. (p. 270)

About 75% of women of childbearing age depend on some form of private insurance to cover reproductive health care, with many requiring Title X funding, which, according to Rowland, is in constant jeopardy due to funding cuts. It is women who bear the physical, social, and emotional brunt of privatized childcare costs in a virtually unresponsive workplace should they decide to have a baby (Smith, 2005, 2017).

Additionally, half of all US pregnancies are unplanned, with nearly a third of pregnancies of married women considered a "surprise" (Joffe, 2011, p. xvi, loc. 83; Rowland, 2004, p. 272). Nearly 60% of women who have an abortion reported using some form of contraception at the time they became pregnant, which is why centrist arguments to outlaw abortion while retaining contraception are flawed strategy (Rowland, 2004, p. 105). Contrary to the image of a young, irresponsible, selfish woman seeking to end a pregnancy so that she can have fun, the majority of abortions performed in the US are for women (married and unmarried) who already have one or more children (Joffe, 2011, p. 145, loc. 1920; Rowland, 2004, p. 294). Even though three fourths of abortions are performed on unmarried women, a good portion of those receiving abortions are married and identify as religious (43% Protestant, 27% Catholic), further eroding media stereotypes (p. 289).

It is no coincidence that abortion and contraception have remained controversial, even though these can be counted among the many safe, routine, medical procedures used by a majority of American women. Rosen (2012) pinpoints the continuing controversy to how women are viewed, with ripple effects stemming from key Court decisions starting in the 1960s:

> For most of human history, sexuality and reproduction have been intricately yoked together. Birth control, particularly the Pill, ruptured that link and gave women the right to enjoy sex without the goal of reproduction. When the Supreme Court formally ratified that rupture by making abortion legal in

Roe v. Wade (1973), many people in this country trembled at the possible changes women's sexual independence might bring. (para. 14)

Indeed, Joffe (2011) locates America's uncomfortable relationship with abortion to a larger uncertainty about sexuality itself. Penny's (2011) insightful framing of prostitution as an economic issue references the societal terror conjured by the "notion of women gaining real sexual control over the proceeds of that labor" (p. 20). Objectification in capitalist society requires that women "remain alienated from our sexuality" despite it being a primary "means of survival in the meat market" (p. 21).

For Rich (1986), another aspect of this discomfort with female-driven sexuality involves society as a whole still dealing with women departing from the biologically determined role of the mother. This mother figure has to be all-suffering and asexual. The removal of that suffering means a severe rupture of social and self-identity, which is not tolerated on the Right. Abortion and contraception represent the ability for women alone (not husbands, fathers, boyfriends, male family members, clergy, police, or politicians) to determine whether or not to have children, and the spacing of those children. Males do not have to be involved in the decision at all, though working-class men also benefit from access to reproductive health care. This is simply not acceptable for the right wing who will continue to do everything in its power to marginalize women and erode working class solidarity through reproductive control.

This chapter dialectically examines, from a Marxist Feminist perspective, a specific ideological development in the abortion/contraction controversy distributed through the media, that of fetal personhood. First, an overview of recent abortion legislation will be presented, highlighting recent personhood bills. Next, the ideology of fetal personhood is examined, along with its legal implausibility. Finally, I present four ways that fetal personhood benefits the ruling class by objectifying women, eroding solidarity, increasing surveillance, and justifying public sector cuts as part of austerity.

ABORTION: AN OVERVIEW

The historical trajectory of abortion legislation has always been contentious, but not necessarily linear. As Casper (1998) explains,

Reproduction is a key site of social control over women and of women's agency, both of which differ by race, ethnicity, class, and sexuality. In the United States and elsewhere, women's reproductive processes are contested and stratified at the interpersonal, biomedical/scientific, cultural, economic, political, and global levels of social life. (p. 10)

Abortion itself was allowable in the early US colonies as well as English common law and the Church prior to the detection of fetal movement, or "quickening" (Rowland, 2004). It was only after the growth of medical knowledge in the 1800s that restrictions against abortion and contraception began to occur, continuing until the first challenge in the form of *Griswold v. Connecticut* in the 1960s, which allowed access to contraception. This paved the way for a further extension of reproductive rights, explored more deeply in Roe v. Wade in 1973.

The Roe decision was ground-breaking, as Rowland (2004) notes:

> From this language came the modern notion of 'reproductive privacy' and a shift in the landscape of women's rights. The decision legalized first-trimester elective abortion, setting forth a cleanly-divided trimester framework to be used by the courts in balancing the rights of women against the interests of states. It was an important intersection of law and medicine. (p. 111)

Immediately after Roe, restrictions began. The most invasive was the *Hyde Amendment* in 1977, which denied federal funding for abortion. The implementation of mandatory waiting periods soon followed. In addition to targeting poor and minority women, laws restricting contraception and abortion services for minors were passed. During this time period of the 1970s and 1980s, women who sought abortions were portrayed as baby-killers, lesbians, and sluts and abortion became a litmus test for conservative politicians. By the 1990s, fetal personhood had already become an integral part of proposed and active legislation, including the 2007 ban on a second-trimester abortion procedure, the first of its kind (Joffe, 2011).

According to Rudolph (2012), the origins of the contemporary opposition to abortion as an organizing feature of the Christian Right wasn't in response to Roe v. Wade at first, but instead had to do with a more obscure reason: protecting the tax-exempt status of religion:

> In the early 1970s, the U.S. government was looking for ways to extend the provisions of the Civil Rights Act of 1964. The IRS opined that any organization that engaged in racial discrimination was not, by definition, a charitable organization and therefore should be denied tax-exempt status... On January 19, 1976, the IRS...revoked Bob Jones University's tax-exempt status. Bob Jones University sued to retain its tax exemption. It eventually lost at the Supreme Court in 1982 and conservative activist Paul Weyrich sensed the electoral potential of enlisting evangelical voters in the conservative crusade. (p. 17)

Led by Weyrich, other pastors spun the ruling against schools that practiced segregation into an attack on states' rights and religious freedom. During the legal battle, because President Carter was for removing the tax-exempt status from Bob Jones University, evangelicals removed their support from him and put it behind Reagan. Eventually, abortion was latched onto as a way to recruit more centrist liberals away from the Democratic Party when original messages such as lower taxes and deregulation had little sway by themselves.

For all of the talk about its "fringe" status, abortion is a key legislative target. In 2011, roughly 40,000 laws and their accompanying provisions were enacted. Close to 1,000 of those restricted access to abortion (Easley, Jones, Haraldsson, & Rmuse,

2013, para. 7). The majority of the legislative activity was at the state level, with 135 of these provisions enacted in 36 states (para. 10). A majority of the provisions restricted abortion services, exceeding all previous statistics on such actions. Of the restrictions, six states enacted bans, three states implemented waiting periods, five states introduced ultrasound requirements, eight states now have bans on insurance coverage for abortion, four states have clinic regulations, and seven states prohibit medication abortion (para. 11).

Baker (2013) notes that ten states have implemented time limits for abortion as low as 20 weeks, based on the notion that fetuses can feel pain (para. 11). Proposals for a 12-week ban are in the works, which would represent the harshest measures to date. Much of this recent legislative activity is due to the outcome of the 2010 midterm elections, where 44 abortion rights supporters in the House were replaced by opponents, with the Senate experiencing seven pro-choice losses (Clark, 2011, p. 28). Added to this is the revised Republican Party platform which states that abortion is opposed in all cases with no exceptions for rape, incest, or risk to the woman's life (Cohen, 2012).

The assault has also targeted poor and working-class women in the form of removal of state funds for abortion services. Currently, 32 states along with the District of Columbia will not allow state monies to be used for abortions, except as a result of incest, rape, or threat to the life of the woman (Smith, S., 2017, p. 21). Those who think that receiving private insurance shields them from these restrictions are wrong, with 11 states enacting restrictions on coverage of abortions (p. 20). This is on top of the 17 states that mandate counseling services prior to an abortion, 27 states requiring waiting periods of 24 hours and 26 states mandating parental consent for minors seeking abortions (p. 22).

Easley and colleagues (2013) readily overturn the notion that the war on women is merely hyperbole or a media stunt by summarizing an array of anti-abortion laws that have been introduced by Republicans: denial of birth control in pharmacies known as *conscience clauses* (HR 1179), prohibition of all abortion except in cases of incest, rape, or health endangerment (HB 2988, Texas); requiring women to attend "spiritual counselling" before obtaining an abortion (HB 1217, South Dakota); mandating that doctors provide misinformation prior to patients receiving an abortion (e.g. that abortions cause suicide ideation or breast cancer; HB 1166, South Dakota, HB 1210 Indiana, Kansas); conditions applied to access to abortion (the "forcible rape" exempt category, HR 3, New Jersey); denial of insurance coverage for birth control and abortion (Senate Bill 438, Georgia; SB 92, Wisconsin), restricting transport to a facility for live-saving procedures (HR 358, Pennsylvania); effectively banning the teaching of abortion methods in medical schools (federal funding House amendment), onerous clinic and personnel requirements including licensure denial (Kansas, Mississippi, Illinois, Virginia, Louisiana, Minnesota); and using austerity as a rationale for ending abortion, including cuts to or defunding of Planned Parenthood (Minnesota, Arizona, Louisiana, Ohio).

153

Many of the anti-abortion laws, whether active or overturned, are directly connected to the fetal personhood strategy (Easley et al., 2013). They include The Pain Capable Unborn Child Protection Act (SB 209, Georgia; Bill 1888, Oklahoma; Nebraska; H.R. 3803, District of Columbia) and the Fetal Pain Bill (House Bill 954, Georgia); Arizona's House Bill 206 which prohibits abortions after 20 weeks (technicalities in the law also classify women as pregnant even prior to conception); Texas' Sonogram Bill (HB 15) which originally required even victims of rape to view images of their wombs prior to receiving an abortion; trans-vaginal ultrasound bills which require women to undergo the procedure before obtaining an abortion (Alaska, Texas, Virginia, Iowa, Alabama); forcing women to watch footage of an abortion before obtaining one (Arizona); outlawing fertility treatments and birth control along with abortion (SB 2771, Mississippi); defending an abortion ban after 20 weeks by viewing a pregnancy as a result of rape or incest as "God's will" (Senate Bill 1165, Idaho); fertilized-egg-as-person bills which would also outlaw contraception (Ohio, Mississippi, Oklahoma); and prohibition of abortion after six weeks (Heartbeat Bill, Ohio).

Some of the legislative actions are directly centered on establishing personhood, such as those in Virginia, Wisconsin, Kansas, and Alabama (Easley et al., 2013). Another strategy is represented by HB1305 in North Dakota, which would make it a Class A misdemeanor for a doctor to perform an abortion based on the gender of a fetus. According to Smith (2013), this is another way of implementing deadlines on seeking abortions (the gender of a fetus can be usually determined at 12 weeks). The fact that these types of laws are often successfully challenged in the courts is beside the point—their very existence shows the continual threat to women's reproductive rights.

Anti-abortion laws and commentary have also begun to traverse the path of establishing punitive consequences for abortion. These include: taxing abortions (H.B. 2598, Kansas); publicly posting identifying information of medical providers and women who have abortions (Life Defense Act, HB 3808, Tennessee); Georgia's illegality of abortions and miscarriages with the death penalty applied for proven violations (amendment to existing state law); women and doctors undergoing abortion as being guilty of committing "feticide" (HB 587, Louisiana; House File 2298, Iowa); a call for public hangings as a "deterrent" for the crimes of abortion, rape, and kidnapping (Representative Larry Pittman, North Carolina); no exceptions for rape, incest or health of the mother who would receive a life sentence with suspicious miscarriages being criminally investigated (House File 2298, Iowa); homicide charges applied to the death of an embryo (House Bill 3517, Tennessee); using ultrasounds to ensure that pregnant rape victims were indeed raped, along with invasive questions by doctors asking about marital and relationship status in the context of the rape (S. 1387, Idaho); forcing women to carry even dead fetuses to term because that's what farm animals do in nature (Georgia Rep. Terry England in support of HR 954 banning abortions after 20 weeks), and legalizing the murder of abortion doctors (South Dakota, Nebraska, Iowa).

Citing "religious liberty" as a justification, opposition to contraception intensified in the wake of the passage of the *Affordable Care Act*, which requires that employers and university health plans cover contraception without copays or deductibles (Baker, 2012). Contraception provisions as part of the Obama Administration's health care reform have been challenged in Nebraska, Florida, Michigan, Ohio, Oklahoma, South Carolina, Alabama, and Texas, on the grounds of inhibiting religious freedom (Easley et al., 2013). Indiana has proposed an especially invasive ultrasound bill that would require women to receive two trans-vaginal probes (before and after) in order to receive the RU-486 pill (Strasser, 2013). The use of probes is medically irrelevant since a blood test could verify that a pregnancy had been ended.

FETAL PERSONHOOD: IDEOLOGY & LAW

A major organizing aspect of the anti-abortion movement is the notion of fetal personhood, which is the justification behind the bulk of recent legislative efforts. It is important to note that religion, while still a primary influencing factor behind the anti-choice movement, is now joined by medicine as a potential ally:

> Part of the reason this has gathered steam in recent decades is something of a convergence of medical science and anti-abortion rhetoric whereby the objective and ostensibly value-free claims of science regarding the fetus are supplementing, even superseding, value-laden religious anti-abortion argumentation. In addition, parental and medical concern for the wanted fetus as patient tends to bolster anti-abortion claims of the personhood, if not primacy, of the fetus. (McCullough, 2012, p. 19)

It is understandable why the notion of fetal personhood has taken a powerful discursive hold in not only the United States, but across the world. What can be more democratic (or even social justice sounding) than everyone enjoying the protections of one's nation, including those most vulnerable and voiceless? To oppose such a thing transforms one into a heartless bully who is no better than the Nazis were, bent on exterminating the "feebleminded" or those not racially fit. Needless to say, when the anti-choice right landed on fetal personhood, they struck gold.

A major factor in the entrenchment of fetal personhood has been medical advances in obstetrics, the use of the ultrasound in particular (Casper, 1998; Joffe, 2011). Joffe (2011) notes the increasingly common practice of parents displaying ultrasound documents as the first pictures of their "baby." Even though most abortions happen in the first trimester with just over 1% occurring after the 20th week (Smith, S., 2017, p. 16), women are given detailed descriptions of fetal development as a potential deterrent, even going as far as mandating the ultrasound procedure as a condition of obtaining an abortion. Further complicating the picture are physicians who belong to pro-life caucuses of organizations such as the American College of Obstetricians and Gynecologists and groups such as the American Academy of Family Physicians.

Joffe points out that some of these physicians do not feel obligated to refer patients to those who might provide abortion and contraception services.

Using fetal personhood logic, pharmacists are also able to enact consciousness clauses, where they can refuse to fill prescriptions for contraceptives (including emergency contraception), viewed as threatening the fetus. Catholic-affiliated hospitals are not allowed to perform life-saving abortions or administer abortion pills to rape survivors (even though, according to Cohen (2012), over 30,000 pregnancies are a result of rape (para. 9) due to the prioritization of the fetus. Ginty (2011) outlines the heroic action of hospital administrator Sister Margaret McBride who approved a life-saving abortion, resulting in her excommunication. Rowland (2004) traces the origins of today's fetal personhood ideology to the struggle over access to contraception. In the Griswold case, doctors asserted that the Fourteenth Amendment applied to those yet "unconceived" and that fetuses had an interest in the outcome of the case.

Casper's (1998) research into the medicalization of the fetus is useful in understanding the trajectory of fetal personhood, as well as who composes the anti-choice movement. She identifies the fetal personhood movement as part of a broader construct of "fetal politics" that includes

> the crafting of a new science called fetology, controversies over fetal tissue research, the emergence of fetal rights in law and ethics, debates about and proscriptions on pregnant women's behavior, a cultural obsession with fetal images, and the relentless pursuit of new reproductive technologies. (p. 4)

Casper explains that success rate of fetal surgeries is extremely low. Of those fetuses that survive and are eventually born, many are maimed for life, assuming that that life is a long one to begin with. There is also a social class dimension to this, as these are extremely expensive procedures that only the wealthiest (and white) can afford. As the media focuses on the miraculous medical achievements of fetal surgery, it also masks the growing heath care crisis as more and more people are unable to achieve basic health services. The cultural myths surrounding motherhood often cover the reality of drastically uneven access to basic prenatal care, for example. As these medical advancements close in on women, rendering them invisible in favor of the fetus, a darker ethics emerge, which Casper (1998) explores. If a woman declines the option of fetal surgery, is she then culpable in the death of her child? Or, harder to consider, is if a woman opts for fetal surgery even knowing that her child will be profoundly disabled the rest of her/his life. Apparently, that type of "choice" is fine with the Right.

New (2013) speculates that attitudes toward abortion are tied to views about the morality of premarital sex, with hardline Catholics and evangelicals taking the most oppositional stances against both. The impossibility of implementing controls over sexuality in the face of a secular society appears to perplex New, who remains against abortion:

I always remind pro-lifers that a promiscuous society will never support significant restrictions on abortion. While pro-lifers are good at talking about fetal development and personal responsibility, we are less comfortable with subjects such as sexual activity and contraception. Indeed, it is doubtless more difficult to advocate for sexual restraint than for the unborn. However, this is a battle in which pro-lifers must continue to engage if we are to succeed in our goal of providing legal protection to all unborn children. (para. 3)

Yet Marty (2013) points to surveys that show that close to 95% of adults have had premarital sex, with a respectable 60% not viewing such relations as sinful. For Marty, the strategy of ending abortion by trying to convince people that premarital sex is wrong seems like a herculean task at best. What is interesting is how New (2013) tentatively acknowledges that it is easier to talk about the fetus than to broach the topic of adult sexual conduct, pointing to some of the psychology behind the anti-abortion movement and reasons for its staying power.

For McCullough (2012), there are only two outcomes of the fetal personhood movement. The first is one where the concept of citizenship becomes so broad as to be rendered null. If eggs and sperm can be human beings entitled to rights, property, etc., then the legal implications lead quickly to inertia and an inability to apply universal definitions of citizenship to a range of situations. The second outcome is one of dystopia aimed at women, along the lines of Margaret Atwood's (1998) *The Handmaid's Tale*. McCullough (2012) describes the aftermath of the fall of communism in Poland and how it contributed to the country making abortion unconstitutional, enacting a "Poland's traumatic transition away from communism played into this portrayal of the fetus as a democratic citizen fetus—a kind of blank-slate citizen, or future citizen, onto which the hopes and dreams of the nation could be projected," (p. 20). McCullough further emphasizes that in the case of Poland, fetuses were not simply transformed into citizens, but the purest form of citizen: the "innocent" person.

Rowland (2004) reviews two clauses of the Fourteenth Amendment relevant to the issue of abortion and women's rights: The Equal Protection Clause and the Due Process Clause. There are two forms of due process, procedural (which has to do with compliance before the intervention of state or federal authorities), and substantive (having to do with previously undefined concepts of liberty). What fetal personhood ideology has done is attempt to extend these same protections to fetuses, embryos, and even eggs. Reacting to these efforts, Crist (2010) distinguishes between "person" and one who is granted constitutional rights, noting that fetal personhood laws fall apart under legal analysis:

Personhood is not a one-dimensional construct. In fact, there are different types of legal personhood, and not all of them fall within the Fourteenth Amendment. In other words, the fetus can be a "person" in some legal ways, but not a "person" of the type contemplated by the Constitution. Thus, we can refer to the fetus as a person without necessarily granting it a constitutional right to life. (p. 862)

Crist distinguishes between natural persons, i.e. human beings viewed as worthy of dignity for simply being human, and juridical persons, non-human entities who are afforded legal protections such as corporations:

> The fetus, like the corporation, is not entitled to protections because of what it is innately. Instead, the law recognizes that there is a natural person, the mother, who has fundamental interests at stake. Her rights are invested in another entity, the fetus. The law gives that entity juridical personhood to ensure that the rights of the mother may be secured, just as the law gives the corporation juridical personhood to protect the rights of the shareholders. (p. 865)

A law can refer to a fetus as a "person" but that doesn't necessarily mean it is granted a right to life via the Constitution.

Crist therefore appears to have full confidence in Roe's standing:

> Even if a legislature wanted to create full fetal personhood, it would be without power to do so. Simply put: fetal laws do not confer personhood upon the fetus because procedurally, they cannot…The Supreme Court has already made clear that the fetus is not a "person"' under the Constitution, and thus is not entitled to protection from deprivation of "life, liberty [or] equal protection of the laws." Legislatures cannot declare otherwise, since this would be in derogation of the Constitution, as interpreted by the Supreme Court in *Roe v, Wade.* Thus, if a legislature attempted to establish natural fetal personhood, its law would simply have no effect unless *Roe's* essential holding was overturned. (p. 867)

This analysis points to a rationale behind attempts to overturn *Roe.* If it were to fall, then the final barrier to fetal personhood would be achieved, and the end of reproductive freedom. Of course, one could argue that the entire purpose of personhood laws is to end abortion, so both means would point to the same end.

Crist (2010) also asserts that there does not have to be a conflict between fetal homicide laws and access to abortion. Much depends on the purpose of the laws. For example, feticide laws are in place because of a recognition of the unique biological situation of a pregnant woman. They are not in place to challenge the right to an abortion (even though supporters for such laws may have that intent in mind). California and Maryland are two states that make it explicitly clear that feticide and abortion are separate situations, with abortion's status remaining legal. There is also the matter of abortion and feticide laws being focused on the rights of the actor (the woman and the attacker, respectively) and not the object of the action (the fetus). Under the law, a woman deciding to obtain an abortion is not held to the same legal consequences as someone who murders a pregnant woman and her fetus:

> If we take this actor distinction one step further, we come to the issue of consent. Forgetting entirely that the fetus even exists, abortion is a medical

procedure performed on the autonomous body of a pregnant woman. Bodily invasion requires consent. This is the very difference between a battery and a hug. When a woman chooses abortion, she consents to the actions taken upon her body. Women do not consent to brutal attacks that end their pregnancies. (p. 882)

The problem with Crist's analysis, however, is that it assumes that the matter of the actor is settled in terms of public perception. For Crist's assurances to hold up, there has to be agreement that consent is the purview of the woman. Yet anti-choicers continually assert a false equivalency of personhood by arguing, "what about the fetus' consent—do they have say?" What anti-abortion activists have essentially done is to craft a fetal separatist movement where not just embryos, but eggs are prioritized over grown women (Burroughs, 2012). Ultimately, relying on *Roe's* legal protections is a shaky proposition in the face of a group that is not really motivated by who is represented in abortion law, but *by limiting women's rights*—a group who has made it clear they will use any form of legislative discourse to achieve that end.

OPPRESSIVE OUTCOMES OF FETAL PERSONHOOD

When approaching history from a dialectical perspective, it becomes clear that rather than remaining static, laws shift and change under capitalism to maintain key benefits for the ruling class (Marx, 1845). In the case of reproductive rights, to a large degree the ruling class appears tolerant of the existence of contraception and abortion on a social level. That doesn't mean, however, that they do not benefit from its continued opposition by conservative groups. For example, the resurrection of attacks on abortion and contraception during the lead up to the passage of the *Affordable Care Act* was utilized by the ruling class who has a key interest in making sure that national single payer healthcare does not happen. This section looks at four key ways that the construct of fetal personhood contributes to the continuing oppression of women, in particular working-class women. These include objectification, erosion of solidarity, increased surveillance, and justification for slashing the public sector.

Objectifying Women

As Rowland (2004) points out, "An independent female sexual identity, one devoid of maternal instincts or disinclined to have heirs, has been perceived throughout history as nothing less than dangerous" (p. xxvii). Fetal personhood represents a powerful form of objectification of women, that of rendering them invisible so as to remove some of that danger. Casper (1998) describes how the fetus being placed front and center has automatically removed the adult woman from the picture:

Like the oversized fetus in *2001: A Space Odyssey*, fetuses are increasingly portrayed as free-floating and larger than life. Where fetuses were once confined to anonymity and invisibility inside pregnant women's bodies, the fetus has now gone solo. Never mind that most fetuses cannot live outside of a woman's body. Contemporary fetal representations routinely erase women's agency and bodies. (p. 16)

Understanding how objectification functions can be helpful in situating the abortion issue. According to Nussbaum (2010), there are seven key ways that people—women especially—can be objectified by those in power. Though Nussbaum was speaking to the objectification of women in Internet forums, these different means of objectification can also be applied to the fetishizing of the fetus over the humanity of the woman. First, is *instrumentality*, where those who do the objectifying envision their victim as nothing more than a means to an end. In the case of the anti-choice concept of pregnancy, women are vessels for carrying the fetus. Second is the *denial of autonomy*, where those who objectify refuse to acknowledge the capability of a woman to make independent decisions. Anti-abortion groups are resistant to the idea of women rationally considering their own bodies in making reproductive health choices, as evidenced by the endless regulations they propose. Third is *inertness*, where women are viewed as passive, waiting to hear what they need to do next. The framing of "alternatives" to abortion, such as crisis pregnancy centers or adoption, operate under the notion that women are frozen in a perpetual state of indecision when it comes to reproductive choices.

Fourth is *fungibility*, where women-as-objects are anonymous and interchangeable with each other. The insistence of the anti-choice movement on women carrying each and every pregnancy to term regardless of context is an example of the anti-choice movement objectifying women as interchangeable entities: all pregnancy is the same pregnancy. All children must be welcomed children. Fifth is *violability* where women who are objectified are viewed as having no boundaries with an assumed permission to invade or destroy. Anti-choice support for trans-vaginal ultrasound bills and denial of abortion in the case of rape are prime examples of violable objectification. Sixth is *ownership*, where women are treated as property. Countless anti-choice propaganda sends the message that women of reproductive age do not fully own their bodies. Instead, those bodies belong to males via the fetus. Finally, the seventh form of objectivity is the *denial of subjectivity*, where the emotions and life experiences of women do not matter. Certainly, this is most characteristic of the conspicuous absence of women to begin with in the abortion conversation.

Nussbaum (2010) goes on to note that there are three additional forms of objectification which include reducing women to body parts (with abortion, women are walking wombs), reduction to appearance (when women are discussed among anti-abortion circles, those who violate the norms of motherhood are "sluts," including rape victims), and silencing (women are not allowed to have a voice in reproductive decision making beyond the range of birthing options). Autonomy can be more than denied; it can be violated, where "the objectifier forcibly removes, or curtails, the woman's autonomy" (p. 72). The ideological invisibility of women in the abortion debate is therefore a particular form of uber-objectification where adult women are forced to the margins of the abortion question. Their presence is unwelcome:

> Arguments against abortion have in common a valuing of the unborn fetus over the living woman…The woman is thus isolated from her historical context as woman; her decision for or against abortion is severed from the peculiar status of women in human history. The antiabortion movement trivializes women's impulses toward education, independence, self-determination as self-indulgence. (Rich, 1986, p. xvi)

An example of objectification in action is noted by Davis (2010), who examined the prevalence of males in the profession of editorial cartooning and how this affected the framing of current issues like abortion. Female political cartoonists such as Jen Sorensen tend to highlight the irony of males making decisions about abortion. By contrast, a content analysis of abortion-related political cartoons created by males from 2005 to 2010 showed no images of a pregnant women speaking: "A common device is for the fetus to speak instead of the mother" (p. 20).

Eroding Solidarity between Women

Fetal personhood is a fundamental attack on the solidarity women can experience through socialist feminist awareness. Sexuality and reproduction are key biological and social ways of shared experience that cut across many boundaries such as age, income, race, ability, and sexual orientation. All humans are sexual beings yet women in particular often bear the brunt of current sexual policies. This is not to say that there are not important differences across these identities when it comes to reproductive rights; just that in the feminist movement of the early 1970s, conversations began to emerge along socialist lines about the need for recognizing that working class women had to maintain control of all decisions regarding their own bodies, regardless of their particular background or identity. This was especially critical in terms of economics. For example, the most economically vulnerable women were the first to be targeted after the gains of *Roe v. Wade*, in the form of the Hyde Amendment (Joffe, 2011; Rowland, 2004; Smith, 2005). As Smith (2017) points out,

> the most typical abortion patient is Black or Latina, in her 20s or 30s, who is living below or slightly below the federal poverty line and already has one or more children. Furthermore, 54% of abortion patients pay for it themselves, without Medicaid or insurance funding. First trimester abortions can cost from $400 to $1500 according to planned parenthood. (p. 16)

Rape is often used as a dividing line between women, with advocates of fetal personhood questioning the long-held notion of rape being an exception to banning abortion even among many anti-abortion advocates. The endless parsing of imaginary categories of rape into "acceptable" and "unacceptable" or "forcible rape" versus some less violent version is a testament to slut shaming at its finest. Former Republican Missouri State Senator Todd Akin's famous quote about legitimate rape and abortion comes to mind: "That's [pregnancy as a result of rape] really rare. If it's a legitimate rape, the female body has ways to try to shut that whole thing down" (Cohen, 2012, paras. 2–3). In 2006, Republican South Dakota State Senator Bill Napoli supported legislation to ban all abortions in the state. When asked if he would allow for any exceptions to the ban, he went into great detail adding conditions to an exception for rape:

> [She] would be a rape victim, brutally raped, savaged. The girl was a virgin. She was religious. She planned on saving her virginity until she was married. She was...sodomized as bad as you can possibly make it, and is impregnated. I mean, that girl could be so messed up, physically and psychologically, that carrying that child could very well threaten her life. (Joffe, 2011, p. 62, loc. 882–886)

These statements carry with them several cultural assumptions about women and sexuality: that somehow rape is more traumatic and unwanted if one isn't a virgin, that extra-vaginal rape is more violating than the "right way" to have sex, that lifestyle choices somehow "bring on" rape, and that pregnancies as a result of rape imply a form of consent on the part of the victim who is therefore selfish for seeking an abortion. The obsession with locating true victimhood is not much different than the quest for the perfect innocent person: the fetus.

Joffe's (2011) interviews with abortion clinic staff and patients revealed heartbreaking accounts of isolation and eroded solidarity between women, particularly patients who considered themselves anti-abortion:

> "I am a Christian-I am not doing this casually," one woman said, clearly suggesting that others in the waiting room were not so thoughtful or moral. Another woman said, "I think that people should be held accountable for their actions, and a lot of times it's the convenience of the situation that makes it easy...to get an abortion, and if I wasn't the person that I was, I mean, this would be real easy, just real simple...I wouldn't support them because...it might become a habit for everyone." (Joffe, 2011, p. 116, loc. 1565–1570)

The anti-choice women had to reconcile the contradiction of their own anti-abortion beliefs and narratives with the stark reality of sitting in the clinic, facing the very situation they had openly derided others for in the past. Many of the women Joffe interviewed already had children. The only way out of their moral contradiction was to distance themselves from other patients by ascribing legitimate reasons to their own choices while framing other women were being promiscuous. For Joffe, this represented manifest shame, in particular as the women often expressed concern that someone might recognize them in the clinic. Indeed, many of the women deliberately chose to travel long distances to ensure that would not happen. After their repeated encounters with anti-choice women, clinic staff wryly described the three exceptions for abortion as being "rape," "incest," and "mine."

The Right has also been using multicultural strategies in their divisive attacks on reproductive rights. Kamoa (2012) provides the example of how homophobic laws and policies are presented as a way to stem the time of "Western" secularism that is targeting "Christian" populations in African countries. This successfully plays on legitimate concerns of the ravages of colonialism on the part of Western nations. Mixed into the message of resisting Western forces, however, is extreme nationalism, as in the case of Zambia's "kill the gays" laws. As Kamoa puts it, "this deep-seated view of LGBT rights as a neocolonial import puts Westerners hoping to stand in solidarity with those under threat for their sexuality in a difficult spot" (p. 15).

A similar tactic occurs with anti-abortion laws and policies being promoted to African-American and Latino/a communities with an anti-eugenicist message through websites like blackgenocide.org and groups such as the National Black Pro-Life Coalition, Blacks for Life, and Human Life International. This decontextualizes the historical and ongoing reality of eugenic overpopulation discourse and policies such as sterilization, overwhelmingly aimed at majority world countries and African-Americans in the US (Rich, 1986). Additionally, Martinez (2002) notes the short-sightedness of mainstream feminist organizations who often assume that women of color are anti-choice or are not interested in reproductive rights issues:

> The problem has often been rooted in a racist arrogance underlying the attitude of many Anglo women toward Latina views on reproductive rights… If we look more closely at Latina views, we find that reproductive freedom is a major concern of Latinas and not some taboo subject or minor matter. In 1977, when Congress ended federal funding of abortions, the first victim was a 27-year-old Chicana—Rosie Jimenez from McAllen, Texas, daughter of migrant workers—who died at the hands of an illegal abortionist after six days of suffering. (p. 273)

These collective efforts of the anti-choice movement see eroded solidarity as a key victory for anti-working-class policies as a whole.

Expanding Surveillance

Marcotte (2013) notes that part of the long-standing strategy of a focus on fetal personhood has been the ability to cultivate sympathy for an embryo without appearing to be too harsh in one's responses to women who seek and obtain abortions, or, as she explains, "Claiming they don't believe that women who get abortions are murderers even while calling abortion "murder" has been a huge part of the anti-choice movement for years" (para. 6). For example, when pressed as to who should be penalized for seeking an abortion if the procedure were to become illegal, the past response was a call for punishing the doctors performing abortions (Rowland, 2004).

163

The woman was carefully avoided as a topic of conversation so as to distance the anti-choice movement from appearing to be anti-woman.

To maintain this line of messaging, the woman, who has no ability to think independently concerning medical decisions (regardless of her age), has to "fall prey" to the malicious intentions of a highly funded abortion network. She should not be to blame, just the liberal, anti-family feminists and the medical establishment who deliberately target the most vulnerable. The default position sustaining this thinking, of course, is that all women "naturally" want to have children so something malicious and out of the ordinary must be at work if a woman seeks an abortion or even oral contraceptives.

However, a recent shift has emerged where we are seeing calls for punitive actions against women who seek abortions (Joffe, 2011; Marcotte, 2013). Marcotte (2013) describes efforts in Iowa to introduce a bill that would define abortion as murder, and require the appropriate legal response aimed at women who engage in such murder. The bill also reaches further by targeting oral contraceptives:

> The point of this bill is, simply put, to throw women in jail for "murder" for deliberately ending pregnancies—and quite possibly for trying to prevent them, as many anti-choicers continue to insist, despite the evidence against them, that the pill and emergency contraception work by "killing" fertilized eggs…The language of this is quite expansive. They're not only counting women who reach out to legal providers for abortion as "murderers," but also women who go online and buy drugs for this purpose. (para. 4)

Marcotte (2013) speculates that this recent attitudinal shift is due to a growing number of women taking matters into their own hands, including seeking in-home use abortion remedies obtained online or traveling to Mexico to have the procedure done. Women have had to do this because of within-state barriers such as mandatory waiting periods, clinic closures, and economic constraints in the wake of the Hyde Amendment (Rowland, 2004). An increasing number of women independently seeking abortions through other means contradict the stereotype of helpless victims who are prey to evil feminist forces and nefarious doctors. It turns out that a significant number of women were not waiting for anti-abortion laws to "change their minds" and are not interested after all in carrying an unintended pregnancy to term, including many women who identify as anti-choice (Joffe, 2011). Marcotte (2013) feels that this has created a gloves-off attitudinal shift in the anti-choice movement, laying bare its deep misogyny in its call for imprisoning women who do not want to be pregnant and insist on defying the natural order of things.

Initially, fetal homicide laws were designed as part of a recognition by law enforcement and social services agencies that pregnant women faced increased crime risk, including domestic violence (Jones, 2013). What has happened instead is that fetal homicide laws have been used punitively against pregnant women, specifically those who are from marginalized groups:

These laws shifted the balance of power in favor of the state and the language of the debate began to change. Developing fetuses so clearly defined by the Justices in *Roe v. Wade* became "unborn children" in need of the protection of the state. Child abuse statutes were used to bully or prosecute women in aggressive, heavy-handed campaigns undertaken—as often, no doubt, in the stated effort to "help people"—as part of a larger political effort intended to change the nation's perspective on "unborn children" by taking aim at the easiest targets: poor, downtrodden, drug-and alcohol-addicted women. (Rowland, 2004, p. 318)

Fetal homicide laws essentially created the category of the unborn human, tried apart from the mother carrying it. What this resulted in was making women subject to the control of the state and their actions placed under intensified surveillance (Jones, 2013).

The problem is that fetal personhood immediately throws us into a competing rights framework where the more rights the unborn receive, the fewer rights the woman carrying the fetus is entitled to (McCullough, 2012). For example, while citizens are afforded protections by the country in which they live, they are also at the same time granting the state access to engage in particular legal behaviors such as surveillance, seizure of property, and access to one's home, etc. Those who propose a fetal personhood legal framework seem to want to transfer all of the protections of citizenship to the fetus, with all of the intrusion-oriented state functions falling to the adult woman who is carrying the fetus. The woman then serves as an appendage whose sole purpose is to absorb the trials of citizenship without question. On the other hand, the fetus experiences no legal sanction whatsoever.

Feticide laws exist in 38 states (Cohen, 2011, para. 11). Of these states, 10 set boundaries at viability while 21 states count the entire pregnancy as prosecutable (Crist, 2010, p. 858). Burroughs (2012) notes, "The state could charge and imprison women who harmed their fetuses by using over-the-counter medications, smoking, or drinking alcohol. The feticide statute could be construed as covering a full range of pregnant woman's behavior" (p. 47). Substance abuse during pregnancy is viewed as grounds for civil convictions in Minnesota, South Dakota, and Washington. More than 200 women have been arrested based on fetal separatist convictions (Rowand, 2004). A majority of these women are minority and poor (Cohen, 2011; Rowland, 2004; Tilly & Albeda, 2002).

Burroughs (2012) and Cohen (2011) relate the situation of Bci Bei Shuai, who had attempted suicide during her pregnancy in reaction to finding out her boyfriend was married and planning to leave her. She was stabilized but her fetus died a few days after being born. Not long after, Shuai was arrested and charged with attempted feticide. Indiana's law recognizes the fetus the same as a person—since Shuai's fetus' death was viewed as a result of her attempted suicide, she is being charged according to the law. The impact of the Shuai case is far-reaching in terms of not only prosecution, but surveillance as a whole. According to Jones (2013), this could create a legal precedent that would make every woman legally responsible for the outcome of her own pregnancy. This could include giving police the authority to determine which miscarriages and stillbirths would garner investigation and possibly arrests. If Roe were to be overturned, women who choose to end their pregnancies by any means necessary would be charged with murder.

McCullough (2012) outlines several examples in New Zealand of personhood actions such as proposing to assign each fetus a registration number tied to the national health care system and child protection alert systems where pregnant women who are victims of domestic violence or take part in harmful behaviors would be placed on a special watch list. Along a similar vein, the high rates of arrest among minority women in the US for fetal harm are not due to minorities using drugs at a greater rate than whites, but because hospitals in poor neighborhoods automatically perform infant toxicology screenings (Cohen, 2011). Rowland (2004) relates an extreme case of fetal privileging in a Massachusetts criminal trial where, as part of the defense strategy, a woman had to stand by and listen as her rapist and kidnapper accused her of being a baby killer because she once attended a pro-life rally.

Increased surveillance also extends to every habit of a pregnant women being placed under intense scrutiny. As Joffe (2011) notes,

> The antiabortion movement has long recognized the power of outing abortion patients as a means of discouraging other potential patients. This explains the movement's numerous efforts to photograph the license plates of cars in clinic parking lots and film those entering and leaving the clinics. (p. 116, loc. 1563–1564)

This form of monitoring has extended into proposed laws, such as the Texas Administrative Code (2012), which requires that abortion providers gather detailed information (assured to remain confidential) from their patients in a 16 point list including date of last menstrual cycle, demographic information, number of previous abortions, and if the patient was given the sonogram results prior to the abortion. Grimes (2013) reports that the Texas Department of State Health Services did not consider the feedback of experts to revise these invasive rules, but instead took action by enacting the Texas Administrative Code, based on the input of 10 individuals, all men, including state legislators and representatives of anti-abortion groups.

The function of fetal personhood laws is also tied to nationalism (McCullough, 2012). As one fights to preserve the national identity of citizens" then the elevated position of the innocent person only aids in the move to a fascist concept of the correct citizen, and the need for outside groups to rush to the aid of the most vulnerable. Cohen (2011) quotes Samuel Casey, who heads the Legal Christian Society:

> In as many areas as we can, we want to put on the books that the embryo is a person...that sets the stage for a jurist to acknowledge that human beings at any stage of development deserve protection—even protection that would trump a woman's interest in terminating a pregnancy. (para. 13)

Indeed, much anti-immigrant rhetoric in the United States refers to declining birth rates of whites as a point of collective anxiety, as in a White Extinction Awareness Blog post linking demographic changes to negative social outcomes (Facts About White Decline, n.d.). The fact that US birth rates across all racial and ethnic groups are dropping overall (Wetzstein, 2013) appears to be missed by contemporary racists who are all too eager to link abortion to social decline.

Ultimately, it becomes difficult to disconnect the use of abortion restrictions to justify increased surveillance of poor women, as Rowland (2004) notes:

> In addition to being written by middle class Americans, these laws are supposed to appeal to middle class Americans. For soccer moms and PTA parents. For the "middle of America" and people who have settled—usually comfortably—into child rearing and, who, therefore, cannot imagine, or don't care to consider, the harsh realities of other people's lives. It is toward these people that state officials have aimed when announcing the prosecutions of poor, urban and mainly minority women for drinking or living out the tragedies of addiction while pregnant. It is for these people—the middle-class parents—that graphic arguments about "partial birth" abortion are made and for whom placards were waved. (p. 331)

As Coontz (1998) has pointed out, any time a social policy is implemented along the lines of moral justification, as in the family values movement's vision for America, the sanctions invariably fall hardest on the most vulnerable, leaving the ruling class relatively unscathed, because exceptions are always granted for their situations or they have the means to locate solutions on their own. In the case of feticide laws, poor and minority women bear the biggest brunt of the sanctions (Tilly & Abeda, 2002).

We are facing a situation where, in an era of intensified privatization, women's reproductive organs are becoming public spaces. As soon as a fetus is defined as a person, women are automatically put under surveillance and control:

> Given that women's reproductive role has long been a basis for inequality and inferiority under the law, a good case can be made that transforming the fertilized egg into a citizen is a way of reinstating at least some of the control over women that has been lost in the wake of the sexual revolution and the pill. Rather than controlling women directly, that control is now exerted on behalf of an innocent fellow citizen. (p. 21)

Thesee (2013) views the panoply of violence against women as "misogynistic tyranny," (p. 192) where the family is the initial portal of control of women. This control is then buttressed through laws and institutions. Fetal personhood is a perfect mechanism for justifying intensified surveillance of women in general, all in the support of the security state as a whole.

Supporting Public Sector Attacks

According to Baker (2012), public sector attacks aimed at women are coming from a variety of fronts, including churches, corporations, conservative politicians at the state level, and high-profile media figures such as Rush Limbaugh and Sean Hannity. For example, Congress aimed to transform Medicaid into block grants, which would result in drastically cutting funding to the program. Medicaid recipients are overwhelmingly women from low-income backgrounds, 70% of recipients, to be exact (p. 31). Fetal personhood is used as a justification for ending access to contraception and abortion, which directly impact women economically:

> Once the government wins the right to deny aid to women who have children while on welfare and to otherwise limit the reproductive rights of poor women, it becomes that much easier to tamper with the reproductive rights of all women. The pattern already exists. Shortly after 1973, when the Supreme Court (in *Roe v. Wade*) granted women the right to an abortion, the right-to-life forces won passage of the Hyde Amendment, which forbids the use of Medicaid dollars for abortions. Since then, abortion foes have successfully limited the reproductive rights of women regardless of their economic class. Welfare reform follows suit. (Abramovitz, 2002, p. 224)

In the United States as well as the rest of the world, women make up the majority of low-wage, no-to-low-benefit, service industry work and public-sector workforces (Madland & Bunker, 2012; Minimum Wage Fact Sheet, 2013; Vivas 2013). Women are also overwhelmingly negatively impacted by cuts to entitlement programs such as social security and welfare (Schilling, 2013; Vivas, 2013). Because cuts to abortion and health care services are often connected to the wider attack on the public sector as a whole, understanding fetal personhood takes on immediate relevance, as Cohen (2011) articulates: "Todays feticide laws extend the assault on reproductive rights just as more and more women face unemployment, eviction, and the slashing of public services—in other words, just as the potential need for abortion grows" (para. 19).

Indeed, the very structure of our privatized health care system contributes to the stigmatization of women who seek abortion services. In the United States, over 90% of abortions occur in clinic type settings, with the remainder happening in hospitals and through private doctors' offices (Joffe, 2011, p. 48, loc. 694). Compounding the problem of access, there has been a drastic reduction in the number of places where women can obtain an abortion. Over 80% of American counties have no abortion provider, even though roughly 33% of women between 15 and 45 live in those counties (Rowland, 2004, p. 288). The Catholic Church operates four out of ten of the largest health care entities in the US, further restricting medical services such as abortion and contraceptives (p. 289). Catholic hospitals are now the largest source of non-profit health care in the US with 1 in 6 patients treated annually (Ginty, 2011, p. 32). Joffe (2011) also notes that many women who do have private health coverage for abortion choose not to use it for fear of leaving a paper trail for others to find out.

In Europe, by contrast, abortion is a routine procedure, occurring in public hospitals insured by national health care systems. Because abortion is automatically part of national health care, harassment is minimal. This points to the emptiness behind Democrats framing abortion as merely a matter of "choice," because women from different income backgrounds do not have the same type of options when it comes to reproductive health care:

> Choice has to include having all the healthcare services and information that enable a woman to make her own decision freely...While a Medicaid-funded abortion may be hard or impossible to get in some states, sterilization services are provided by states under Medicaid, and the Federal government reimburses states for 90% of those expenses. (Martinez, 2002, p. 273)

Much of the discourse surrounding the controversy that emerged after the passage of the Affordable Care Act in the US focused (in varying degrees of severity and insult) on the construct of decent, hard-working, middle class Americans having to support the sexual peccadillos of poor, slutty women who were a burden on the system. Joffe (2011) explains how this plays out against the larger context of a declining social safety net for the working class as a whole:

> Women who otherwise have a great deal in common-because of the failures of both government and the private market to meet many families' needs-are separated by their positions on abortion. Even people who are profoundly anti-choice don't have health insurance and are losing their pensions and can't send their kids to college...conservatives' focus on abortion and 'bad mothers' has led to a situation where it is more acceptable to deny welfare to 'bad mothers' and where it is more acceptable to have the U.S. be the only industrialized country without paid parental leave. (pp. 141–142, loc. 1876–1880)

It becomes all too clear that the nuclear family construct is no longer sustainable for a growing number of women (Coontz, 1998; Smith, 2005). Yet Kandiyoti (2002) speculates that the motivation of a good number of female anti-abortion activists is due to their resistance to separating sexuality from reproduction because they feel this separation lets men off the hook in terms of family responsibility. In the absence of a supportive public sector (such as childcare), many women attempt to resurrect the nuclear family instead as a solution to the problem of men who abandon their children.

Kaplan (2002) identifies nostalgia for the nuclear family and "good mothers" as going hand in hand with an intensified decrease in the interest of existing children—particularly children from lower income backgrounds—along with hostility toward their mothers. The pro-life position apparently does not extend to poor women's rights to have children. Additionally, "good families" are those families who do not bother the rest of society with their economic problems. Good families take on all expenses silently and without complaint. Joffe (2011) notes how compared to other countries which view childcare as a socialized duty, a virtual consensus exists in the

US that only people of means should have children. Rich (1986) expresses the grave limitations of this perspective:

> A movement narrowly concerned with pregnancy and birth which does not ask questions and demand answers about the lives of children, the priorities of government; a movement in which individual families rely on consumerism and educational privilege to supply their own children with good nutrition, schooling, health care can, while perceiving itself as progressive or alternative, exist only as a minor contradiction within a society most of whose children grow up in poverty and which places its highest priority on the technology of war. (p. xii)

CONCLUSION

On May 15, 2019, Alabama Governor Kay Ivey signed the most restrictive anti-abortion law in over 40 years. Citing God as leading her to decide to sign, the law would make abortion a felony, with no exceptions in the cases of rape or incest (Madani, 2019). It is way past time for us to act. With this in mind, a starting point for responding to the assault on reproductive freedom is militancy, not compromise. With the recent connection of the #MeToo movement and the Women's March to larger issues like reproductive rights, racism, police brutality, workers' rights, and the LGBTQ community, a more direct, insistent discourse is saying, "enough is enough." Even with the Democratic Party finally openly defending abortion and reproductive rights, largely as a response to the Trump administration, women remain unrepresented and relegated to "fringe issue" status in mainstream politics, especially poor and working-class women. Because reproductive laws do not remain static nor adhere to linear notions of progress, access to contraception and abortion remain vulnerable (Rich, 1986). Militancy is therefore necessary.

Planned Parenthood's disastrous decision to "tone down" their language used in advertising and promotions by removing "pro-choice" is an example of how the right wing has successfully eroded reproductive freedom (Abortion Shouldn't be a Dirty Word, 2013; Smith, S., 2017). Because of the ideological (and sometimes actual) attacks on Planned Parenthood clinics, the organization had assumed that a simple removal of terminology would reduce these assaults. This pragmatic approach only emboldens rightist responses and does nothing to ease legal actions on the part of anti-choice groups. Rowland (2004) expresses concerns about this strategy of civility:

> Genteel. Polite. With battles that are carefully chosen and calmly planned by a close circle of highly celebrated and roundly educated women who have tended to take the high road. All seem to agree that it is a nice way to handle it: not to stoop to "their level." The problem with this approach, however, is that the high road is rapidly leading women to defeat. (p. 757)

Joffe (2011) asserts that the contradiction between public discourse on abortion and contraception and polling which consistently shows that majorities believe both should remain legal, is due more to people not wanting to stir up controversy than to any sustained opposition on moral grounds. This leads to the increased stigmatization of abortion and contraception in the media that does not reflect reality as well putting the lives of poor, working-class and disabled women on the line. Since most of the recipients of Planned Parenthood rely on Medicaid public health and Medicaid funding, for this service to end would mean no options for safe reproductive health services (Smith, S., 2017).

In June 2013, Texas women turned the genteel approach on its head. In response to a special session to discuss draconian anti-abortion legislation which would criminalize all abortions after 20 weeks of pregnancy, hundreds of reproductive rights activists (including males in solidarity) gathered at the state capitol to protest the actions of legislators (Culp-Ressler, 2013). Even though Democrats brought legal challenges to the proposed bill, the street action inside and outside the Capitol was the remarkable highlight of the story:

> All this led to the "people's filibuster" on the final day of the special session on June 24, in which protesters in the gallery and the Capitol rotunda took over for a filibuster by Democratic Sen. Wendy Davis and yelled at the top of their lungs long enough to prevent the bill from passing by the midnight deadline.

> Undeterred this outpouring of protest, Perry quickly called another special session to try to pass the bill. Though many people were no doubt exhausted from the activism during the first special session, pro-choice activists continued to come out in droves during the second special session. They arrived at the Capitol before dawn to fill the House and Senate galleries, they shared their personal experiences about abortion at committee hearings, and they attended rallies and marches throughout the session. (Taylor, 2013, para. 8–9)

Immediately Wendy Davis and her supporters were portrayed as unreasonable, unfeminine, and as not being "respectful" of those in power, even dangerous. The tone policing didn't work. Protests were ramped up after attempts were made to silence the women, with police responding by going as far as disallowing tampons in the legislature (though firearms were apparently fine). This only resulted in a more abysmal image for the Republican Party, whose support among women was already on shaky ground.

Even though the bill still passed, an important lesson was learned. Fighting back still means something and being loud is the way to get things done. The Texas legislature had assumed that the feminist movement was docile, irrelevant, and too afraid to appear militant or even…feminist! They were wrong. Unmoved by a fetus baiting counter-rally which featured a bussed-in audience and the reality television mega-sized Duggar family, Texas women and others around the country took organizing and protest to a whole new level, using multiple strategies, none of which involved compromise or toning down the message. Taylor (2013) quotes one of the activists who had obviously had enough and didn't care about appearing "angry":

> It's infuriating and insulting to watch the past 40 years of progress be so aggressively rolled back by those least affected by a bill like House Bill 2. I went to the Capitol not because I believed we could stop the bill from passing, but because I felt the spark of a new movement for reproductive justice, and I wanted to be a part of that energy.

> Also, I was really mad, and I wanted to yell. A lot. I wanted the senators of the Texas legislation to hear the enraged voices of the people they so carelessly disregarded. If this bill was passing, it wasn't passing quietly. (para. 25–26)

With the recent resurgence of authoritarian populism and fascism, we can expect an urgent need for more of this type of active resistance.

CHAPTER 7

IN DEFENSE OF SCIENCE, THE PRESS AND EXPERTISE FOR THE PUBLIC GOOD

INTRODUCTION

Two contradictory phenomena are happening within media discourse. The first is the rapid rise of the Internet and social media, which has vastly increased the reach of ideas. At the same time, because of search tracking and the revenue models of social media such as click through ads, people are increasingly isolated within narrow thought collectives, only receiving information tailored to their indicated interests and viewpoints. Truth becomes more elusive, and not in a fun, playful postmodern way (DeVega, 2017). The interaction of these two aspects has shaped how people approach truth and reality, creating openings for those in power to exploit vulnerabilities (Illing, 2017a; Pomeranstev & Weiss, 2014; Starbird, 2017).

Once viewed as democratizing and liberating, it has become clear that the Internet and social media are just as subject to the ruling ideas of the capitalist class as any other endeavor. Pomeranstev and Weiss (2014) note that political leaders no longer have to rely on manifest oppression, they can "manipulate from the inside" by exploiting "the idea that 'truth' is a lost cause and that reality is essentially malleable" (p. 17). Because the Internet facilitates the distribution of copies of copies without much fact checking, it is fertile soil for these efforts. Additionally, the data produced from interactions on the Internet has caught the attention of private companies who regularly contract with governments, corporations, political campaigns, etc. to analyze such data to optimize influencing (Shaw, 2018).

The power of the "big lie" that is often attributed to Hitler and Goebbels has far outgrown its original constraints, such as they were. In the past, propaganda would be distributed with a specific message or set of ideas meant to shape public perception. Today, the *lie itself* is the goal:

> We live in a time when intentional, systematic, destabilizing lying—totalitarian lying for the sake of lying, lying as a way to assert or capture political power— has become the dominant factor in public life in Russia, the United States, Great Britain, and many other countries in the world…engaging with these lies is unavoidable and even necessary. (Gessen, 2018, para. 15)

It is fast becoming clear that even efforts at using leftist alternative media have not been able to penetrate "how information is shared and consumed, and, more profoundly…how narratives around that information are shaped and by whom" (Starbird, 2017, p. 1).

In the recent past, concepts that were considered too outlandish and unacceptable for mainstream journalistic discourse have now been given a hearing in those venues. As Goldberg (2018) notes, "an opinion section that truly captured the currents of thought shaping our politics today might include Alex Jones, the conspiracy-mad Sandy Hook truther; the white nationalist Richard Spencer; and CliffsNotes fascist Steve Bannon" (para. 11). This is the culmination of "the coming of a networked society" much heralded by the left in the early days of the Internet, where traditional journalism would be unseated by more democratically produced, leaderless crowdsourcing and just-in-time-content (Nagle, 2017a, p. 3). Unfortunately, "this network has indeed arrived, but it has helped to take the right, not the left, to power" (p. 27). In all of the excitement over the Internet, people failed to see that the *content* of what was being distributed does indeed matter.

Added to this is a profound dialectical-materialist disconnect between people and the views that they hold. This starts with a misunderstanding about the source of one's beliefs, which do not simply originate within one's self apart from external factors:

> An individual's ideology doesn't come from inside them, but is an effect of time and place. But it's much easier to understand how this was true of some stranger in the distant past than to accept it about yourself—that you're a product of the social processes of your time, and your ideas are not crystals of pure rationality, but the residue of these processes. (Winant, 2017, para. 1)

An example of this is the lack of political engagement about the very beliefs that people claim to have, which leads to not being politically informed. When asked to situate themselves along a continuum of government providing more social services on the left to reducing spending on the right, 15% of respondents declined to answer because "they have not thought about it" (The Power of Groupthink, 2017, para. 8). The same percentage will indicate where they appear on the continuum, but are not able to correctly place Democratic or Republican party platforms. This means one third of the electorate has a profound misunderstanding where the politicians they vote for stand regarding the role of the state (para. 4).

At this point it should be pretty clear that we have moved far beyond Karl Rove's Bush-era declaration of an empire creating its own reality into there being no reality at all unless it meets the approval of Trump and his supporters:

> Trumpland…knows no national loyalties and recognizes no transcendent or democratic values beyond power and profit. Trumpland is post-truth and lives on the propagation of fake news. For Donald Trump himself, discourse serves the interests of Trumpland and has no relation to truth and falsity. (Kellner, 2017, p. 100)

At the same time, much of the left clings to the futile hope that simply repeating facts at the right wing will disrupt their efforts at misinformation (Cloud, 2018). This chapter presents five primary ways that the right wing has attempted to manage perceptions related to their dismantling of the public good and eroding rational thought. These include an attack on the notion of expertise, reviving pseudoscience around race and gender, manufacturing fake news, promulgating both-sides-ism in the press and intensifying the spread of conspiracy theories.

ATTACK ON EXPERTISE

As discussed in Chapter 2, anti-intellectualism has long been a hallmark of right-wing populist and fascist movements. However, rightist discourse has more recently moved into a more intense focus on a particular facet of intellectualism: expertise (DeVega, 2017; T. Nichols, 2017). Trump and his supporters regularly portray experts as elitist, out of touch, and purveyors of leftist bias. Experts are bogged down by an adherence to tedious, time-wasting details when what is needed is a man (it is always a man) who will get down to business. Dworkin (2017) includes an excerpt from a right-wing blog which encapsulates this hostility toward expertise:

> Trump is slaying sacred cows…The only thing anybody knows is that the things we are seeing have never been done before and Donald Trump is refusing to follow any of the proper conventions…Think of the glory of it all. This is the fight we have been waiting for. This is the turmoil we need. The president is making common sense policy decisions that don't need the backing of long reports authored by "experts"…It is almost as if he thinks the people should rule, not supposed expertise…This will undoubtedly result in pushback from bureaucrats and "experts," and timid culture warriors who apparently enjoy self-emasculation or have realized (incorrectly) that they have more to gain from maintaining the status quo. (para. 11)

What this blog post illustrates is that the right-wing view of expertise is also highly gendered, with common sense and "gut instinct" being masculinized, and experts relegated to the realm of the feminized. Disruption is also valued, especially if it stops experts who spend too much time thinking when they should be acting—in right-wing directions, of course. The irony is that while the right-wing continually complains about overly sensitive liberals, their discourse runs entirely on appeals to emotion, such as the talking points surrounding Brexit in 2016. Despite warnings from economists, proponents of England remaining in the EU were portrayed as "enemies of the ordinary voter" or fearmongers (T. Nichols, 2017, p. 209). Michal Gove, one of the key figures behind the Brexit movement, "argued that facts were not as important as the feelings of the British voter" (p. 209).

It is also contradictory that expertise is seen as being out of touch with reality, when what expertise involves is a series of reflections on lived experiences and integrating those reflections into one's practice and existing set of content knowledge (T. Nichols, 2017). This is the key difference for the right—experience is rarely reflected upon—and it becomes a form of dogma which reinforces existing prejudices. The idea is to barge ahead and act in-the-moment with the resolve of a heat-seeking missile.

Within anti-expertise frameworks, the mediocre is elevated and becomes a celebrated value. Sartre's (1976) analysis of anti-Semitism found that its anti-intellectual adherents, far from being humble and "just regular folks," were the embodiment of arrogance: "there is a passionate pride among the mediocre, and anti-Semitism is an attempt to give value to mediocrity as such, to create an elite of the ordinary. To the anti-Semite, intelligence is Jewish; he can thus disdain it" (p. 16). Dorfman (2017) sees the Trump administration as equating expertise with liberalism. Therefore, experts are replaced by "know-nothing fundamentalists" who represent industry and seek to defund public programs and agencies (para. 6). As T. Nichols (2017) notes, "the public space is increasingly dominated by a loose assortment of poorly informed people, many of them autodidacts who are disdainful of formal education and dismissive of experience" (p. 14).

Under these conditions, the nature of education itself is radically altered, where patriarchal hierarchies are valorized and expressed in narrow, all-male terms. Loyalty, in particular, is held above all other values, with curriculum and messaging stressing concepts like reverence and respect for those holding the appropriate values, over time-tested expertise (Theweleit, 2010b). Sartre (1976) sees this as a manifestation of "a longing for impenetrability" that is held up as an important personality characteristic (p. 12). The anti-expert has to develop this survival strategy in order to "choose to reason falsely" (p. 12). Sartre locates the fear of truth not in the content of that truth (what is usually dismissed as unimportant), but in the various forms that truth can take, which are harder to control.

The attack against experts is accompanied by a resentment of any type of oversight, which is built into professional structures and credentialing. Though imperfect, these protective structures exist to maintain the integrity of the profession and to ensure that ethical standards are being met (T. Nichols, 2017). Jones (2015) relates the views of education privatizer Wendy Kopp, founder of Teach for America when asked to comment on hiring less-experienced teachers instead of veteran ones:

> There's also a power in inexperience—that it can make a huge difference to channel the energy of young people, before they know what's "impossible" and when they still have endless energy, against a problem that many have long since given up on. They can set and meet goals that seem impossible to others who know more about how the world works. (p. 81)

It is important to note, however, that right-wing resentment of professionals is *not* applied to conservative wealthy people (DeVega, 2017). Combined with the disdain for professional expertise is a desire to aspire to be rich and ambitious, but still retain one's folksy, populist values.

Part of what contributes to a hostility toward experts is that much of the systematic problem-solving processes they use are not easily seen and can be shrouded in mystery. T. Nichols (2107) points out how the multiple revisions that are part of professional communities take place outside of the public eye where all that is visible is the final result. And even then, it's not as apparent unless something malfunctions. In the case of repealing the *Affordable Care Act*, it is difficult for people to conceptualize the degree of economic impacts that a repeal could have, even if they have some vague ideas. Society is also structured in such a way that people are alienated from the processes that produce most of the artifacts of modern life. This can lead people to think, "how hard can that be?" when contemplating the role of expertise (para. 13). A lack of transparency also applies to how projects like think tanks are funded and the impact of the private sector on shaping laws (Pomeranstev & Weiss, 2014). It is no surprise that political leaders take advantage of an overall lack of political knowledge to create messaging in support of right-wing ideas like Brexit that fall apart under scrutiny (T. Nichols, 2017).

There is also a cognitive aspect to anti-expertise thinking, involving confirmation bias and reasoning shortcuts (Ehrenreich, 2017; T. Nichols, 2017). All people, including experts, have to grapple with how to explain phenomena and start with a set of assumptions; otherwise nothing would get done. While strategies like shortcuts can assist with decision-making, they can also be misleading and end up reinforcing one's own prejudices. Confirmation bias also tends to involve critique-averse concepts that are not falsifiable. Ehrenreich (2017) explains that people tend to "underestimate the risks of events that unfold slowly and whose consequences are felt only over the long term (think *global warming*) and overestimate the likelihood of events that unfold rapidly and have immediate consequences (think *terrorist attacks*) (para. 11). Laypeople also tend to conflate experts' errors with systemic error, and point to instances of experts being wrong in order to reject, across the board, findings they don't agree with (T. Nichols, 2017).

Contrary to the arbitrariness that is often associated with experts, Santer (2017) recounts the thought processes involved with scientific expertise, from the perspective of being a climate scientist:

You put in a long apprenticeship. You spend years learning about the climate system, computer models of climate and climate observations. You start filling a tool kit with the statistical and mathematical methods you'll need for analyzing complex data sets. You are taught how electrical engineers detect signals embedded in noisy data. You apply those engineering insights to the detection of a human-caused warming signal buried in the natural "noise" of Earth's climate. Eventually, you learn that human activities are warming Earth's surface, and you publish this finding in peer-reviewed literature. (para. 4)

Part of this process involves extensive peer review and assessments, along with a deliberate decision to consider one's own bias, hold up a range of scientific findings against your own, and work within the limits placed by industry and government.

On top of this careful practice, climate scientists deal with constant criticism of their findings and are held up to extremely rigorous standards. Yet their conclusions, like those of other experts, are dismissed as "opinion."

It should come as no surprise that educational institutions and professionals are the continual target of right-wing discourse opposing expertise. At a recent Trump rally, Donald Trump Jr. directed young conservatives to "keep up that fight, bring it to your schools. You don't have to be indoctrinated by these loser teachers that are trying to sell you on socialism from birth" (Mazza, 2019, para. 3). Not limiting their wrath to public schools, early 60% of Republicans see universities as negatively contributing to US society, marking the first time a majority of conservatives viewed postsecondary education in this light (Sitrin, 2017, para. 2). Trump's election and the strident anti-expertise thinking that comes with it has impacted conservatives, 54% of them who as recently as 2015 viewed universities as having a positive impact on the country (para. 2). One contributing aspect of the backlash is the fact that Trump is actively resisted on college campuses and the loyalty aspect of anti-expertise thinking kicks in.

Jones (2015) also connects recent hostility toward teachers to an overall de-professionalization of teaching, where teachers are expected to align themselves with the business world and "willingly agree to repeal tenure, give up collective bargaining, and accept job performance evaluation based largely on student test scores, and support merit pay" (p. 36). Jones also notes how notions about expertise surrounding the saying "those who can't do, teach" have long been a part of the teaching profession, hinting at the perceived lesser quality of teachers who couldn't survive in more prestigious professions. The irony is that the increased surveillance and rigidity of evaluation schemes paired with lower salaries and no workplace protections that conservatives advocate for would *not* be tolerated by higher-paid professionals.

Ultimately, anti-expertise thinking occurs against a backdrop of overall distrust of government and any kind of public service, including education. "Education reformers" and others with an interest in eroding expertise, "draw upon the economic understanding and political will of a sizable number of citizens and politicians that has taken shape since the economic downfall of 2008 and the rise of the Tea Party" (Jones, 2015, p. 9). This contributes to an attitude of "cutting the waste," the waste being experts who are blamed for social problems. Dorfman (2017) recalls more dire consequences of this line of thinking in 1973 Chile:

> Books were turned to ashes, musicians were shot, scientists and educators were tortured. Meanwhile, the military, inspired by the same fundamentalism and loathing that had raged in Franco's Spain, derided intelligence and reveled in death. The intelligentsia, they insisted, was to blame for Chile's upheavals and supposed decline. (para. 3)

McCandless' (2017) investigative piece on the city of Von Ormy provides a recent case study of the consequences of rejecting expertise. Back in 2006, a few residents were hostile to the idea of the city becoming annexed by San Antonio as well as resistant to any solution that involved formal roles of government. The libertarian mayor, Arturo Martinez de Vara, floated the idea of Von Ormy becoming a "liberty city," essentially "a stripped-down, low-tax, low-government version of municipal government" touted by the Texas Tea Party (para. 6). According to the plan, the town would first collect property and sales taxes, but eventually the property tax would be reduced to zero.

To make up for the revenue loss, residents were promised that businesses would be attracted to the low tax base and eventually only sales taxes would be needed to support the city. Martinez de Vara attempted to recruit major chains but immediately ran into a problem because there was no sewer system in Von Ormy and connecting to San Antonio's was too expensive. The City Administrator suggested accepting a bond, which most cities do when faced with major expenses. Martinez de Vara turned down this advice since liberty cities were supposed to stand on their own without assistance.

By 2011, Texas Republicans took notice and began to tout the city as an impressive example for other smaller localities, recruiting Martinez de Vara to serve as chief of staff to Representative John Garza and later Senator Konni Burton. However, an attempt to pass Senate Bill 710, recognizing the liberty city concept as an official category of municipal government never made it out of committee. The promised businesses never materialized. By 2016, the police and fire departments had to close down. City officials ended up bickering over who was supposed to be police chief, with the new mayor attempting to fire the existing police chief who was accused of misrepresenting his law enforcement resumé. Three city council members were arrested on the assumption that they violated the Open Meetings Act and others kept things at a standstill by refusing to show up to vote for important measures. Essentially, the only thing left in the town was enough blame to go around (McCandless, 2017).

PSEUDOSCIENCE

Feeding off of anti-expertise sentiment, pseudoscience uses a different strategy by presenting itself as connected to the scientific community while using superficial markers of science as a way to obfuscate and insert confusion surrounding important public health issues. Pseudoscience practitioners use visual and discursive symbols of academic science as a way to add credibility to their messaging while supporting science in the service of capital. Currently, there are three primary approaches that are part of pseudoscience. First is the presentation of flat-out false or unscientific ideas under the guise of science. Second includes the tactic of using different means to interfere with or suppress the development and distribution of scientific knowledge. Finally, a third way that pseudoscience is promoted involves the selective support and funding of science projects that can be monetized in a capitalist system while ignoring projects for the common good.

The Guise of Science

Regarding the first approach, Trump's election, friendliness toward white supremacists and receptivity to pseudoscientific thinking has revived debunked concepts such as race realism and evolutionary psychology, which uses academic language to carry racism, sexism, and homophobia to the mainstream. Additionally, movements like the flat earthers and anti-vaxxers often use scientific-sounding arguments to support faulty reasoning, creating just enough confusion while taking advantage of the both-sides-ism of the media. For Gaspar (2018), concepts like scientific racism, though regularly refuted, have to be repeatedly debunked because the inequality that feeds these ideas has never really gone away. In other words, "because scientific racism is driven not by scientific evidence but by the racial animus of some and the unexamined assumptions of others, these hopes have not yet come to fruition" (p. 104).

A hallmark of pseudoscience is pointing to indirect evidence that is neither refutable nor testable, such as attributing differences to specific genetic traits (Gaspar, 2018; Penny, 2018). Science often gets mixed together in a hodgepodge of religious assertions, as Penny (2018) colorfully explains:

> The simultaneous appeal to both science and religious mysticism, to God-and-or-genetics, is an ingenious arse-covering mechanism: if God didn't strictly say he created man to compete in a series of vicious status battles and fuck the other guy, then genetics probably did, and any blue-haired social justice neuroscientists popping up to explain that that's really not how gene expression works simply haven't grasped the larger cosmic context. If there's no actual scientific evidence for it, then it's all a metaphor. It's a prosperity gospel for toxic masculinity, *The Art of the Deal* via the Book of Leviticus. (para. 48)

To support pseudoscientific notions of race, past research such as the classic twin studies (where identical twins are raised separately yet have similar personality traits) are often cited (Gaspar, 2018). The problem with these studies is that the socio-environmental conditions where the twins were raised are just as identical as the twins themselves.

Gaspar (2018) notes that pseudoscience's preoccupation with genetic causation is ultimately connected to right-wing efforts to end social programs that are designed to ameliorate poverty. He presents the case of childhood asthma, which is almost entirely environmental, yet funding continues to prioritize genetic studies. Even when motivations are more positive, such as including non-white patients in medical research, they end up reinforcing flawed thinking about race and genetics. For example, white medical students often hold false beliefs about Black patients, including that they process pain differently or that their blood coagulates faster (para. 109). Likewise, despite evidence that the environment is a more significant shaper of intelligence than genetics, beliefs about biological differences in intelligence between whites and minorities persist in differing degrees of intensity (Hatewatch Staff, 2018).

The interconnection between white supremacist groups and race realism is represented by figures like Sam Harris and Jared Taylor, who are able to appeal to the more secular, non-religiously-based demographic known as "skeptics." On the Daily Stormer, a white supremacist website, Taylor is cited by one out of five members as having introduced them to white nationalism (Hatewatch Staff, 2018, para. 29). During one podcast, Harris used flawed data to assert that Muslim bans were rational because of their inherently violent traits and stressed that "this is not an expression of xenophobia; this is the implication of statistics" (para. 30). Similar pseudoscientific speculations are regularly broadcast on the news media to imply that immigrants from southern hemispheric nations are genetically and culturally inferior to whites, along with harboring diseases (Dorfman, 2017).

Torres (2017) explains that in communities that authentically value rationality, those who might not have the expertise tend to take a wait and see attitude when it comes to more complex scientific issues. Pseudoscientists like Sam Harris or Jordan Peterson violate this epistemic protocol by immediately declaring that characteristics related to race and gender are genetically based. In turn, they get rewarded by those in the right-wing atheist community for being bold and edgy and are in turn cited by other conservatives. Because of their atheism, they feel insulated from their views being critiqued for their religiosity, as often happens with Christian pseudoscience practitioners. Torres also sees an ethical violation in their taking up the question of the inferiority of races and genders to begin with, especially when members of those groups are often the most vulnerable to the consequences of those ideas taking hold in society as white supremacists become empowered. The irony is that by alienating women and minorities, right-wing atheists lose a significant number of allies in confronting the excesses of religiosity.

Interfering with Science

The second approach to pseudoscience involves direct interference with scientific work. This can take several forms including appointing corporate cronies to scientific posts, censorship of data that doesn't conform to right-wing policies, and harassment of scientists who work in fields that challenge profit. These strategies often occur in combination. A recent example is the Trump administration's Scott Pruitt not renewing the contracts of Environmental Protection Agency scientists involved with oversight of research and development and then replacing these positions with oil and gas industry representatives (Geiling, 2017; Dorfman, 2017). The rationale provided? "EPA advisory boards did not include a diversity of views and therefore frequently presented a biased perspective on issues before them" (para. 5). In other words, the EPA scientists were not exclusively promoting research to prop up energy companies and were therefore "biased."

While it isn't possible to outright ban scientific research, private sector companies know that it is relatively easy in a nation with low scientific literacy (Miller, 2016) to introduce just enough industry-friendly perspectives under the guise of scientific-sounding language to create confusion:

> Both mistrust of scientists and other "experts" and mistrust of the mass media that reports what scientists and experts believe have increased among conservatives (but not among liberals) since the early '80s. The mistrust has in part, at least, been deliberately inculcated. The fossil fuel industry publicizes studies to confuse the climate change debate; Big Pharma hides unfavorable information on drug safety and efficacy; and many schools in conservative areas teach students that evolution is "just a theory." The public is understandably confused about both the findings and methods of science. (Ehrenreich, 2017, para.7)

During the 1990s when the tobacco industry was facing increased scrutiny, Philip Morris funded the Orwellian astroturf group, The National Smokers Alliance, and distributed newsletters to cigarette consumers (Halpern, 2015, p. 8). Tobacco companies also created legal entities, the American Smoker's Rights Foundation and American Smokers Alliance used to delay the legal process and produce publications.

Scientists are also directly harassed by well-funded organizations and corporations, specifically by the use of public records laws such as the *Freedom of Information Act* (FOIA) (2016). These laws were originally intended to promote open inquiry and discourse on a variety of important topics and were meant to provide an important check against harmful research. Currently, they have been seized upon by conservatives as an important tactic (Kurtz, 2017). Public universities, which use taxpayer funds, are especially subject to FOIA requests (Halpern, 2015). Nearly 66% of these requests are from private organizations with the goal of targeting researchers whose work presents a threat to their profits (p. 4). Essentially, conservatives have gone beyond using public records to gain an advantage in scientific knowledge to weaponizing FOIA. Examples that Halpern shares includes groups publishing contact information of scientists, including their home location and private phone numbers, which has led to cyber-mobbing and death threats.

A specific example that Halpern provides is the Wisconsin Republican Party using FOIA to obtain the email correspondence of a history professor, William Cronon, who was researching labor history and collective bargaining, topics hostile to Governor Scott Walker's efforts to squelch labor. Around the same time, another industry group in Michigan targeted three other professors who specialized in labor studies (p. 9). Emails have become a specific goal of conservatives because most communication now occurs in this fashion:

> Snooping on researchers' emails has become the twenty-first-century equivalent of tapping their phone lines or bugging a lab's water cooler. Further, social expectations around transparency are shifting. More and more, hackers are

illegally obtaining private information—from emails to intellectual property to credit card files—from major corporations, government agencies, and scientific institutions and disclosing it online. (p. 2)

The scope of who is targeted can also exceed the researchers themselves. Markowitz and Rosner's (2013) book on the history of industrial pollution and how chemical industries intentionally suppress environmental impact research resulted in conservatives attacking their reputation as researchers. Lawyers working for chemical companies not only legally harassed the original authors, but sent subpoenas to those who peer reviewed the book. Eventually, "industry representatives later used a FOIA request to the National Science Foundation to seek "all records relating to research conducted by David Rosner and/or Gerald Markowitz on the history of lead that has been funded by NSF" (p. 4).

These types of efforts do result in pushback by scientists and concerned citizens. Williams (2017) points to the creation of Alt-National Park Service Facebook and Twitter pages to directly share scientific information with the public as a countermeasure to the Trump administration. Large-scale marches for science occur annually, with protest signs indicating a more systemic critique of how science serves profit over people (Molteni, 2018). Another issue that people are mobilizing around is how anti-immigration policy in the form of travel bans harms science, since 20% of scientists working in the US are not native-born (Williams, 2017, p. 35).

Science for Profit

The final approach to pseudoscience is the privileging of scientific development and research with the most potential for monetization over projects that have less of an immediate profit potential. An example would be funding science in support of smaller-scale alternative energy companies or carbon tax schemes rather than putting the full weight of scientific knowledge behind confronting climate change as a whole. While not attempting to mislead or interfere with the scientific process like the first two forms of pseudoscience discussed above, this third form has larger and more dangerous implications. By failing to examine science in dialectical materialist terms, the default position remains limited by what can or can't produce profit. This starts with the funding of public universities, which has dropped to states only funding 19% of expenses and public universities receiving fewer federal grants than private ones (Halpern, 2015, p. 2).

The question of how to address pseudoscience must be approached within a dialectical materialist frame. Galileo is often held up in a limited way as an example of how new scientific ideas are penalized. Williams (2017) points out how Galileo's confrontation with the Catholic church is often presented as a matter of religion's censorship of science. In actuality, there were more far-reaching issues at play, not unlike our current era:

> Galileo's conflict with the Papacy was, in fact, just as rooted in material considerations of political power as it was with ideas about the nature of the solar system and our place within it…Under pressure from what came to be known as the Thirty Years' War raging across central Europe between Catholic and Protestant armies, Urban was attempting to shore up and re-establish the might of Rome though the Inquisition, racking up massive Papal debt from increased military spending, while promoting rampant nepotism and corruption. (p. 34)

This example is important because it highlights how science does not exist apart from social forces nor does it come down to simple binaries of "either religion or science." There are additional factors that work against science serving human need.

Advocating for science by itself is no guarantee that it will serve in the public's interest because currently the majority of scientific efforts take place within a capitalist system that prioritizes profit over human need. On the one hand, it is clear that science itself has been under attack by both religious and right-wing secular forces. Yet at the same time, science is a field that exists within a class society, so it is going to reflect the interests of the capitalist class to begin with. As Williams (2017) notes, "Trump is not telling businesses to stop doing science. He wants the federal government to stop doing science in the public interest. He wants to end fact-based discourse wherever the facts run counter to right-wing ideology" (p. 37). For Gaspar (2018), defeating pseudoscience necessitates taking on capitalism and its utilization of racism and sexism.

FAKE NEWS

On July 4, 2017, National Public Radio (NPR) continued its nearly 30-year practice of highlighting the Declaration of Independence, that year using the format of Tweeting line-by-line excerpts. Immediately, NPR was attacked on Twitter by angry Trump supporters, accusing the media organization of fomenting rebellion and spreading propaganda (Rosario, 2017). The fact that they assumed the line "A Prince, whose character is thus marked by every act which may define a Tyrant, is unfit to be the ruler of a free people" referred to Trump was telling enough, but "what leapt out…is the fact that Trump supporters are so detached from reality that they literally thought NPR was openly calling for a violent overthrow of the President of the United States" (para. 2).

Additionally, only one fourth of those who voted for Trump believe that climate change has been impacted by humans and just over 40% of Republicans acknowledge human evolution (Ehrenreich, 2017, para. 2). After the inauguration, even when shown photographs comparing Trump's and Obama's inauguration crowds, nearly 1 out of every 6 Trump voters declared that Obama's inauguration crowd was smaller (para. 3). Further edging into the terrain of the unreal, 66% of conservatives believe that Sharia law is being practiced in US courts and just under half "either thought that

Hillary Clinton was connected to a child sex trafficking ring run out of the basement of a pizzeria in Washington, D.C., or weren't sure if it was true" (para. 3). And for those who argue that this is just a phenomena among the less educated, "college-educated Republicans are actually more likely than less-educated Republicans to have believed that Barack Obama was a Muslim and that "death panels" were part of the Affordable Care Act." (Ehrenreich, 2017, para. 5).

Narayanan et al. (2018) identify five characteristics of fake news: (1) not using proper journalistic standards such as citations; (2) style that includes hyperbole, emotionally charged language, misspellings, communication via memes; (3) spreading of conspiracy theories and self-referential evidence; (4) partisan reporting, and (5) using counterfeit tactics like pretending to be an academic site. If distributed information includes three of these characteristics, it is likely to be fake news. In Starbird's (2017) analysis of fake news sites, much of the discourse was not limited to traditional political frames such as liberal/conservative, but instead floated stories related to anti-globalism (closely tied to anti-Semitic conspiracy theories) and criticisms of Western governments in general. These sites present themselves as "an alternative to mainstream media" whom they label as "fake news" (p. 9).

A general distrust in traditional media has been growing, particularly since the exposure of the manufactured evidence leading the invasion and occupation of Iraq and Afghanistan (Narayanan, 2018; Pomerantsev & Weiss, 2014). Trump himself has made it his mission to dismantle the media, mostly as a form of revenge for it not providing non-stop positive coverage of him and his administration. This is ironic considering the free and mostly positive coverage he received during his campaign, exceeding that of any prior candidate (Kellner, 2017; Illing, 2017a).

T. Nichols (2017) also views American skepticism toward the media is part of a larger tendency to not trust anything anymore—or at the very least people more intensely distrust sources that tell them things they don't like to hear. Even though just over 60% of Americans view news organizations as inaccurate, that number is reduced to 30% when people are asked about the sources that they use the most (p. 158). National media distrust is also divided along partisan lines, with a 10/85 approval/disapproval split for Republicans, beating out labor unions which stand at 33/46 (Kilgore, 2017, para. 5). As a contrast, nearly 45% of Democrats and Independents see the media as a positive entity, an increase of 11 points since 2016 (Sitrin, 2017, para. 7).

The media itself has been the single biggest contributing factor to Trump's rise, starting with a decades-long right-wing talk radio onslaught, culminating in Fox News 24/7 echo chamber of misinformation (DeVega, 2017). Pomeranstev and Weiss (2014) see the liberal ethos of stepping back and letting the viewers make up their minds as having created a major vulnerability that the right wing eagerly exploited:

Freedom of information and expression are sacrosanct in Western culture. They are key to any idea of globalization based on liberal democracy. The more freedom of information we have, the thinking goes, the greater the debate, and the greater the common good. But what if a player uses the freedom of information to subvert its principles? To make debate and critical thinking impossible? Not to inform or persuade, but as a weapon? (p. 14)

Making this situation even more urgent is that the very people who see themselves as highly informed and above the fray in avoiding the mainstream media are the *most* receptive to fake news, representing "an abandonment of objectivity that precludes and abandonment of accuracy" (p. 35).

A key driver of fake news has been emotion, closely followed by group membership, which are prioritized over evidence. Coupled with a lack of clarity regarding the political process, people are able to now receive immediate validation on social media, "a projection of themselves" where "they're wedded to the notion that they are the peer of the person they're talking to" (DeVega, 2017, para. 24–25). Emotion and loyalty can be easily used to walk around inconvenient facts, such as evangelicals viewing Obama as the antichrist and Trump a God-fearing Christian (The Power of Groupthink, 2017, para. 10). Which attributes are prioritized is another aspect of the psychology of right-wing media, with conservatives more highly rating conformity, tradition and authority while dismissing kindness, fairness, and ambiguity as evidence of weakness (Ehrenreich, 2017).

The manipulability of emotion has not gone unnoticed. Shaw (2018) recounts the investigation into Cambridge Analytica and their use of behavioral and psychological research to influence not only elections in places like Nigeria in 2007, but the 2016 US election by distributing targeted inflammatory fake news. Global Science Research, another company associated with Cambridge Analytica, utilized an app that collected data from Facebook users via a personality quiz, under the guise of academic research. However, the app also gathered data from Facebook friends of the quiz takers, who never consented to having their data harvested. Only after it became known that Cambridge Analytica was contacted to work with the State Department and the Pentagon did the story break.

However, Shaw outlines how the connections between psychological research and warfare is nothing new:

> Much of the classic, foundational research on personality, conformity, obedience, group polarization, and other such determinants of social dynamics—while ostensibly civilian—was funded during the cold war by the military and the CIA. The cold war was an ideological battle, so, naturally, research on techniques for controlling belief was considered a national security priority. (para. 6)

Other civilian programs utilizing behavioral research include the Well Being Institute, focused on developing characteristics like "resilience" and "optimism" to work hand-in-hand with big data so that employees will become more productive and less resistant to the neoliberal workplace (para. 11). Essentially, behavioral science is being used to prioritize the manipulability of people over fostering rationality.

Fake news is therefore the manifestation of the transformation of journalism from a profession that distributes information meant to benefit people into a form of public relations (PR) (West, 2016). This branding-focused PR is hyper-targeted toward different interest groups, a form of micro-individualism:

> What once called itself a provider of news now sees itself exclusively as a platform for a plurality of (pre-approved) "voices" and identities, all marching to the beat of same consumer ethos: "do you," "be one of a kind," "be together, not the same"...where the power of something like criticism...is overtaken by the more pressing desire to confirm one's mind, one's self, as it is, and to guarantee its equal representation in the cultural and political marketplace. (Alvarez, 2017, para. 2)

In one example, West (2016) describes an online platform Kinja, where commenters start blogs hosted by Gawker, the content of which is "mined for re-posting on the main sites" (p. 115). The fact that salaried journalists would be working alongside "the anonymous ramblings of the unpaid commentariat" (p. 116) is cause for concern but not surprising considering how there are now nearly five PR people for every one journalist in the US (Pomeranstev & Weiss, 2014, p. 34). This, against a backdrop of a 33% reduction in journalistic personnel since 2006 (p. 34).

The social media model for news has worked in tandem with the PR approach, especially since 67% of Americans now receive at least some of their news from platforms such as Facebook and Twitter (Shearer & Gottfried, 2017, para. 1). While reputable news outlets are on these platforms, they are mixed in with an array of fake news sites, often incidentally popping up in the form of ads or links during a search. Narayanan (2018) notes how highly targeted algorithms used on social media platforms are able to gather information about users and the type of information they share, so it was only a matter of time until the discovery that this feature could be used for a variety of political purposes, including Russia's use of automated accounts and bots. The hyper-polarization of media discourse leading up to 2016 is locked into a cyclical relationship with the social media model which feeds the discourse, to the point where it is hard to know where it begins or ends.

Narayanan (2018) tracked the spread of computational propaganda and identified two primary distributors of fake news, the Trump Support Group and the Conservative Media Group, both with coverage rates in the mid-90% range (p. 4). The Trump Support Group alone spread more fake news than all of the other groups reviewed put together. Far from being a "both sides do it" activity, Narayanan found that there was limited overlap between the sources that Democrats and Republicans shared on social media, with Democrats preferring mainstream media sites and Republicans preferring fake news sites. The one exception is the Occupy-related sites which have significant overlap with conspiracy-theory sites.

A recent example of fake news cutting out the middleman is the Trump TV endeavor, in particular its purposefully Orwellian-named Real News Update series. Overseen by Lara Trump, Trump's daughter in law who once produced *Inside Edition*, Trump TV operates out of Trump Tower yet presents itself as a legitimate television news network (Illing, 2017a). Trump TV is supported by Trump's reelection fund and is for all intents and purposes a state-owned propaganda arm no different than those in authoritarian regimes. Illing points to the cable channel GOP TV in 1995 as an earlier example of rightwing propaganda, but whose reach was nothing like today where information is distributed openly vs. the underground networks of video cassettes in the 1990s used to recruit younger media conservatives.

The benefit of the hermeneutically closed-loop nature of Trump's base regarding the media they consume is that there appears to be no combination of actions that is enough to budge their support, with 20% of his supporters declaring unconditional loyalty (The Power of Group Think, 2017, para. 5). Further, because the Republican Party depends on this same base for political survival, they have taken no actions to censure Trump, despite the growing evidence of collusion with Russia, obstruction of justice, and fraud, let alone sexual assault (Kellner, 2017). This then sets the bar for what Trump and the GOP are able to get away with. A major contributor to the extreme loyalty of Trump's base is the construct of fake news and the projection of the fake news accusation onto any source that attempts to criticize Trump and his actions (Kilgore, 2017). Such critics are dismissed as being politically biased, even if evidence is presented, creating an impasse:

> You cannot reach out and find common ground with people who do not acknowledge reality in any way. There is literally no amount of evidence that can persuade them once Fox News, AM Hate Radio and Breitbart sell them the lie. Every word Trump speaks is infallible and if he directly contradicts himself, the fake new media is guilty of taking his statements out of context. (Rosario, 2017, para. 8)

BOTH-SIDES-ISM

The centrist counterpart of fake news, *both-sides-ism*, advances the claim that if a liberal or leftist perspective is included in journalistic media, then other perspectives must be included for balance. This is embodied in Fox News' original motto of "fair and balanced," (which has now tellingly been dropped) the idea being that there is such a preponderance of liberal values within the media that a marginalized and powerless right wing has to endlessly struggle for survival in order to gain a hearing. Reality paints a different picture with conservative leaders of major media outlets, such as the broadcast company Sinclair, which owns the largest number of TV stations in the US (Graves, 2017).

Even in cases where the leadership of these companies and their programming may accommodate centrist or even liberal perspectives, they fully support and privilege capitalism and discourse friendly to it. Far from there being a clandestine conspiracy among right-wing media owners to target liberals, suppression of leftist views in the media are baked into the formula by default:

> It is enough that corporate-inspired ideologies pervade a society and that corporate ownership ensures that decision-making positions are filled with those who hold to some variant of prevailing ideologies or are inclined to play it safe by cautiously remining within acceptable boundaries. The mass media will then simply reflect these dominant ideologies, and continual repetition through multiple mass-media outlets reinforces the ideologies, making them more pervasive until the emergence of a significant countervailing pressure. (Dolack, 2017b, p. 35)

The two-part rationale supporting both-sides-ism is the idea that a) all opinions are of equal weight and value and b) all opinions have the imperative to be heard. A key problem with this is the notion of automatic protective rights surrounding opinions, or the idea of entitlement to one's opinions, which "devalues the ways that opinions are supposed to *earn* serious consideration through logical argumentation, persuasion, rigorous research, and expertise" (Alvarez, 2017, para. 6). Within media outlets, it doesn't take long for this entitlement rationale to slip into demands to "respect" opinions, which means protecting opinions from external challenge. Because of the highly individualized nature of opinions ("it's *my* opinion!"), it serves as an automatic shield from critical discourse, as if those interrogating opinions are violating some sort of sacred space and veering into personal attack (Goldberg, 2018).

The pressures then mount for centrist media spaces to not be closed-minded and to find aspects of individualized opinions (that cannot be challenged) to hold up for discussion, thus giving some sort of serious weight by merely being mentioned in a publicized and prestigious format (Ganz, 2018). It's important to note that invariably these demands come from conservative groups. What ends up happening is that the news stories which prop up dominant discourses are covered more frequently and for longer time periods, thus magnifying conservative and pro-capitalist ideologies. At the same time, "stories that are ideologically inconsistent are reported briefly, often without context, then quickly dropped" (Dolack, 2017b, p. 35). It then becomes easier for both-sides-ism to reinforce right-wing views under the veneer of an open and tolerant democratic ethos, which gives it deeper cover.

This is illustrated by the actions of the *Atlantic* magazine's recent hire of anti-choice advocate Kevin Williamson, who advocated abortion be treated as premeditated homicide. Though eventually fired after public outcry, the idea that a mainstream outlet would feel pressured to incorporate someone with Williamson's views when there are many conservative media outlets available to him is troubling (Goldberg, 2018). The blurred lines and deliberate destabilization generated by fake news and its insertion of doubt has apparently hit moderate outlets who seem incapable of reaching a basic level of consensus.

Alvarez (2017) presents an overview of other mainstream elite outlets like the *New York Times* who hired climate-change denier Bret Stephens as a regular columnist. A frightening rationale for hiring Stephens was provided by the *Times'* editorial page editor, who claimed "there are millions of people who agree with him" (para. 13). CNN used a similar justification for hiring commentators Jeffery Lord and Corey Lewandowski because of their "expertise." Alvarez concludes:

> In one sense, it's baldly a question of money and ratings—news outlets maximize their chances of drawing in bigger audiences by giving platforms to a more "diverse" range of opinions. In another sense, though, this rationale takes for granted that the job of a news outlet is not so much to present consumers with "truth" as to represent an array of rigid viewpoints with which consumers can potentially identify. (para. 13)

However, media consumers can fight back in a big way. In October 2018, *The New York Review of Books* (NYRB) decided to publish an essay by Jian Ghomeshi, a Canadian broadcaster who was accused, and later acquitted, of seven counts of sexual assault, including choking, by several women (Gollom, 2016). The essay appeared without any accompanying information about the charges or responses from any of the women who had accused him. In the essay, Ghomeshi (2018) briefly summarizes how he was accused of "criminal charges including hair-pulling, hitting during intimacy in one instance, and—the most serious allegation—non-consensual choking while making out with a woman on a date in 2002" (p. 29). That pretty much ends any mention of his actions as he proceeds to go into a litany of rationalizing, free from the constraints of any sort of counter-perspective, which is how both-sides journalism actually operates.

Referencing his celebrity status, Ghomesh and that "I was the guy everyone hated first" (p. 29). Ghomeshi then dismisses the importance of public apology because he himself had always doubted other men who had publicly apologized after being accused, and because the response to being accused of sexual assault is too all-encompassing to really be able to sincerely atone in that manner. He also explains how apologies are not a reliable way to ensure the whole mess gets turned around in one's favor: "What you truly fear in the first days after being publicly accused is fear and anger, in that order" (p. 29). If the apology could make the whole thing go away, then it might be a worthwhile thing to do.

What is remarkable is how, over several paragraphs, Ghomeshi proceeds to detail *his* suffering, such as being afraid to leave the house, losing friends, being attacked online, and stereotyped with other rapists. This entire account is made rhetorically possible by his brief and breezy dismissal of the accounts of the women involved early on in the essay. Their absence makes his essay plausible at first glance. Immediately, he pivots to his supporters, who over time, are less likely to vouch for him: "as the storm grew, many backed away, too scared or conflicted or shocked at the headlines to make a public stand" (p. 30). The phrase "as the storm grew" is more accurately a stand-in for his female friends probably reading the actual testimony from several women and having second thoughts, not so much them being afraid or shocked at the scandal itself as he claims.

The essay ends with Ghomeshi describing an anonymous conversation he had with a woman on a train about music. His account has him resisting impulses to tell her about his notoriety, the overall message being "she just liked me for ME and not because of my fame." The reader is apparently supposed to be impressed that he didn't give in to his former ways and has now reformed. What is the most striking about Ghomeshi and others like him is the expectation that they should not only continue to have a normal life, but also get to parlay their experiences into a revival of their careers, with a nice glossing over of the women involved and a silencing of their voices. The media is a direct partner in these efforts.

After facing an outcry by regular subscribers, feminist groups, and academics, The NYRB published an extensive "letters to the editor" section in the following issue, thinking that would hold back the heat. Taken together, these letters serve as a critical corrective to the account Ghomeshi provides and reveals both-sides-ism for the hollow farce that it is. The reader is immediately struck by the collective characteristic of the writing in the letters, far exceeding the quality of Ghomeshi's essay. Collectively, the letter writers made it clear that this goes way beyond a free speech issue (as it is often reduced to), but an issue of *editorial discretion*, considering that publications do not have to print everything they receive, as Meghan G.'s response summarizes:

> By publishing this, you are telling us that the people who violated us can get away with it, relatively unscathed. Hell, they can even write an article about the difficulty of leaving the house post-persecution. You tell us that our security, safety, and lives mean less than those who harmed us. (Responses, 2018, p. 58)

One of the best letters was written by Joanne O., who was victimized by Ghomeshi in 2013. She viewed the decision to publish his essay as having consequences reaching far beyond just telling his side of the story. By a respected publication such as the NYRB giving legitimacy to Ghomeshi and not including any contextual information, it served as a public reminder that his story would be believed, and the victims' accounts wouldn't. His story was therefore worth more as well as getting a double hearing, the first being in court. Joanne then took on the usual media tactic of questioning women's own experiences with sexual assault and the notion of them imagining things:

> My experience is so similar to other women's you may think we must have colluded. But no, we don't have to speak to one another to know how this reality feels because this reality is so common for far too many of us...our stories are rarely ever heard beyond a sensational article in which we rip ourselves open to expose our wounds for the salacious reader. (Responses, 2018, p. 54)

Linda Redgrave, another letter writer, notes how Ghomeshi's essay may have been an attempt on his part to put a career back together, but that it is not sufficient and he now must face "the court of public opinion" which is "a very large court, and we are trauma-informed judges" (Responses, 2018, p. 54).

Since the NYRB wasn't able to do some basic journalistic follow-up on the essay's claims, Lisa Guenther's letter stepped up to the task:

> The fact that you published Ghomeshi's point of view on the numerous allegations against him without minimal fact-checking is reprehensible. For one thing, he was not fired by the CBC because of "allegations circulated online" by an ex. He was fired because he literally showed CBC brass photos of a woman he had beat the hell out of, and tried to pass it off as "rough sex." Oh, and there are no such things as charges of hair-pulling, etc., not even in Canada. (Responses, 2018, p. 54)

One letter writer, Lester Bergquist, simply quoted an excerpt from the trial transcripts of one of the victims, letting the account speak for itself: "I'm terrified. I don't know why he's doing this, I don't know if he's going to stop…And my ears are ringing, and I felt like I was going to faint. I'm going to end up passed out on his floor" (Responses, 2018, p. 56).

Some readers extended their critique of the essay's publication to the larger systemic lack of diversity of the NYRB, connecting the decision to publish the essay with the idea that even a mediocre essay from a male celebrity broadcaster is more important than the voices of women and minorities. Rohan Maitzen takes on the common tactic of an organization referencing their "quality" standards as a rationale for not having diverse writers. If "quality" was the primary criteria driving the decision to publish, then how to explain the NYRB publishing such a mediocre essay?

> Diversity is an aspect of quality, and the apparent recalcitrance of the NYRB's editors in the face of reasonable pressure to feature a wider range of voices in its prestigious pages has been an ongoing disappointment…that you have room for his story but are indifferent to the lack of wider representation in your pages is frankly shocking to me. (Responses, 2018, p. 58)

Elizabeth Wurtzel wrote to suggest that instead of just sitting back and waiting for women and minorities to magically appear, the editorial staff needs to be actively seeking them out, including mentoring up-and-coming writers. Other letters also echoed continued disappointment at the publication not featuring diverse writers and more inclusive perspectives.

Taken together, the letters provide a damning critique of the both-sides-ism of today's press and how people are beginning to speak back against it. In particular, Bridget V.'s response takes aim at the social media model of reporting in its eroding public journalism while upholding edginess as the supreme value:

> Perhaps this piece is tailored to appeal to an imagined readership of intellectually lazy men looking to indulge their narcissism. Maybe it's for the thousands of

rage-clicks readers will inevitably give you to see what this trash pile consists of. Maybe you truly and honestly think you're showcasing a subversive new perspective on a subject. Regardless, you're reinforcing the notion that men who abuse women still have a place in their professional field. (Responses, 2018, p. 55)

Similarly, Leanna Brodie's letter posed some wry questions regarding the intellectual laziness that is both-sides-ism:

Can we expect an upcoming guest editorial from Harvey Weinstein on the art of pitching woo; the cops who beat Rodney King on their contributions to the civil rights movement; or Kevin Spacey swearing that from now on he will always check ID? Or can we agree that widely known sexual predators and the beneficiaries of miscarriages of justice have forfeited the public perks of celebrity, as well as the considerable prestige of your publication? (Responses, 2018, p. 56)

Building on this, Elizabeth Wurtzel declares "no, men do not have a side in this. That is like white supremacists saying white lives matter too" (Responses, 2018, p. 57). When one thinks about the amount of time wasted parsing the basic boundaries of what is considered "up for debate," one starts to realize the deliberateness of keeping people mired in such enterprises. Maybe it is time for centrist and liberal media to stop doing the right wing's work for them.

CONSPIRACY THEORIES

Defining what constitutes a conspiracy theory, let alone determining which are or are not legitimate conspiracy theories, has been a source of ongoing disagreement. Since this section is primarily focused on the political and personal functions of conspiracy theories as part of a larger capitalist effort to destabilize social institutions, a basic definition can be helpful. Sunstein and Vermeule (2009) conceptualize conspiracy theories as "an effort to explain some event or practice by reference to the machinations of powerful people, who attempt to conceal their role (at least until their aims are accomplished)" (p. 205). This is echoed by Ellis' (2018) definition of conspiracy theories as "an unfounded, deeply held alternative explanation for how things are—often invoking some shadowy, malevolent force masterminding the coverup" (para. 2). The unfounded component is critical because this differentiates conspiracy discourse from actual documented events of the powerful operating in often protected or concealed ways to harm the powerless, as in government-sponsored medical and military projects.

There is no doubt that conspiracy discourse has become increasingly mainstream, especially as distributed through the media. Figures such as Curt Schilling and Roseanne Barr regularly post conspiracy theories on social media and in televised interviews. Fox News' Sean Hannity and Alex Jones weave conspiracy theories into their discussions of current events (Chang, 2018). Republican politicians regularly distribute conspiracy theories as current events talking points, including former Trump administration national security advisor Michael Flynn who made conspiracy theories a regular part of his communication, "ranging from stories that Hillary Clinton "is involved with child sex trafficking and has secretly waged war on the Catholic Church, as well as charges that Obama is a 'jihadi' who 'laundered' money for Muslim terrorists" (Kellner, 2017, p. 69). Of course, Trump himself is one of the most prolific conspiracy distributors, considering the power of his political office and use of Twitter. The "birther" conspiracy theory—that President Obama could not produce a birth certificate documenting his US citizenship—was a key factor leading to Trump's candidacy for president.

Of all of the strategies of the right discussed so far, conspiracy theories present the most challenging to dislodge. Part of this is due to the features built into the structure of conspiracy narratives, which requires three interconnected elements of vastness (too big to comprehend, but not to speculate on), multi-level infiltration (they are all in on it), and a sense of urgency (if we don't reveal the conspiracy, their plan will succeed) (Kimmel, 2017). This relates to Muirhead and Rosenbulm's (2018) conceptualization of "conspiracism," which is an apt term for describing a worldview as well as the overall practice of integrating conspiracy theories into all aspects of public life. They acknowledge that while the practice of conspiracism has been seen before, "the conspiracism we see today does introduce something new—conspiracy without the theory" (para. 2).

In its more mainstream networks of adherents, conspiracy without the theory is more about innuendo and less about complicated narratives that one might see from more dedicated adherents (Muirhead & Rosenblum, 2018). The phrase "people are saying" is a way to safely distance one's self from originating or taking part in the narrative: "The manner of coy insinuation that marks the new conspiracism both absolves the speaker of responsibility for the charge he's putting forth and invites endless investigation" (para.10). For example, when the political usefulness of the birther conspiracy expired, a new talking point emerged on the right that it was *Hillary Clinton* who originated the birth certificate story, not Trump (Prokop, 2016).

Conspiracism is also a form of conspiracy for its own sake and serves different aims, such as the birther movement seeking to delegitimize Obama's presidency or interrupting climate science work by claiming that government climate data is made up to enhance the urgency of global warming (Muirhead & Rosenblum, 2018). This illustrates that conspiracy theory adherents have existing political beliefs that seek out self-affirming conspiracy narratives. For example, Trump supporters unequivocally reject actual acts of collusion, such as energy companies suppressing research that illustrates their role in climate change. When given a choice between two narratives, one of which has energy companies being motivated to suppress climate science because of potential profit loss or a group of climate scientists banding together to seek fame, the former narrative is rejected in favor of the latter conspiracy theory.

In particular, after 9/11, conspiracy discourse intensified its right-wing talking points to create a special sub-category known as "conspiranoia" (Weinberg, 2010, para. 6). This resembles the constructs of superstition, which is rife with confirmation bias and common-sense notions that are difficult to disprove through traditional means (T. Nichols, 2017). As T. Nichols explains, "each rejoinder or contradiction only produces a more complicated theory. Conspiracy theorists manipulate all tangible evidence to fit their explanation, but worse, they will also point to the absence of evidence as even stronger confirmation" (p. 55). In other words, the only thing that can defeat a conspiracy theory is a bigger conspiracy theory.

In the past, the potential reach of conspiracy theories was limited to brochures, books, video recordings and public talks. There was also more of an underground element to conspiracy theories, where tight-knit groups would form to share evidence (Ellis, 2018). With the advent of social media, conspiracy theories have added to the issue of increased reach an important participatory element, which further binds proponents to the narrative as it evolves over time. In some cases, older conspiracy theories, like UFOs or the Kennedy assassination, can find renewed interest by the ability of adherents to archive publicly available materials on websites and blogs. These can then be linked to and shared quite easily.

Several websites devoted to the distribution of conspiracy theories include beforeitsnews.com, nodisifo.com and veteranstoday.com and these are linked to Twitter posts, often generated by bots (Westneat, 2017). This creates "strange clusters of wild conspiracy talk, when mapped, point to an emerging alternative media ecosystem on the web of surprising power and reach" (para. 10). As one example, Alex Jones Infowars.com has the same number of page views as the Chicago Tribune (para. 13). What ends up happening is that a person visiting these websites sees the same conspiracy theory referred to by different sites and in different forms, which gives it "the false appearance of source diversity" (Starbird, 2017, p. 9).

There are two aspects to conspiracy theories that are important to examine. The first is the political function of conspiracy theories, or that the spread of these narratives assists the ruling class in various ways. This is often uncovered through noting the common themes or threads that run through conspiracy discourse, which "pretends to own reality" while carrying us "beyond partisan polarization to epistemic polarization, so that Americans are in conflict about nothing less than what it means to know something" (Muirhead & Rosenblum, 2018, para. 12).

A second key aspect is the personal enhancement that conspiracy theories offer to proponents. This includes a sense of participating in a conspiracy narrative as it unfolds, made possible by social media and the Internet as well as the concept that you are "in the know" unlike the rest of the population who unquestioningly follow along. It is important to note that both of these larger aspects regularly interact with each other and never occur in isolation. For the conspiracy theory to have power, it has to have both political and personal functions.

Political Functions

Far from being relegated to the fringe, conspiracy theories have important political functions that help to propel and make mainstream anti-expertise and fake news narratives. These functions are part of conceptualizing all of history itself through the lens of conspiracy rather than understanding that "it is political economy, not conspiracy theory, that explains what is fundamentally wrong with society" (Weinberg, 2010, para. 1). The first political function of conspiracy theories is that by serving up the target of the "big entity"—whether it is a powerful wealthy person, group of wealthy people (often Jewish), multinational corporation, or government—this serves to conveniently take the pressure off of capitalism and its functions. Weinberg views conspiracy theories as serving a compensatory function, much as fascism giving "the little man" superficial changes or scapegoats instead of fundamentally confronting oppression.

The big entity can be utilized in various ways. With events like the Boston Marathon bombing, airline disasters or mass shootings where causation is pretty clear, more elaborate rumors immediately surface assigning blame to those other than the perpetrators in order to create the false flag or crisis actor type of conspiracy narrative (Starbird, 2017). This delegitimizes efforts like legislation controlling access to lethal firearms or associate liberals or the Democratic Party with terrorist activities. Another political function of the big entity is that it serves to divert attention to more fringe groups like the Illuminati or Trilateral Commission rather than the larger military infrastructure or capitalism (Weinberg, 2010). This is different than traditional notions of propaganda which is to shape thinking around a specific topic. The idea of the big entity is "to keep the viewer hooked and distracted, passive and paranoid, rather than agitated to action" (Pomeranstev & Weiss, 2014, p. 11).

A second political characteristic of conspiracy theories is their attack on the global, usually partnered with classic anti-Semitic talking points such as the Rothschilds, Protocols of the Elders of Zion and, more recently, George Soros. It is important to note that the anti-globalization sentiment of these conspiracy narratives is always bounded by the "big entity" and never moves toward a critique of capitalism, other than to add descriptors like "global capitalism," as if the problem is its international status or multiculturalism. Westneat (2017) finds that anti-globalist conspiracy theory adherents are also "anti-mainstream media, anti-immigration, anti-science, anti-US government, and anti-European Union" (para. 20). Trump continually uses anti-globalist talking points in order to cement connections with his nationalist base (Muirhead & Rosenbulm, 2018).

As with the big entity, anti-globalization serves to divert attention from capitalism's role in the current economic condition. For example, almost one third of people in the US think a global elite is attempting to take over the world, with 15% believing that the government, working in tandem with this global elite, has installed mind-controlling devices into televisions and broadcasts (T. Nichols, 2017, p. 59). For these individuals, the problem isn't capitalism, it is that a small number of Jewish elites are attempting to take over. Weinberg (2010) notes how the conspiracy theory of history has right wing nationalistic and xenophobic roots going back the 18th century and continuing through The Protocols of the Elders of Zion, and eventually adopted by Hitler. The same can be said for anti-Muslim conspiracy theories emerging after 9/11 and The Money Masters DVD which exposes a cabal of international bankers. Most anti-globalist conspiracy theory sites never fail to track George Soros and the Rothschilds, more recently connecting them to global pedophile rings (Starbird, 2017).

Third, related to the attack on the global is the messaging of distrust in "big government" or any type of structural social program. Instead, the emphasis is on individual, isolationist, and nationalist solutions. Again, this helps to take the focus off of capitalism and place it onto efforts to support politicians who advocate for dismantling the social safety net. It is pretty easy to see how this serves as a major benefit to the capitalist class, since "the ultimate consequence of the new conspiracism is the destruction of the administrative state, a state with the capacity to design and implement long-term policy" (Muirhead & Rosenblum, 2018, para. 13). Conspiracy theories serve to "obscure any perception of governmental integrity" and "feeds the assumption that the government is staffed by those who are actively hostile to the common interest" (para. 13). In terms of partisan politics, the majority of big government conspiracy theories attempt to tie the Democratic Party to efforts to allow minorities to take over, as in the notion that undocumented immigrants are voting in large numbers.

The fourth political characteristic of conspiracy theories is to foster a hostility toward experts, specifically around important issues of public health, climate, education, and science. Conspiracy theories also help promote a distrust in the media, with everything except the conspiracy narrative viewed as "fake news" or being in on the coverup:

> The effect of conspiratorial thinking…is delegitimation. The new conspiracist accusations seek not only to unmask and disempower those they accuse but to deny their standing to argue, explain, persuade, and decide. Conspiracism rejects their authority. In the end, the consequences of delegitimation are not targeted or discrete but encompassing. (Muirhead & Rosenblum, para. 8)

This has been assisted by the decline in the number of professionally trained journalists and "the work of gatekeeping shifting to end-users" (Starbird, 2017, p. 2). Profit-driven social media information distribution models have become conduits for content, which has "challenged the traditional authority of journalists, both directly and indirectly" (p. 2).

An additional outcome of hostility toward expertise is evidenced by the inability of the mainstream media to intervene by fact checking or other forms of debunking conspiracy narratives. Within the conspiracy mindset, fact checks only serve to further adhere followers to the conspiracy narrative: if the media is debunking us, then what we believe must be true (Westneat, 2017). This provides "the ultimate bulwark against expertise" because any knowledgeable professional is automatically a part of the larger conspiracy (T. Nichols, 2017). At the same time, mainstream media *are* referred to for evidence in support of the conspiracy narrative when the opportunity arises (Starbird, 2017). Oxenham (2017) found that the only way to counteract conspiracy thinking was to "inoculate" people with more rational assertions prior to them being exposed to conspiracy theories, "before they have the opportunity to take hold in the wild" (para. 7).

Personal Functions

Though powerful enough on their own, the political functions of conspiracy theories do not by themselves serve as a sufficient means of attracting and retaining adherents. There also have to be aspects of the conspiracy theory experience that personally bonds proponents to the narrative and to its further distribution and construction. This is incredibly important as the conspiracy discourse descends further into the realm of implausibility. You have to have such a degree of loyalty to the narrative that it approaches religious fervor in order to sustain it:

> Paranoid politics is thus a psychological disposition—projecting one's problem onto the fiendish machinations of others, so as both to uphold one's own purity and goodness and simultaneously to identify the source of the problem. As with many projects that rely on psychological displacement, the groups often produce the very thing the most fear. (Kimmel, 2017, p. 230)

The first key personal function is the participatory nature of conspiracy theories, especially within the context of social media where responses to one's contributions can happen in a fraction of a second. Chang (2018) and Starbird's (2017) tracking of online conspiracy networks is invaluable in understanding the relevance of participation. In particular, Chang (2018) examines the QAnon conspiracy cascade (Sunstein & Vermuele, 2009), which emerged in cyberspace. Essentially, proponents of QAnon assert that both Trump and Robert Mueller are collaborating to reveal a group of pedophiles that are funded by the Democratic party. Chang (2018) traces the narrative to a poster on 4chan who claimed to have "Q-level security clearance" and became known as simply "Q." Eventually, conversation about the conspiracy moved to the/r/greatawakening subreddit where participation jumped.

Because of his obvious need for anonymity, Q would post vague statements that kept the online community constantly speculating, such as telling posters "to follow former Clinton staffer Huma Abedin and to figure out why billionaire George Soros donated all his money recently" (Chang, 2018, para. 23). These and other "bread crumbs" would become increasingly cryptic and mysterious, leaving the subreddit community (known as "bakers") to be the ones to propel the narrative. As Chang explains, "this community…has turned an internet conspiracy theory into a live-action role-playing game. *They* are the main characters — except they don't think it's a game; they believe this conspiracy is real" (para. 15). As the participation reached a fever pitch, QAnon proponents compared themselves to the reporters who broke the pedophilia story about the Catholic Church.

Eventually, Trump supporters appeared at his rallies wearing QAnon t-shirts, prompting further investigation of the conspiracy theory. Chang (2018) and his associates conducted a cyber content analysis to track the network of/r/ greatawakening users and found that the majority of them were not hard-core adherents. In other words, support for Trump is what drove them to participate in the QAnon conspiracy, along with other factors like cryptocurrency, men's rights, and martial arts, often associated with white males (para. 10). The bulk of the content was generated by only one fourth of the commenters, or about 200 posters (para. 11). Chang found that 700 other users contributed another fourth of the comments. The rest of the participants on the subredit (11,000 commenters/42,000 lurkers) were just "along for the ride" (para. 12).

Starbird (2017) gathered conspiracy theory tweets on Twitter, focusing on mass shootings. The research group then tweeted the URLs of the stories to recreate a quantitative visual of the network accompanied by a qualitative analysis of the different themes that arose from the networks. Results indicated that conspiracy theory adherents build connections across different conspiracy sites "in a mutually reinforcing manner," such as retweeting sites that reinforced existing political beliefs (p. 5). Additionally, much of the retweeted material was attributed to bots, with the most activity around The Real Strategy, a fake news site: "The temporal signature of tweets citing this domain reveals a consistent pattern of coordinated bursts of activity at regular intervals generated by 200 accounts that appear to be connected to each other…and coordinated through an external tool" (Starbird, 2017, pp. 5–6).

A second personal function of conspiracy narratives is the allure of being among the few who are "in the know." Being in the know serves to set you and your fellow adherents apart from the masses of people who are duped into believing what the government or other big entity wants you to believe. DeVega's (2017) interview with Tom, a conspiracy theory adherent, reveals this enjoyment of conspiracy narratives:

> Yes—they are fun. Yes—it's empowering. It tells you that you are one of the people who has the secret knowledge of what is really going on. It makes you feel superior to other people. It makes you feel good; it's self-actualization. (DeVega, 2017, para. 21)

This form of wheel spinning is of enormous benefit to the capitalist class because to them, nothing is better than people being kept safely tucked away thinking they are "in the know" when all along they are happily accomplishing their work for them.

One study involving 238 participants from the US completed a survey that measured their "need for uniqueness" by indicating the degree to which they agreed or disagreed with various statements (Oxenham, 2017, para. 2). After completing the instrument, participants noted which common online conspiracy theories they believed in from a list of 99 possibilities. Researchers found that belief in one conspiracy theory was correlated with beliefs in others as well as a stronger endorsement of the conspiracy theories correlated with a need for uniqueness (para. 2).

In one of the more dramatic examples of the need to be in the know, an experiment was conducted where researchers made up a conspiracy theory related to smoke detectors creating a dangerous hard-to-detect sound (Oxenham, 2017). Half of the participants were told that over 80% of Germans believed in the conspiracy with the other half of participants told that over 80% doubted the theory (para. 4). Just knowing the conspiracy theory was popular tended to impact the strength of the belief of those prone to conspiracy narratives:

> Their belief in the made-up smoke detector conspiracy was enhanced on average when the conspiracy was framed as a *minority* opinion. Just as people are known to stop liking a band as soon as it becomes popular or "mainstream," it appears conspiracy theorists can behave in a very similar fashion upon learning about the next big new conspiracy theory. (para. 5)

A final revealing finding occurred after the participants were debriefed by the researchers about the conspiracy theory being created for the study. One fourth of the participants refused to recognize that the theory was researcher-generated and became even *more* attached to it, rejecting all efforts to convince them otherwise.

The third personal function of conspiracy theories is they provide proponents with a sense of being in control and channel the desire to bring order to chaos through the conspiracy narrative (T. Nichols, 2017). For this reason, conspiracy theories tend to intensify during times of great historical and political upheaval (DeVega, 2017; Sunstein & Vermeule, 2009). Because the large, imposing problems facing neoliberal society can often cause a sense of helplessness, the conspiracy theory provides a sense of relief because you can finally "see it all" and structure some semblance of order to chaos. This can go in both optimistic and pessimistic directions:

> When conspiracists attribute intention where in fact there is only accident and coincidence, reject authoritative standards of evidence and falsifiability, and seal themselves off from any form of correction, their conspiracism can seem like a form of paranoia—a delusional insistence that one is the victim of a hostile world. (Muirhead & Rosenblum, 2018, para. 6)

Of course, the irony is that the real, evidence-based problems that are happening within capitalism are totally rejected in favor of an alternative narrative that will never really address the situation. This, too, benefits the capitalist class because instead of taking to the streets in mass actions that could change things, that energy is spent on further refining and adding details to the conspiracy theory's tenets. Ultimately, conspiracy theories also take the energy that could be spent developing dialectical materialist skepticism and channels it into unproductive, formless skepticism that discourages acting on knowledge to change the status quo.

CONCLUSION

While nowhere near the dangerous levels of nationalism that countries such as Brazil are experiencing, we can safely say that the United States is currently in the grips of direct, sustained attacks on reason, knowledge, and the notion of truth (Dorfman, 2017). The hostility toward facts and lack of critical thinking we currently see reflects a profound failure of schools to educate for the protection of democracy, in a time when no one appears to be able to hold Trump and his administration accountable (Kellner, 2017). Ganz (2018) speculates that the historical era that we are in could easily be called the Age of the Charlatan:

> Everywhere you turn there seems to be some kind of quack or confidence man catering to an eager audience: Fox News hosts like Sean Hannity have moved from pushing ill-informed opinion to flat-out conspiracy mongering; pickup artists sell "tried and true" methods for isolated young men to seduce women; and sophists pass off stale pedantries as dark and radical thought, selling millions of books in the process. (para. 1)

The attraction to charlatans and what they offer seems to happen during times of immense change, when it is more challenging to handle the sheer amount of information appearing at any given time. Fake news and conspiracy theories provide convenient narratives that self-reinforce existing political beliefs and notions of common sense, along with providing the illusion that we are taking action.

When feelings become the barometer for truth, dangerous things can happen. This is especially the case where the feelings of those in power and their supporters are prioritized. For example, Trump's Tweets continuously validate the feelings of white males who are troubled by women and minorities refusing to stay quietly tucked away. As Penny (2018) points out, "Just because young white men are experiencing hurt feelings does not make those hurt feelings rational, or reasonable, or a sound basis for policy-making. It certainly doesn't oblige anyone to dignify those hurt feelings with the status of cosmic wisdom" (para. 36).

It is pretty obvious that finding a way out is going to be a challenge, especially when the ruling class has unprecedented access to the media and routinely uses strategies like fake news, both-sides-ism, pseudoscience, and conspiracy theories. The deployment of these attacks has real consequences, especially for the Earth's climate, where capitalists "can deny, delay, defund, distort, dismantle" and "fiddle while the planet burns" (Santer, 2017, para. 10). We are going to have to mobilize, and before we do, we have to face some important dialectical truths:

> There are a number of claims circulating in political culture with no basis in reality that are persuasive nonetheless. They are largely impervious to challenges based on empirical evidence…the left, armed with science, history, and buckets full of facts, attempts to speak truth to power. In other words, we

assume that in any controversy, the person who has the truth on their side will eventually win the day. Here's the uncomfortable part: this assumption is just not true. The truth does not necessarily set us free; indeed, the powerful often control the circulation and authority of what counts as truth. (Cloud, 2018, para. 15)

CONCLUSION

Enough Is Enough

At the time of writing this conclusion, an impeachment inquiry of Trump is underway, prompted by anonymous whistleblower accounts of his threatening to cut off funding for Ukraine unless officials agreed to investigate Joe Biden, a 2020 Democratic presidential candidate. The impeachment inquiry is accompanied by a daily rundown of subpoenas, arrests, and investigative reporting, revealing the increasingly deep and complex networks of corruption, a hallmark of both right-wing populism and fascist governments. In the September 26, 2019 House Intelligence Committee hearing, acting director of national intelligence, the perpetually incompetent Joseph Maguire, faced what appeared to be two radically different groups of questioners. One group, the Democrats, posed direct and intense questions, related to the contents of the whistleblower report and transcript of the phone call between Trump and the Ukrainian president. The other group, the Republicans, wrapped conspiracy theory talking points in question form, peppered with constant genuflecting to Maguire's military service and aggrieved whataboutism in attempts to deflect onto Democrats. Enough is enough.

As momentum for impeachment builds, the GOP, much of its membership compromised if not complicit in what we are only beginning to understand as their monumental, global corruption, continues to present conspiracy theories as official statements. They fully understand that their base of support relies only on Trump and the true believers in his flailing administration for sources of truth and have crafted specific messaging to solidify the closed information loop. One could even argue that the entire motivation for threatening the Ukraine was itself based on a conspiracy theory that they had a secret server with information about the Bidens. At the advent of key conspiracy talking points being invalidated by Trump's own actions along with individual refutations, new ones emerge to take their place. With the 2020 election ramping up, these talking points are infiltrating Trump campaign ads on social media with Facebook privileging profit over truth by refusing to take down ads with false claims. This renders their earlier promises of a "crackdown" on fake news hollow and irrelevant. Enough is enough.

Social media has also facilitated dangerous misogynist and violent verbal attacks on Congresspersons of color, including "the squad" Alexandria Ocasio-Cortez, Rashida Tlaib and Ayanna Pressley and Ilhan Omar. The presence of these four women in positions of power have fuelled the rage of white males' sense of aggrieved entitlement, to the point of their unleashing death threats on and outside of social media, all while claiming to be victims. At a Minneapolis rally, Trump extended his attacks on Tlaib to targeting Somali immigrants and citizens in order

© KONINKLIJKE BRILL NV, LEIDEN, 2020 | DOI: 10.1163/9789004424531_009

to create intimidation and fear. Sixteen-year-old climate activist Greta Thunburg has been regularly attacked, from her autism being made fun of, to grown men claiming that if she is old enough to speak her mind, then she should be old enough to consent to sexual activity. Because all of these women are extremely savvy with social media, their ability to talk back and engage in public pedagogy while attracting an increasing following continues to perplex and frustrate the alt-right who will likely escalate their rhetoric. Enough is enough.

Early abortion bans, ranging from six to twelve weeks, have passed in several states. Alabama passed the most restrictive law, with a total ban on abortion unless the woman's health is at risk. Though these are likely to be overturned in the courts, they demonstrate the extension of misogyny into the control of women's bodies. They also represent cynical and deliberate attempts to get the Supreme Court to revisit abortion, especially since the GOP was able to recently confirm two right-wing judges. The irony is the level of evangelical support for Trump, who has marshalled love and devotion of his religious followers who never seem to extend such a degree of forgiveness to those outside of their narrow fellowship. Apparently, women who seek abortions are "sluts" while no one is supposed to point out the hypocrisy of Trump's past sexual conduct because "God has forgiven him." Enough is enough.

Finally, the 2020 election features more progressive Democratic candidates this go-round than just Bernie Sanders. This is due to there being more demands placed on centrist Democrats like Joe Biden by voters who are frankly fed up. When a Democratic candidate hedges on single payer health care, they are immediately confronted on social media and at public appearances. It is no longer tolerable to defend the detention of immigrants and our existing immigration policy as a whole. Women in particular are seeking to build on the electoral anger of the midterm elections to not only vote, but to run for office. Activism continues apace with mobilizations growing and increasing in diversity. Though there may still be attempts at colorblind class rhetoric this election cycle, the white male working class meme has lost its power. Let's hope that enough is enough.

REFERENCES

Abrams, R., & Gebeloff, R. (2017, June 25). In towns already hit by steel mill closings, a new casualty: Retail jobs. *The New York Times*. Retrieved from https://www.nytimes.com/2017/06/25/business/economy/amazon-retail-jobs-pennsylvania.html

Achcar, G. (2018, Spring). Morbid symptoms: What did Gramsci mean and how does it apply to our time? *International Socialist Review, 108*, 30–37.

Afonso, A. (2017, March 17). The far right's leftist mask. *Jacobin*. Retrieved from https://www.jacobinmag.com/2017/03/far-right-ukip-fn-welfare-immigration-working-class-voters/

Aftab, A. (2017, Summer). Visibility or complicity: Western capitalism gets its hands on the hijab. *Bitch, 75*, 33–36.

Alt Right: A primer. (2019). *Anti-defamation league*. Retrieved from https://www.adl.org/resources/backgrounders/alt-right-a-primer-about-the-new-white-supremacy

Alvarez, M. (2017, August 2). Cogito zero sum. *The Baffler*. Retrieved from https://thebaffler.com/the-poverty-of-theory/cogito-zero-sum-alvarez

Anderson, C. (2017, August 5). The policies of white resentment. *The New York Times*. Retrieved from https://mobile.nytimes.com/2017/08/05/opinion/sunday/white-resentment-affirmative-action.html?smid=tw-nytopinion&smtyp=cur&referer=https%3A%2F%2Ft.co%2FmyKGxYJo9r%3Famp%3D1

Ansara, M. (2016, November). The lousy reason I didn't vote in 1968 and why Sanders' supporters shouldn't fall for it. *Z Magazine, 20*(11), 20–25.

Apple, M., & Whitty, G. (2002). Structuring the postmodern in education policy. In D. Hill, P. McLaren, M. Cole, & G. Rikowski (Eds.), *Marxism against postmodernism in educational theory* (pp. 67–87). New York, NY: Lexington Books.

Armstrong, E. (2020). Marxist and socialist feminism. *Study of Women and Gender: Faculty Publications*. Retrieved from https://scholarworks.smith.edu/cgi/viewcontent.cgi?article=1014&context=swg_facpubs

Arnove, A. (2018, Summer). How Marx became a Marxist. *ISR, 109*, 82–91.

ARoamingVagabond. (2018, January 15). An investigation into red-brown alliances: Third positionism, Russia, Ukraine, Syria, and the western left. *Ravings of a Radical Vagabond*. Retrieved from https://ravingsofaradicalvagabond.noblogs.org/post/2018/01/15/an-investigation-into-red-brown-alliances/

Auerbach, D. (2017, September 17). The sci-fi roots of the far right: From 'Lucifer's Hammer' to Newt's moon base to Donald's wall. *The Daily Beast*. Retrieved from http://www.thedailybeast.com/from-lucifers-hammer-to-newts-moon-base-to-donalds-wallthe-sci-fi-roots-of-the-far-right?source=twitter&via=desktop

Bachtell, J. (2017, December 14). 'Voting lesser evil' is no way to think about elections. *People's World*. Retrieved from https://www.peoplesworld.org/article/voting-lesser-evil-is-no-way-to-think-about-elections/

Bacon, D. (2018, December). Immigration is a form of fighting back: Looking at the root causes of migration. *Z Magazine*, 29–35.

Barlow, J. (1996). *A declaration of the independence of cyberspace*. Retrieved from https://www.eff.org/cyberspace-independence

Beauchamp, J. (2016, November 4). White riot: How racism and immigration gave us Trump, Brexit, and a whole new kind of politics. *Vox*. Retrieved from http://www.vox.com/2016/9/19/12933072/far-right-white-riot-trump-brexit

Beauchamp, Z. (2019, April 23). Our incel problem. *Vox*. Retrieved from https://www.vox.com/the-highlight/2019/4/16/18287446/incel-definition-reddit?fbclid=IwAR0tTSOWGcKxMVkXSFcrOq-WqNRgUDIWTVTPuQfZiMbsEk3iGqn5dRI2SdY

REFERENCES

Beauchamp, Z. (2018a, September 13). It happened there: How democracy died in Hungary. *Vox*. Retrieved from https://www.vox.com/policy-and-politics/2018/9/13/17823488/hungary-democracy-authoritarianism-trump

Beauchamp, Z. (2018b, September 28). Lindsey Graham, Brett Kavanaugh, and the unleashing of white male backlash. *Vox*. Retrieved from https://www.vox.com/policy-and-politics/2018/9/28/17913774/brett-kavanaugh-lindsey-graham-christine-ford-backlash

Bello, W. (2018, October 8). Understanding the global rise of the extreme right. *Counterpunch*. Retrieved from https://www.counterpunch.org/2018/10/08/understanding-the-global-rise-of-the-extreme-right/

Benkler, Y., Faris, R., Roberts, H., & Zuckerman, E. (2017, March 3). Breitbart-led right-wing media ecosystem altered broader media agenda. *Columbia Journalism Review*. Retrieved from https://www.cjr.org/analysis/breitbart-media-trump-harvard-study.php

Bernstein, J. (2017, October 5). Alt-white: How the Breitbart machine laundered racist hate. *BuzzFeed News*. Retrieved from https://www.buzzfeed.com/josephbernstein/heres-how-breitbart-and-milo-smuggled-white-nationalism?utm_term=.hiee8LmlD9#.dbBB2KxD0P

Bevins, V. (2018, October 12). Jair Bolsonaro, Brazil's would-be dictator. *The New York Review of Books Daily*. Retrieved from https://www.nybooks.com/daily/2018/10/12/jair-bolsonaro-brazils-would-be-dictator/?utm_medium=email&utm_campaign=NYR%20Precision%20Paul%20Simon%20Brazil&utm_content=NYR%20Precision%20Paul%20Simon%20Brazil+CID_aaf20d7627fc49965 65b281048474141&utm_source=Newsletter&utm_term=Jair%20Bolsonaro%20Brazils%20Would-be%20Dictator

Blair, E. (2019, June 27). Fighting for her life. *New York Review of Books, 66*(11), 28–32.

Blanchard, D. (2018, Fall). Lessons from the teachers' strike wave. *ISR, 110*, 8–28.

Bode, K. (2018, April). Community owned internet. *Z Magazine, 32*(24), 10–11.

Bohrer, A. (n.d.). Intersectionality and Marxism: A critical historiography. *Historical Materialism, 26*(2). Retrieved from http://www.historicalmaterialism.org/articles/intersectionality-and-marxism

Bonefield, W. (1992). *Open Marxism 1: Dialectics and history*. New York, NY: Pluto Press.

Bonilla-Silva, E. (2018). *Racism without racists: Color-blind racism and the persistence of racial inequality in America*. New York, NY: Rowman & Littlefield.

Bouie, J. (2017, April 18). Fake working class. *Slate*. Retrieved from http://www.slate.com/articles/news_and_politics/politics/2017/04/the_response_to_the_retail_apocalypse_shows_which_workers_count_in_trump.html

Brady, D., Finnigan, R., & Hubgen, S. (2018, February 10). Single mothers are not the problem. *The New York Times*. Retrieved from https://www.nytimes.com/2018/02/10/opinion/sunday/single-mothers-poverty.html

Bray, M. (2015). Rearticulating contemporary populism: Class, state, and neoliberal society. *Historical Materialism, 23*(3), 27–64.

Brecher, J. (2017, April). Social self-defense, part two. *Z Magazine, 30*(4), 40–45.

Brenner, J., & Fraser, N. (2017, Spring). What is progressive neoliberalism? A debate. *Dissent*, 130–140.

Britt, L. (2003). *Fourteen defining characteristics of fascism*. Retrieved from https://rense.com/general37/char.htm

Browning, C. (2017, April 20). Lessons from Hitler's rise. *The New York Review of Books, 64*(7), 10–14.

Browning, C. (2018, October 25). The suffocation of democracy. *The New York Review of Books, 65*(16), 14–17.

Brum, E. (2018, October 6). How a homophobic, misogynistic, racist 'thing' could be Brazil's next president. *The Guardian*. Retrieved from https://www.theguardian.com/commentisfree/2018/oct/06/homophobic-mismogynist-racist-brazil-jair-bolsonaro?CMP=share_btn_tw

Burns, B. (2017, July/August). Feminist revolution and climate. *Z Magazine, 30*(7–8), 35–38.

Burns, K. (2017, June 27). The strange, sad case of Laci Green: Feminist hero turned anti-feminist defender. *The Establishment*. Retrieved from https://theestablishment.co/the-sad-case-of-laci-green-feminist-hero-turned-anti-feminist-defender-322515344297

Burton, T. (2018a, June 1). The religious hunger that drives Jordan Peterson's fandom. *Vox*. Retrieved from https://www.vox.com/2018/6/1/17396182/jordan-peterson-alt-right-religion-catholicism

Burton, T. (2018b). The GOP can't rely on white evangelicals forever. *Vox.* Retrieved from https://www.vox.com/2018/11/7/18070630/white-evangelicals-turnout-midterms-trump-2020

Camacho, D. (2016, December 26). Fascism can't be stopped by fact-checking. *The Christian Century.* Retrieved from https://www.christiancentury.org/blog-post/fascismfactchecking

Camfield, D. (2013, February 27). Why socialists need feminism. *Solidarity.* Retrieved from https://solidarity-us.org/why_socialists_need_feminism/

Carter, J. (2014). *A call to action: Women, religion, violence, and power.* New York, NY: Simon & Schuster.

Carter, Z. (2018, August 19). For fancy racists, classical liberalism offers respect, intrigue. *Huffington Post.* Retrieved from https://www.huffingtonpost.com/entry/racists-classical-liberalism-classic-rock-fraud_us_5b6b232ee4b0fd5c73dff019

Catte, E. (2018, Fall). Grassroots organizing in Appalachia. *ISR, 110,* 70–77.

Chacon, J. A. (2017, Summer). From 'deporter-in-chief' to xenophobia unleashed: Immigration policy under Trump. *International Socialist Review, 105,* 28–42.

Chadwick, A., & Stromer-Galley, J. (2016). Digital media, power, and democracy in parties and election campaigns: Party decline or party renewal? *The International Journal of Press/Politics, 21*(3), 283–293.

Chang, A. (2018, August 8). We analyzed every QAnon post on Reddit: Here's who QAnon supporters really are. *Vox.* Retrieved from https://www.vox.com/2018/8/8/17657800/qanon-reddit-conspiracy-data

Cheng, J., Bernstein, M., Danescu-Niculescu-Mizil, C., & Leskovec, J. (2017, February–March). Anyone can become a troll: Causes of trolling behavior in online discussions. *CSCW.* Retrieved from https://files.clr3.com/papers/2017_anyone.pdf

Chomsky, A. (2017, June). Deportation. *Z Magazine, 30*(6), 31–35.

Chretien, T. (2018, July 4). Getting organized for a socialist future. *SocialistWorker.org.* Retrieved from http://socialistworker.org/2018/07/04/getting-organized-for-a-socialist-future

Cloud, D. (2018). *Reality bites: Rhetoric and the circulation of truth claims in U.S. political culture.* Columbus, OH: Ohio State University Press. [Kindle Edition]

Cole, P. (2018, October). A tribute to Ron Dellums, radical. *Z Magazine,* 2–4.

Collins, M. (2015, February 4). Wall Street and the financialization of the economy. *Forbes.* Retrieved from https://www.forbes.com/sites/mikecollins/2015/02/04/wall-street-and-the-financialization-of-the-economy/#7767a54f5783

Communications Decency Act. (1996). Pub. L. No. 104-104 (Tit. V), 110 Stat. 133 (Feb. 8, 1996), *codified at* 47 U.S.C. §§223, 230.

Connor, W. R. (2018, July 31). A vacuum at the center. *The American Scholar.* Retrieved from https://theamericanscholar.org/a-vacuum-at-the-center/#.W2DMRfZFxzq

Coutts, S. (2017, August 28). How hate goes mainstream: Gavin McInnes and the proud boys. *Rewire.* Retrieved from https://rewire.news/article/2017/08/28/hate-goes-mainstream-gavin-mcinnes-proud-boys/

Crane, B. (2018, Fall). More than a ballot line: The Democratic Party, class struggle, and the socialist left today. *ISR, 110,* 29–46.

Daguerre, A. (2019, January 10). The Gilets Jaunes: The good, the bad, and the ugly. *The London School of Economics and Political Science.* Retrieved from https://blogs.lse.ac.uk/europpblog/2019/01/10/the-gilets-jaunes-the-good-the-bad-and-the-ugly/

Daher, J. (2017, Fall). Marxism, the Arab Spring, and Islamic fundamentalism. *International Socialist Review, 106,* 90–113.

Daniels, J. (2009). *Cyber racism: White supremacy online and the new attack on civil rights.* New York, NY: Rowman and Littlefield Publishers.

Davidson, N. (2017, Spring). Choosing or refusing to take sides in an era of right-wing populism: Part one. *International Socialist Review, 104,* 53–73.

Del Valle, G. (2018, November 16). The real reason conservative critics love talking about Alexandria Ocasio-Cortez's clothes. *Vox.* Retrieved from https://www.vox.com/the-goods/2018/11/16/18099074/alexandria-ocasio-cortez-clothes-eddie-scarry

REFERENCES

Demeter, H. (2016, November 29). It's not economic insecurity: Quit peeing on my leg and telling me it's raining. *Hecatedemeter*. Retrieved from https://hecatedemeter.wordpress.com/2016/11/29/its-not-economic-insecurity-quit-peeing-on-my-leg-and-telling-me-that-its-raining/

Der Spiegel Staff. (2018, June 13). Rise of the autocrats. *Der Spiegel*. Retrieved from http://www.spiegel.de/international/world/trump-putin-and-co-liberal-democracy-is-under-attack-a-1212691.html

DeVega, C. (2016, December 6). If you think you can start a dialogue with Trump supporters, wake up. *Alternet*. Retrieved from http://www.alternet.org/election-2016/if-you-think-you-can-start-dialogue-trumps-supporters-wake

DeVega, C. (2017, July 31). The triumph of the idiocracy: How narcissism, stupidity, and the internet got us Donald Trump, an accidental president. *Alternet*. Retrieved from http://www.alternet.org/news-amp-politics/tom-nichols-how-trump-won#.WYD8J6-4d9R.twitter

DeVega, C. (2018, August 1). White Americans support welfare programs: But only for themselves says new research. *Salon*. Retrieved from https://www.salon.com/2018/08/01/white-americans-support-welfare-programs-but-only-for-themselves-says-new-research/

DiAngelo, R. (2006). My class didn't trump my race: Using oppression to face privilege. *Multicultural Perspectives, 8*(1), 51–56.

DiMaggio, A. (2017, August 15). Fascism here we come: The rise of the reactionary right and the collapse of 'the left.' *Counterpunch*. Retrieved from https://www.counterpunch.org/2017/08/15/fascism-here-we-come-the-rise-of-the-reactionary-right-and-the-collapse-of-the-left/

Dittmar, K. (2016, October). Watching election 2016 with a gender lens. *American Political Science Association, 49*(4), 807–812. Retrieved from https://www.cambridge.org/core/journals/ps-political-science-and-politics/article/watching-election-2016-with-a-gender-lens/52C22A77D82A3B0E74F50420747FB869/core-reader#

Dolak, P. (2017a, July/August). Housing is a human right. *Z Magazine, 30*(7–8), 13–18.

Dolak, P. (2017b, November). An honest conversation about Vietnam. *Z Magazine, 30*(11), 34–36).

Dorfman, A. (2017, October 12). Trump's war on knowledge. *The New York Review of Books*. Retrieved from http://www.nybooks.com/daily/2017/10/12/trumps-war-on-knowledge/?utm_medium=email&utm_campaign=NYR%20Orthodox%20marriage%20war%20on%20knowledge&utm_content=NYR%20Orthodox%20marriage%20war%20on%20knowledge+CID_860e0c001b2558123ae3e076fa3b5fb5&utm_source=Newsletter&utm_term=Trumps%20War%20on%20Knowledge

Draitser, E. (2017, July 28). Enough nonsense! The left does not collaborate with fascists. *Counterpunch*. Retrieved from https://www.counterpunch.org/2017/07/28/enough-nonsense-the-left-does-not-collaborate-with-fascists/

Dworkin, G. (2017, August 2). Abbreviated pundit roundup: Trump takes a darker turn in response to losing bigly. *Daily Kos*. Retrieved from https://www.dailykos.com/stories/2017/8/2/1685984/-Abbreviated-Pundit-Round-up-Trump-takes-a-darker-turn-in-response-to-losing-bigly?detail=emaildkre

Ehrenreich, J. (2017, November 9). Why are conservatives more susceptible to believing lies? *Slate*. Retrieved from http://www.slate.com/articles/health_and_science/science/2017/11/why_conservatives_are_more_susceptible_to_believing_in_lies.html?wpsrc=sh_all_dt_fb_bot

Ellis, E. (2018, October 5). Online conspiracy theories: The Wired guide. *Wired*. Retrieved from https://www.wired.com/story/wired-guide-to-conspiracy-theories/

Farrell, H. (2018, May 10). The "intellectual dark web" explained: What Jordan Peterson has in common with the alt-right. *Vox*. Retrieved from https://www.vox.com/the-big-idea/2018/5/10/17338290/intellectual-dark-web-rogan-peterson-harris-times-weiss

Fassler, J. (2017, August 2). The left needs to acknowledge its sexism, part two: Kamala Harris edition. *The Daily Banter*. Retrieved from https://thedailybanter.com/2017/08/left-needs-to-acknowledge-its-sexism-kamala-harris/

Feist, S. (2019, January 28). Why the Constitution makes a third-party presidency extremely difficult. *CNN Politics*. Retrieved from https://www.cnn.com/2019/01/28/politics/howard-schultz-electoral-college-difficulty/index.html?utm_medium=social&utm_source=fbCNNp&utm_term=link&utm_content=2019-01-28T20%3A40%3A06

Fierro, C., & Vasco, P. (2019, Spring). The struggle for abortion rights in Argentina. *ISR 112*. 34–45,

Fletcher, B. (2016, December). Quick reflections on the November 2016 elections. *Z Magazine, 20*(12), 10–11.

Foderaro, L. (2018, August 10). Alexandria Ocascio-Cortez likens $10,000 debate offer by conservative columnist to catcalling. *The New York Times.* Retrieved from https://www.nytimes.com/2018/08/10/nyregion/alexandria-ocasio-cortez-debate-catcalling-ben-shapiro.html

Forsetti. (2016, November 14). On rural America: Understanding isn't the problem. *Forsetti's Justice.* Retrieved from http://forsetti.tumblr.com/post/153181757500/on-rural-america-understanding-isnt-the-problem

Foster, J. B. (2017, April). Neofascism in the White House. *Monthly Review, 68*(11). Retrieved from https://monthlyreview.org/2017/04/01/neofascism-in-the-white-house/

Fraser, N. (2017, January 2). The end of progressive neoliberalism. *Dissent.* Retrieved from https://www.dissentmagazine.org/online_articles/progressive-neoliberalism-reactionary-populism-nancy-fraser

Freedland, J. (2016, October 19). Why is Assange helping Trump? *The New York Review of Books.* Retrieved from http://www.nybooks.com/daily/2016/10/19/wikileaks-why-is-assange-helping-trump/

Freedom of Information Act. (2016). 5 U.S.C. § 552.

Freedom Socialist Party Platform. (n.d.). Retrieved from https://socialism.com/about-fsp/

Fung, B. (2019, October 14). Elizabeth Warren escalates Facebook ad feud. *CNN.* Retrieved from https://www.cnn.com/2019/10/13/politics/elizabeth-warren-facebook-feud/index.html

Gallagher, T. (2016, February). Feeling the Bern: An analysis of the Bernie Sanders phenomenon. *New Labor Forum.* Retrieved from http://newlaborforum.cuny.edu/2016/02/10/the-sanders-movement/

Gallant, C. (2018, Summer). Word travels: The social network sex workers built. *Bitch, 79,* 35–39.

Gans, J. (2018, June 12). Why we are so vulnerable to charlatans like Trump. *The New York Times.* Retrieved from https://www.nytimes.com/2018/06/12/opinion/trump-jordan-peterson-charlatans.html

Gaspar, P. (2018, Fall). Critical thinking: The return of scientific racism. *ISR, 110,* 103–112.

Geiling, N. (2017, June 21). EPA accelerates purge of scientists. *Think Progress.* Retrieved from https://thinkprogress.org/epa-dismisses-more-scientists-pruitt-trump-7530dc37dcf

Gessen, M. (2018, June 10). How George Orwell predicted the challenge of writing today. *The New Yorker.* Retrieved from https://www.newyorker.com/news/our-columnists/how-george-orwell-predicted-the-challenge-of-writing-today

Gessen, M. (2017, August 29). Trump's hoodlums. *New York Review Daily.* Retrieved from http://www.nybooks.com/daily/2017/08/29/trumps-hoodlums/?utm_medium=email&utm_campaign=NYR%20Memory%20Kenya%20Trumps%20hoodlums&utm_content=NYR%20Memory%20Kenya%20Trumps%20hoodlums+CID_e0763e3a451279fddbca4f7cfac4bd66&utm_source=Newsletter&utm_term=Trumps%20Hoodlums

Giroux, H. (2016, December 14). War culture, militarism and racist violence under Trump. *Truthout.* Retrieved from http://www.truth-out.org/news/item/38711-war-culture-militarism-and-racist-violence-under-donald-trump

Gnomeshi, J. (2018, October 11). Reflections from a hashtag. *The New York Review of Books, 65*(15), 29–33.

Godwin, M. (2018, June 24). Do we need to update Godwin's Law about the probability of comparison to Nazis? *Los Angeles Times.* Retrieved from https://www.latimes.com/opinion/op-ed/la-oe-godwin-godwins-law-20180624-story.html

Goldberg, M. (2018, March 30). Affirmative action for reactionaries. *The New York Times.* Retrieved from https://www.nytimes.com/2018/03/30/opinion/affirmative-action-diversity.html

Gollom, M. (2016, February 1). Jian Ghomeshi was 'punching me in the head, multiple times,' witness says. *CBC.* Retrieved from https://www.cbc.ca/news/canada/toronto/jian-ghomeshi-trial-charges-sexual-assault-1.3418856

Goodman, D. (2016). *Women fight back: The centuries-long struggle for liberation.* San Francisco, CA: Liberation Media.

Gopnik, A. (2016, May 20). The dangerous acceptance of Donald Trump. *The New Yorker.* Retrieved from http://www.newyorker.com/news/daily-comment/the-dangerous-acceptance-of-donald-trump

REFERENCES

Gramsci, A. (1999). *Selections from the prison notebooks.* London: The Electric Book Company, Ltd. Retrieved from http://abahlali.org/files/gramsci.pdf

Graves, L. (2017, August 17). This is Sinclair: 'The most dangerous US company you've never heard of.' *The Guardian.* Retrieved from https://www.theguardian.com/media/2017/aug/17/sinclair-news-media-fox-trump-white-house-circa-breitbart-news

Gulliver-Needham, E. (2018, February 22). Adam Smith to Richard Spencer: Why libertarians turn to the alt-right. *Medium.* Retrieved from https://medium.com/@elliotgulliverneedham/why-libertarians-are-embracing-fascism-5a9747a44db9?fbclid=IwAR2LsSXYANXBUoKJRhrEuAnkDivmn2-vHV8CW1p7TUSi8u_B-KpcfQX8Vik

Halpern, M. (2015, February). Freedom to bully: How laws intended to free information are used to harass researchers. *Union of Concerned Scientists.* Retrieved from http://www.ucsusa.org/sites/default/files/attach/2015/09/freedom-to-bully-ucs-2015-final.pdf

Hamilton, S. (2016, December 19). What those who studied Nazis can teach us about the strange reaction to Donald Trump. *Huffington Post.* Retrieved from http://www.huffingtonpost.com/entry/donald-trump-nazi-propaganda-coordinate_us_58583b6fe4b08debb78a7d5c

Halpern, S. (2017, July 13). The nihilism of Julian Assange. *The New York Review of Books.* Retrieved from http://www.nybooks.com/articles/2017/07/13/nihilism-of-julian-assange-wikileaks/?utm_medium=email&utm_campaign=NYR%20Assange%20Matisse%20Oliver%20Stone&utm_content=NYR%20Assange%20Matisse%20Oliver%20Stone+CID_840ef13586cf43f48b54763bdc542f47&utm_source=Newsletter&utm_term=The%20Nihilism%20of%20Julian%20Assange

Halpern, S. (2019, January 17). Apologize later. *The New York Review of Books, 56*(1), 12–14.

Hardt, M., & Negri, A. (1994). *Labor of Dionysus: A critique of the state form.* Minneapolis, MN: University of Minnesota Press.

Hatewatch Staff. (2018, April 19). McInnes, Molyneaux, and 4chan: Investigating pathways to the alt-right. *Southern Poverty Law Center.* Retrieved from https://www.splcenter.org/20180419/mcinnes-molyneux-and-4chan-investigating-pathways-alt-right

Heilbrunn, J. (2017, December 21). Donald Trump's brains. *New York Review of Books.* Retrieved from http://www.nybooks.com/articles/2017/12/21/donald-trump-brains/?utm_medium=email&utm_campaign=NYR%20Trump%20Peres%20May&utm_content=NYR%20Trump%20Peres%20May+CID_584efa14a1859b76989b3d77b6b19a31&utm_source=Newsletter&utm_term=Donald%20Trumps%20Brains

Hill, D., Sanders, M., & Hankin, T. (2002). Marxism, class analysis and postmodernism. In D. Hill, P. McLaren, M. Cole, & G. Rikowski (Eds.), *Marxism against postmodernism in educational theory* (pp. 159–194). New York, NY: Lexington Books.

Illing, S. (2017a, August 9). Media scholar on Trump TV: "This is Orwellian, and it's happening right now, right here." *Vox.* Retrieved from https://www.vox.com/conversations/2017/8/9/16112430/donald-trump-tv-kayleigh-mcenany-state-propaganda-lara-trump

Illing, S. (2017b, September 19). The woman at the center of #Gamergate gives zero fucks about her haters. *Vox.* Retrieved from https://www.vox.com/culture/2017/9/19/16301682/gamergate-alt-right-zoe-quinn-crash-override-interview

Isenberg, N. (2018, June 28). Left behind. *The New York Review of Books, 65*(11), 16–20.

Jacobs, T. (2018, February 15). Inside the minds of hardcore Trump supporters. *Pacific Standard.* Retrieved from https://psmag.com/news/inside-the-minds-of-hardcore-trump-supporters

Jaffe, S. (2017, June 20). America's massive retail workforce is tired of being ignored. *Racked.* Retrieved from https://www.racked.com/2017/6/20/15817988/retail-workers-unions-american-jobs

Johnson, M. (2016, August 9). One year later: BLM protestor who interrupted Bernie Sanders' rally discusses the moment and the movement. *The Root.* Retrieved from https://www.theroot.com/1-year-later-blm-protester-who-interrupted-bernie-sand-1790856353

Jones, S. (2016, November 17). J.D. Vance, the false prophet of blue America. *The New Republic.* Retrieved from https://newrepublic.com/article/138717/jd-vance-false-prophet-blue-america

Jones, S. (2017, October 25). Why conservatives blame poverty on the poor. *The New Republic.* Retrieved from https://newrepublic.com/article/145504/conservatives-blame-poverty-poor

Jones, S. P. (2015). *Blame teachers: The emotional reasons for educational reform*. Charlotte, NC: Information Age Publishing, Inc.

Jotanovic, D. (2018, Summer). The future is fembot: Can we change the direction of gendered AI? *Bitch, 79*, 30–33.

Khan, C. (2019, March 6). How many tampons do you need? This man will explain. *The Guardian*. Retrieved from https://www.theguardian.com/society/shortcuts/2019/mar/06/how-many-tampons-do-you-need-this-man-will-explain

Kellner, D. (2016). *American nightmare: Donald Trump, media spectacle, and authoritarian populism*. Rotterdam, The Netherlands: Sense Publishers.

Kellner, D. (2017). *American horror show: Election 2016 and the ascent of Donald J. Trump*. Rotterdam, The Netherlands: Sense Publishers.

Kelly, J. (2002). Women, work and the family: Or why postmodernism cannot explain the links. In D. Hill, P. McLaren, M. Cole, & G. Rikowski (Eds.), *Marxism against postmodernism in educational theory* (pp. 211–235). New York, NY: Lexington Books.

Kilgore, E. (2017, July 11). Trump's biggest political asset is supporters who believe any negative news is fake news. *Daily Intelligencer*. Retrieved from http://nymag.com/daily/intelligencer/2017/07/trumps-biggest-asset-fans-who-think-negative-news-is-fake.html?utm_campaign=nym&utm_source=fb&utm_medium=s1

Kilpatrick, C. (2016, May 13). Burying white workers. *Jacobin Magazine*. Retrieved from https://www.jacobinmag.com/2016/05/white-workers-bernie-sanders-clinton-primary-racism/

Kimmel, M. (2017). *Angry white men: American masculinity at the end of an era*. New York, NY: Nation Books.

Kumar, D., Trogo, G., Tylim, Natalia, C. J., & Jaffe, S. (2019, Spring). The global struggle against the war on women. *ISR, 112*, 20–33.

Kurtz, L. (2017, Spring). The application of open records laws to publicly funded science. *Natural Resources and Environment, 31*(4). Retrieved from http://columbiaclimatelaw.com/files/2017/04/The-Application-of-Open-Records-Laws-to-Publicly-Funded-Science-_-Section-of-Environment-Energy-and-Resources.pdf

Leavy, P., & Harris, A. (2019). *Contemporary feminist research from theory to practice*. New York, NY: The Guilford Press.

Lee, C. (2017, August 11). I'm a woman in computer science. Let me ladysplain the Google memo to you. *Vox*. Retrieved from https://www.vox.com/the-big-idea/2017/8/11/16130452/google-memo-women-tech-biology-sexism

Leonard, S. (2017, January 16). The nihilistic purity of the far left will kill us all. *ExtraNewsFeed*. Retrieved from https://extranewsfeed.com/the-nihilistic-purity-of-the-far-left-will-kill-us-all-54169b25e3a8

Link, T. (2018, August 26). Milo Yiannopoulos attacks his fans for failing to support him emotionally and financially. *Salon*. Retrieved from https://www.salon.com/2018/08/26/milo-yiannopoulos-attacks-his-fans-for-failing-to-support-him-emotionally-and-financially/

Lively, S., & Abrams, K. (2002). *The pink swastika: Homosexuality in the Nazi party*. Sacramento, CA: Veritas Aeterna Press.

Loofbourow, L. (2018, September 18). Men are more afraid than ever. *Slate*. Retrieved from https://slate.com/news-and-politics/2018/09/brett-kavanaugh-christine-blasey-ford-assault-me-too.html?wpsrc=sh_all_dt_tw_ru

Lopez, G. (2017, January 4). Study: Racism and sexism predict support for Trump much more than economic dissatisfaction. *Vox*. Retrieved from http://www.vox.com/identities/2017/1/4/14160956/trump-racism-sexism-economy-study

Lynd, S., & Grubacic, A. (2008). *Wobblies and Zapatistas: Conversations on anarchism, Marxism and radical history*. Oakland, CA: PM Press.

Lyons, M. (2017, May 2). The alt-right hates women as much as it hates people of colour. *The Guardian*. Retrieved from https://www.theguardian.com/commentisfree/2017/may/02/alt-right-hates-women-non-white-trump-christian-right-abortion?CMP=twt_gu

REFERENCES

Madani, D. (2019, May 15). Alabama governor signs controversial abortion ban bill into law. *NBC News*. Retrieved from https://www.nbcnews.com/politics/2020-election/alabama-governor-signs-controversial-abortion-ban-bill-law-n1006211

Maisano, C. (2017, Summer). The new "culture of poverty." *Catalyst, 1*(2). Retrieved from https://catalyst-journal.com/vol1/no2/new-culture-of-poverty-maisano

Malik, N. (2018, June 7). Islam's new 'native informants.' *New York Review of Books*. Retrieved from https://www.nybooks.com/daily/2018/06/07/islams-new-native-informants/?utm_medium=email&utm_campaign=NYR%20Turkey%20Kobayashi%20India&utm_content=NYR%20Turkey%20Kobayashi%20India+CID_d86f43bbaae92d2cae27593d57a7a691&utm_source=Newsletter&utm_term=Islams%20New%20Native%20Informants

Mandelbaum, R. (2017, August 13). By all means, compare these shitheads to the Nazis. *Gizmodo*. Retrieved from https://gizmodo.com/godwin-of-godwins-law-by-all-means-compare-these-shi-1797807646

Marantz, A. (2017, October 16). Birth of a white supremacist. *New Yorker*. Retrieved from https://www.newyorker.com/magazine/2017/10/16/birth-of-a-white-supremacist

Markowitz, G., & Rosner, D. (2013). *Deceit and denial: The deadly politics of industrial pollution*. Los Angeles, CA: University of California Press.

Marsha, A. (2018, January 9). What's the deal with men's rights activists and Asian fetishes? *Vice*. Retrieved from https://www.vice.com/en_id/article/9kqqn3/whats-the-deal-with-mens-rights-activists-and-asian-fetishes?utm_campaign=sharebutton

Martinot, S. (2000, Spring). The racialized construction of class in the United States. *Social Justice, 27*(1), 43–60.

Mason, P. (2016, November 9). Globalisation is dead, and white supremacy has triumphed. *The Guardian*. Retrieved from https://www.theguardian.com/commentisfree/2016/nov/09/globalisation-dead-white-supremacy-trump-neoliberal

Matthews, D. (2016, October 15). Taking Trump voters seriously means listening to what they're actually saying. *Vox*. Retrieved from http://www.vox.com/policy-and-politics/2016/10/15/13286498/donald-trump-voters-race-economic-anxiety

Mazza, E. (2019, February 12). Don Jr. gets an 'f' on Twitter after slamming 'loser teachers' at campaign event. *Huffington Post*. Retrieved from https://www.huffingtonpost.com/entry/donald-trump-jr-loser-teachers_us_5c626b08e4b028d5431768c8

McAuley, J. (2019, March 21). Low visibility. *The New York Review of Books, 67*(5), 58–62.

McCandless, J. (2017, July 31). The rise and fall of the 'freest little city in Texas.' *Texas Observer*. Retrieved from https://www.texasobserver.org/the-rise-and-fall-of-the-freest-little-city-in-texas/

McElwee, S., & McAuliffe, C. (2018, July 2). The more people vote, the more progressives win. *Vice*. Retrieved from https://www.vice.com/en_us/article/zm8ppx/democrats-can-win-in-2018-by-raising-turnout

McEwan, M. (2017a, April 24). The movement against smart women. *Shakesville*. Retrieved from http://www.shakesville.com/2017/04/the-movement-against-smart-women.html?m=1

McEwan, M. (2017b, August 3). "Sanders democrats" don't own the left. *Shakesville*. Retrieved from http://www.shakesville.com/2017/08/sanders-democrats-dont-own-left.html?m=1

McLaren, P. (2016, December 31). A message to social studies educators of the US in the coming Trump era. *Truthout*. Retrieved from http://www.truth-out.org/opinion/item/38926-a-message-to-social-studies-educators-of-america-in-the-coming-trump-era

McLaren, P., & Farahmandpur, R. (2002). Breaking signifying chains: A Marxist position on postmodernism. In D. Hill, P. McLaren, M. Cole, & G. Rikowski (Eds.), *Marxism against postmodernism in educational theory* (pp. 35–66). New York, NY: Lexington Books.

McMorris-Santoro, E. (2016, January 29). The Bernie bros are a problem and the Sanders campaign is trying to stop them. *BuzzFeed*. Retrieved from https://www.buzzfeednews.com/article/evanmcsan/the-bernie-bros

McRae, E. G. (2018). *Mothers of massive resistance: White women and the politics of white supremacy*. New York, NY: University of Oxford Press.

Meyerson, H. (2016, Summer). The Democrats after Bernie. *Dissent*, 26–34.

Miller, J. (2016, June 15). *Civic scientific literacy in the United States.* Retrieved from https://smd-prod.s3.amazonaws.com/science-red/s3fs-public/atoms/files/NASA%20CSL%20in%20 2016%20Report_0_0.pdf

Miocci, A., & DiMario, F. (2017). *The fascist nature of neoliberalism.* New York, NY: Routledge.

Mishra, P. (2018, March 19). Jordan Peterson & fascist mysticism. *The New York Review of Books.* Retrieved from https://www.nybooks.com/daily/2018/03/19/jordan-peterson-and-fascist-mysticism/

Molteni, M. (2018, April 13). How the march for science became a movement. *Wired.* Retrieved from https://www.wired.com/story/mos-movement/

Moody, K. (2018, Summer). The changing working class: Challenges and new potentials. *ISR, 109,* 50–60.

Morris, C. D. (2010, Spring/Summer). Why misogynists make great informants: How gender violence on the left enables state violence in radical movements. *Make/Shift Magazine.* Retrieved from https://incite-national.org/2010/07/15/why-misogynists-make-great-informants-how-gender-violence-on-the-left-enables-state-violence-in-radical-movements/?fbclid=IwAR33gDDvfQH52Tuz cqgvZcGlsJLggcl5RHnqDM7n6Ur9I2s3kmAFeSaxSTo

Muirhead, R., & Rosenblum, N. (2018, Winter). The new conspiracists. *Dissent.* Retrieved from https://www.dissentmagazine.org/article/conspiracy-theories-politics-infowars-threat-democracy

Myerson, J. (2017, May 8). Trumpism: It's coming from the suburbs. *The Nation.* Retrieved from https://www.thenation.com/article/trumpism-its-coming-from-the-suburbs/

Nagle, A. (2017). *Kill all normies: Online culture wars from 4chan and Tumblr to Trump and the alt-right.* Winchester, UK: Zero Books.

Narayanan, V., Barash, V., Kelly, J., Kollanyi, B., Nuedert, L., & Howard, P. (2018, February 6). Polarization, partisanship and junk news consumption over social media in the U.S. *Comprop Data Memo,* 1–6. Retrieved from http://comprop.oii.ox.ac.uk/wp-content/uploads/sites/93/2018/02/ Polarization-Partisanship-JunkNews.pdf

Neiwert, D. (2017). *Alt-America: The rise of the radical right in the age of Trump.* New York, NY: Verso.

Nichols, A. (2017, July 14). Stop patronizing the working class. *The Outline.* Retrieved from https://theoutline.com/post/1916/stop-patronizing-the-working-class?utm_ source=FB&zd=2&zi=bqozsiyq

Nichols, T. (2017). *The death of expertise: The campaign against established knowledge and why it matters.* New York, NY: Oxford University Press.

Nicol, J. (2016). Sexual assault: Where do we go from here? *Herizons.* Retrieved from https://herizons.ca/ node/597

Niman, M. (2019, April 5). Weaponized social media is driving the explosion of fascism. *Truthout.* Retrieved from https://truthout.org/articles/weaponized-social-media-is-driving-the-explosion-of-fascism/

Nowak, M., & Prashad, V. (2016, December 20). The essentials of socialist writing. *Jacobin Magazine.* Retrieved from https://www.jacobinmag.com/2016/12/socialist-writing-publishing-books-reading/ ?utm_campaign=shareaholic&utm_medium=facebook&utm_source=socialnetwork

O'Hagan, E. M. (2019, March 8). Feminism without socialism will never cure our unequal society. *The Guardian.* Retrieved from https://www.theguardian.com/commentisfree/2019/mar/08/celebrate-international-womens-day-why-not-join-union?CMP=fb_gu&fbclid=IwAR0Dp2cybLqA76zzzuLX MiToNKvHkIrZBj_1YxQSmT5eD9_5Ls4I-kJnrxo

Olson, D. (2014, December 22). The mods are always asleep. *Medium.* Retrieved from https://medium.com/ @FoldableHuman/the-mods-are-always-asleep-7f750f879fc

Oxenham, S. (2017, September 1). Believing widely doubted conspiracy theories satisfies some people's needs to be special. *Research Digest.* Retrieved from https://digest.bps.org.uk/2017/09/01/believing-widely-doubted-conspiracy-theories-makes-some-people-feel-special/

Packer, G. (2016, February 14). Turned around: Why do leftists move to the right? *The New Yorker.* Retrieved from https://www.newyorker.com/magazine/2016/02/22/why-leftists-go-right

Paquette, D. (2017, June 29). Analysis: Trump's tweet about Mika Brzezinski's 'bleeding' face was way more than just an insult. *Washington Post.* Retrieved from http://www.msn.com/en-us/news/us/ analysis-trump%E2%80%99s-tweet-about-mika-brzezinski%E2%80%99s-%E2%80%98bleeding% E2%80%99-face-was-way-more-than-just-an-insult/ar-BBDsCWx?li=BBmkt5R&ocid=spartanntp

Penny, L. (2011). *Meat market: Female flesh under capitalism.* Winchester: Zero Books.

REFERENCES

Penny, L. (2017a, February 21). On the Milo bus with the lost boys of America's new right. *PacificStandard*. Retrieved from https://psmag.com/on-the-milo-bus-with-the-lost-boys-of-americas-new-right-629a77e87986

Penny, L. (2017b, September 11). You are not a rebel. *The Baffler*. Retrieved from https://thebaffler.com/war-of-nerves/you-are-not-a-rebel

Penny, L. (2018, July). Peterson's complaint. *Longreads*. Retrieved from https://longreads.com/2018/07/12/petersons-complaint/amp/?__twitter_impression=true

Petersen, B. (2017, August 14). Cloudfare is helping defend a neo-Nazi website from hackers, even as Google and GoDaddy are distancing themselves from it. *Business Insider*. Retrieved from http://www.businessinsider.com/cloudflare-defends-nazi-website-from-hackers-godaddy-cancels-services-2017-8

Piascik, A. (2018, December). Working people will make a better world: An interview with labor historian Priscilla Murolo. *Z Magazine*, 22–28.

Piepzna-Samarasinha, L. (2017, Summer). A modest proposal for a fair trade emotional labor economy. *Bitch, 75*, 21–26.

Poland, B. (2016). *Haters: Harassment, abuse, and violence online*. Lincoln, NE: Potomac Books.

Pomerantsev, P., & Weiss, M. (2014). The menace of unreality: How the Kremlin weaponizes information, culture and money. *The Interpreter, 22*. Retrieved from https://imrussia.org/media/pdf/Research/Michael_Weiss_and_Peter_Pomerantsev__The_Menace_of_Unreality.pdf

Post, C. (2017, Spring). We got Trumped: Results and prospects after the 2016 election. *International Socialist Review, 104*, 34–52.

Prokop, A. (2016, September 16). Trump fanned a conspiracy about Obama's birthplace for years. Now he pretends Clinton started it. *Vox*. Retrieved from https://www.vox.com/2016/9/16/12938066/donald-trump-obama-birth-certificate-birther

Quan, J., & Ryshina-Pankova, M. (2016). "Let me tell you…": Audience engagement strategies in the campaign speeches of Trump, Clinton, and Sanders. *Russian Journal of Linguistics, 20*(4), 140–160.

Rader, B. (2017, September 1). I was born in poverty in Appalachia: 'Hillbilly Elegy' doesn't speak for me. *The Washington Post*. Retrieved from https://www.washingtonpost.com/opinions/i-grew-up-in-poverty-in-appalachia-jd-vances-hillbilly-elegy-doesnt-speak-for-me/2017/08/30/734abb38-891d-11e7-961d-2f373b3977ee_story.html?tid=ss_fb&utm_term=.3d57d280d5b3

Rasmus, J. (2018a, August). U.S. government survey on "precarious" jobs. *Z Magazine*, 32–35.

Rasmus, J. (2018b, December). Comparing crises: 1929 with 2008 and the next. *Z Magazine*, 36–41.

Rehmann, J. (2016). Bernie Sanders and the hegemonic crisis of neoliberal capitalism: What next? *Socialism and Democracy, 30*(3), 1–11.

Renton, D. (2017, July 25). Convergence on the right. *Rs21*. Retrieved from https://rs21.org.uk/2017/07/25/convergence-on-the-right/

Renton, D. (2019, Spring). What is different about today's far right? *ISR, 112*, 78–91.

Resnikoff, N. (2017, January 6). The center has fallen and white nationalism is filling the vacuum. *Think Progress*. Retrieved from https://thinkprogress.org/the-center-has-fallen-and-white-nationalism-is-filling-the-vacuum-beb0611dfe94#.otqfsj2sz

Responses to 'Reflections from a Hashtag.' *The New York Review of Books, 65*(16), 54–58.

Richards, J. (2017, June 21). *The privilege discussions we need to have*. Retrieved from http://www.joannarichards.com/new-blog/2017/6/21/the-privilege-discussions-we-need-to-have

Roediger, D. (2017). *Class, race, and Marxism*. New York, NY: Verso Press.

Roesch, J. (2019, Spring). The new women's movement. *ISR, 112*, 8–19.

Romano, A. (2016, December 14). How the alt-right's sexism lures men into white supremacy. *Vox*. Retrieved from http://www.vox.com/culture/2016/12/14/13576192/alt-right-sexism-recruitment

Roose, K. (2019, June 8). The making of a YouTube radical. *The New York Times*. Retrieved from https://www.nytimes.com/interactive/2019/06/08/technology/youtube-radical.html?fbclid=IwAR0k_O52y5z8lUYeZL3BkbGUVDsylJg6rmCtVin80-ZwCE-i0y0RtrEVE1M

Rose, R. (2014, January 13). Man poses as a woman on online dating site; Barely lasts two hours. *Jezebel*. Retrieved from https://jezebel.com/man-poses-as-woman-on-online-dating-site-barely-lasts-1500707724

Rösner, L., & Krämer, N. C. (2016, July–September). Verbal venting in the social web: Effects of anonymity and group norms on aggressive language use in online comments. *Social Media + Society*, 1–13.

Rothkopf, D. (2017, August 8). Decoding the ancient logic of the Google bro. *The Washington Post*. Retrieved from https://www.washingtonpost.com/news/global-opinions/wp/2017/08/08/decoding-the-ancient-logic-of-the-google-bro/?tid=sm_fb&utm_term=.3b39b1ee19e6

Rottenberg, C. (2018). *The rise of neoliberal feminism*. New York, NY: Oxford University Press.

Rosario, J. (2017, July 5). The right's NPR freakout shows a political movement consumed by insanity. *The Daily Banter*. Retrieved from https://thedailybanter.com/2017/07/right-wingers-be-crazy/

Rosenbaum, S. (2017, July 2). The legacy of 'swiftboat.' *Huffpost*. Retrieved from https://www.huffingtonpost.com/entry/the-legacy-of-swiftboat_us_5959206ae4b0326c0a8d118a

Ryan, M. (2016, December 28). How Trump and his army beat us online. *Ctrl Alt Right Delete*. Retrieved from https://medium.com/@melissaryan/how-trump-and-his-army-beat-us-online-8be518306b35#.x7kqrw71k

Sanders, D. (2018, August). Let's get real about the democratic party. *Freedom Socialist Party*. Retrieved from https://socialism.com/fs-article/lets-get-real-about-the-democratic-party/

Sanders, J. (2017, Fall). Expensive denial: The rising cost of ignoring climate change. *Bitch, 76*, 19–22.

Santer, B. (2017, July 5). I'm a climate scientist and I'm not letting trickle-down ignorance win. *The Washington Post*. Retrieved from https://www.washingtonpost.com/news/posteverything/wp/2017/07/05/im-a-climate-scientist-and-im-not-letting-trickle-down-ignorance-win/?tid=ss_fb&utm_term=.0dbf39b2c988

Sartre, J. P. (1976). *Anti-Semite and Jew: An exploration of the etiology of hate*. New York, NY: Random House.

Schulte, E. (2018, Spring). The year of #MeToo: Pulling back the curtain on women's oppression. *International Socialist Review, 108*, 16–29.

Sedillo, M. (2017, August 29). Chris Hedges is a public menace. *The Southwest Political Report*. Retrieved from https://thesouthwestpoliticalreport.com/2017/08/29/chris-hedges-is-a-public-menace/

Selfa, L. (2012). *The democrats: A critical history*. Chicago, IL: Haymarket Books.

Selfa, L. (2017, Summer). Donald Trump's first 100 days. *International Socialist Review, 105*, 1–11.

Sen, R. (2018, January 9). The lefty critique of #TimesUp is tired and self-defeating. *The Nation*. Retrieved from https://www.thenation.com/article/the-lefty-critique-of-timesup-is-tired-and-self-defeating/

Shaw, T. (2018, March 21). The new military-industrial complex of big data psy-ops. *New York Review of Books*. Retrieved from https://www.nybooks.com/daily/2018/03/21/the-digital-military-industrial-complex/?utm_medium=email&utm_campaign=NYR%20Wolves%20Orban%20Cambridge%20Analytica&utm_content=NYR%20Wolves%20Orban%20Cambridge%20Analytica+CID_54761ca178aa65ea5c4a4410b9616c02&utm_source=Newsletter&utm_term=The%20New%20Military-Industrial%20Complex%20of%20Big%20Data%20Psy-Ops

Shearer, E., & Gottfried, J. (2017, September 7). News use across social media platforms 2017. *Pew Research Center*. Retrieved from http://www.journalism.org/2017/09/07/news-use-across-social-media-platforms-2017/

Shenk, T. (2017, February 7). Booked: Capitalizing on rural resentment. *Dissent*. Retrieved from https://www.dissentmagazine.org/blog/booked-katherine-cramer-politics-resentment-rural-wisconsin-scott-walker-trump

Siegel, H. (2017, September 17). The tech giants promise to heal themselves, but the internet was built to hate. *The Daily Beast*. Retrieved from http://www.thedailybeast.com/the-tech-giants-promise-to-heal-themselves-but-the-internet-was-built-to-hate?source=twitter&via=desktop

Silverman, J. (2017, May12). Julian Assange and the banality of access. *The Baffler*. Retrieved from https://thebaffler.com/the-future-sucked/julian-assange-banality-of-access

Simon, S. (2017, May). Drugs, migration, and NAFTA. *Z Magazine, 30*(5), 35–40.

Sitrin, C. (2017, July 10). Most republicans now think colleges are bad for America. *Vox*. Retrieved from https://www.vox.com/policy-and-politics/2017/7/10/15947954/republicans-think-colleges-bad-for-america-media-pew-study

SJWiki. (n.d.). *Brocialists and tankies*. Retrieved from https://www.sjwiki.org

REFERENCES

Slaughter, J. (2017, December). Low-wage harassment. *Z Magazine, 30*(12), 10–12.

Smith, A. (2017, Summer). Trump and the crisis of the neoliberal world order. *International Socialist Review, 105*, 43–60.

Smith, D. N., & Hanley, E. (2018). The anger games: Who voted for Donald Trump in the 2016 election and why? *Critical Sociology, 44*(2), 195–212.

Smith, S. (2017, Summer). Fighting for reproductive rights in the age of Trump. *International Socialist Review, 105*, 12–27.

Sobieraj, S. (2017, July 13). Bitch, slut, skank, cunt: Patterned resistance to women's visibility in digital publics. *Information, Communications, and Society*. Retrieved from http://www.tandfonline.com/doi/abs/10.1080/1369118X.2017.1348535?journalCode=rics20

Solnit, R. (n.d.). Whose story (and country) is this? *Literary Hub*. Retrieved from https://lithub.com/rebecca-solnit-the-myth-of-real-america-just-wont-go-away/

Solod, L. (2017, June 1). The silencing of the Hillary Clinton supporter. *Dame*. Retrieved from https://www.damemagazine.com/2017/06/01/silencing-hillary-clinton-supporter

Solomon, N. (2018, December 18). Beto, we hardly knew ye. *Common Dreams*. Retrieved from https://www.commondreams.org/views/2018/12/18/beto-we-hardly-knew-ye

Stan, A. (2017, February 24). CPAC dispatch: How Donald Trump killed movement conservatism. *Moyers & Company*. Retrieved from http://billmoyers.com/story/cpac-dispatch-donald-trump-killed-movement-conservatism/

Stanley, M. (2018, Spring). Capital offenses: Hillbilly Elegy and anti-worker mythologies. *International Socialist Review, 108*, 38–56.

Starbird, K. (2017). Examining the alternative media ecosystem through the production of alternative narratives of mass shooting events on Twitter. *Association for the Advancement of Artificial Intelligence* (Paper). Retrieved from http://faculty.washington.edu/kstarbi/Alt_Narratives_ICWSM17-CameraReady.pdf

Starr, T. (2017, July 19). Bernie Sanders' black woman problem. *The Root*. Retrieved from https://www.theroot.com/bernie-sanders-black-women-problem-1796995081?utm_medium=sharefromsite&utm_source=The_Root_facebook

Sunshine, S. (2017, July 14). Islamophobia is the glue that unites diverse factions of the far right. *Truthout*. Retrieved from http://www.truth-out.org/news/item/41265-islamophobia-is-the-glue-that-unites-diverse-factions-of-the-far-right

Sunstein, C., & Vermeule, A. (2009). Conspiracy theories: Causes and cures. *The Journal of Political Philosophy, 17*(2), 202–227.

Surin, K. (2018, April). Extreme poverty in the U.S. is a political choice of the powerful. *Z Magazine, 32*(24), 7–10.

Sustar, L. (2018, Summer). The future of class struggle in the US: A radical road to labor's revival? *ISR, 109*, 25–48.

Sykes, C. (2017, November 10). Year one: The mad king. *New York Review of Books*. Retrieved from http://www.nybooks.com/daily/2017/11/10/year-one-the-mad-king/?utm_medium=email&utm_campaign=NYR%20Milosz%20Persian%20art%20local%20news%20resistance&utm_content=NYR%20Milosz%20Persian%20art%20local%20news%20resistance+CID_53c5f8974f87366b31fcc861f996d10e&utm_source=Newsletter&utm_term=Year%20One%20The%20Mad%20King

Szalavitz, M. (2017, July 5). Why do we think poor people are poor because of their own bad choices? *The Guardian*. Retrieved from https://www.theguardian.com/us-news/2017/jul/05/us-inequality-poor-people-bad-choices-wealthy-bias?CMP=share_btn_fb

Szoldra, P. (2016, April 1). The Anonymous 'war' on Donald Trump is a complete disaster. *Tech Insider*. Retrieved from http://www.businessinsider.com/anonymous-war-donald-trump-fail-2016-4

Taibbi, M. (2018, January 23). How Donald Trump's schizoid administration upended the GOP. *Rolling Stone*. Retrieved from https://www.rollingstone.com/politics/news/taibbi-trump-schizoid-administration-up-ended-gop-w515787

Tax, M. (2017, December). United fronts. *Z Magazine, 30*(12), 21–24.

Terzakis, E. (2018, Summer). Marx and nature. Why we need Marx now more than ever, *ISR, 109*, 103–123.

The power of groupthink. (2017, July 1). *The Economist*. Retrieved from https://www.economist.com/news/special-report/21724115-observers-donald-trumps-presidency-who-hope-politics-will-eventually-return

Theweleit, K. (2010a). *Male fantasies, volume 1: Women, floods, bodies, history*. Minneapolis, MN: University of Minnesota Press.

Theweileit, K. (2010b). *Male fantasies: Male bodies: Psychoanalyzing the white terror* (Vol. 2). Minneapolis, MN: University of Minnesota Press.

Thier, D. (2018, Fall). What's the matter with the Israeli working class? *ISR, 110*, 113–137.

Thier, H. (2019, Spring). Ten years since the great recession. *ISR, 112*, 92–103.

Thompson, D. (2016, December 5). The dangerous myth that Hillary Clinton ignored the working class. *The Atlantic*. Retrieved from https://www.theatlantic.com/business/archive/2016/12/hillary-clinton-working-class/509477/

Thorton, T. (2016, November 10). I'm a coastal elite from the Midwest: The real bubble is rural America. *Roll Call*. Retrieved from http://www.rollcall.com/news/opinion/im-a-coastal-elite-from-the-midwest-the-real-bubble-is-rural-america

Tolentino, J. (2018, May 15). The rage of the incels. *The New Yorker*. Retrieved from https://www.newyorker.com/culture/cultural-comment/the-rage-of-the-incels?mbid=contentmarketing_facebook_citizennet_paid_culture_the-rage-of-the-incels%3Fsource%3D_3-visit

Torres, P. (2017, July 29). From the Enlightenment to the Dark Ages: How "new atheism" slid into the alt-right. *Salon*. Retrieved from http://www.salon.com/2017/07/29/from-the-enlightenment-to-the-dark-ages-how-new-atheism-slid-into-the-alt-right/

Traister, R. (2018, September 17). And you thought Trump voters were mad: American women are furious and our politics and culture will never be the same. *The Cut*. Retrieved from https://www.thecut.com/018/09/rebecca-traister-good-and-mad-book-excerpt.html?utm_campaign=nym&utm_medium=s1&utm_source=fb

Trudell, M. (2016, April 4). Sanders, Trump and the US working class. *International Socialism*. Retrieved from http://isj.org.uk/sanders-trump-and-the-us-working-class/

Ullrich, V. (2016). *Hitler: Ascent 1889–1939*. New York, NY: Alfred A. Knopf.

Ullrich, V. (2017, February 1). Wait calmly. *Zeit Online*. Retrieved from http://www.zeit.de/wissen/geschichte/2017-02/adolf-hitler-chancellor-appointment-anniversary/komplettansicht?print

Vance, J. D. (2016). *Hillbilly elegy: A memoir of family and culture in crisis*. New York, NY: Harper.

Vanderbeck, R. M. (2006). Vermont and the imaginative geographies of American whiteness *Annals of the Association of American Geographers, 96*(3), 641–659.

Waas, M. (2019, April 26). Mueller prosecutors: Trump did obstruct justice. *New York Review of Books*. Retrieved from https://www.nybooks.com/daily/2019/04/26/mueller-prosecutors-trump-did-obstruct-justice/

Wagner, J. (2019, January 22). Alexandria Ocasio-Cortez a popular choice for president even though she is too young to serve. *The Washington Post*. Retrieved from https://www.washingtonpost.com/politics/alexandria-ocasio-cortez-a-popular-choice-for-president--even-though-shes-too-young-to-serve/2019/01/22/05cb590c-1e43-11e9-8e21-59a09ff1e2a1_story.html?utm_term=.3e65f770ebaa

Waldman, K. (2018, July 23). A sociologist examines the "white fragility" that prevents white Americans from confronting racism. *The New Yorker*. Retrieved from https://www.newyorker.com/books/page-turner/a-sociologist-examines-the-white-fragility-that-prevents-white-americans-from-confronting-racism

Walters, S. (2017). In defense of identity politics. *Signs*. Retrieved from http://signsjournal.org/currents-identity-politics/walters/

Wang, T. (2012). *The politics of voter suppression: Defending and expanding Americans' right to vote*. Ithica, NY: Cornell University Press.

Ward, B. (2018, October 22). You don't fight racists with racist junk science. *SocialistWorker.org*. Retrieved from https://socialistworker.org/2018/10/22/you-dont-fight-racists-with-racist-junk-science

Warner, B., Galarza, R., Coker, C., Tschirhart, P., Hoeun, S., Jennings, F., & McKinney, M. (2017). Comic agonism in the 2016 campaign: A study of Iowa caucus rallies. *American Behavioral Scientist*, 1–20.

REFERENCES

Weida, K. (2017, September 29). The forgotten Hillary Clinton voter: A profile of the not-so-silent majority. *Rantt*. Retrieved from https://rantt.com/the-forgotten-hillary-clinton-voter-a-profile-of-the-not-so-silent-majority-5e903b846643

Weinberg, B. (2010, December 31). The conspiracy industry and the lure of fascism. *GrafbeyondGraf*. Retrieved from http://grafbeyondgraf.blogspot.com/2010/12/conspiracy-industry-and-lure-of-fascism.html

West, L. (2016). *Shrill*. New York, NY: Hachette Books.

West, L. (2017, July 12). Real men might get made fun of. *The New York Times*. Retrieved from https://mobile.nytimes.com/2017/07/12/opinion/real-men-might-get-made-fun-of.html?smid=fb-share&referer=http%3A%2F%2Fm.facebook.com

Westneat, D. (2017, March 28). UW professor: The information war is real and we're losing it. *The Seattle Times*. Retrieved from http://www.seattletimes.com/seattle-news/politics/uw-professor-the-information-war-is-real-and-were-losing-it/

Wilkinson, A. (2016, November 15). We need to talk about the online radicalization of young, white men. *The Guardian*. Retrieved from https://www.theguardian.com/commentisfree/2016/nov/15/alt-right-manosphere-mainstream-politics-breitbart

Williams, C. (2017, April). Scientists and politics. *Z Magazine, 30*(4), 33–39.

Wilz, K. (2016). Bernie bros and woman cards: Rhetorics of sexism, misogyny, and constructed masculinity in the 2016 election. *Women's Studies in Communication, 39*(4), 357–360.

Winant, G. (2017, June 27). The new working class. *Dissent*. Retrieved from https://www.dissentmagazine.org/online_articles/new-working-class-precarity-race-gender-democrats

Windham, L. (2017, June). Working-class feminism. *Z Magazine, 30*(6), 9–11.

Wise, T. (2016, December 8). Alt+right+delete: The disingenuous and contradictory nature of white nationalism. *Rawstory*. Retrieved from http://www.rawstory.com/2016/12/altrightdelete-the-disingenuous-and-contradictory-rhetoric-of-white-nationalism/

Wolcott, J. (2017, March 3). Why the alt-left is a problem, too. *Vanity Fair*. Retrieved from http://www.vanityfair.com/news/2017/03/why-the-alt-left-is-a-problem

Wolff, M. (2018). *Fire and fury: Inside the Trump White House*. New York, NY: Henry Holt and Company.

Wrigley-Field, E. (2019, March 20). What socialists can learn from #MeToo. *Socialist Worker*. Retrieved from https://socialistworker.org/2019/03/20/what-socialists-can-learn-from-metoo

Young, D. (2016, November 23). Mark Lillia's "The End of Identity Liberalism" is the whitest thing I've ever read. *VSB Newsletter*. Retrieved from http://verysmartbrothas.com/mark-lillas-the-end-of-identity-liberalism-is-the-whitest-thing-ive-ever-read/

INDEX

2016 Election, 5, 6, 10, 14, 21, 31, 61, 77, 100, 132, 135

A

abortion, 4–6, 13, 14, 97, 106, 141, 149–164, 166–171, 189, 204
activism, 3, 5–9, 13, 15, 28, 64, 68, 74, 77, 81, 85–88, 90, 91, 126, 137, 171, 204
affirmative action, 70, 75, 107
aggrieved entitlement, 9, 10, 46, 68, 138, 203
alt-right, 4, 27, 29, 31, 32, 34, 35, 48, 56–59, 89, 126, 131–140, 142, 145, 204
anti-semitism, 39, 47, 50, 57, 176
authoritarianism, 7, 33, 41, 44, 45, 56, 57, 104, 137

B

birth control, 150, 153, 154
Black Lives Matter, 18, 90, 91, 98, 106
blackpilling, 143
both-sides-ism, 2, 175, 180, 188, 189, 191–193, 201
bots, 92, 134, 147, 187, 195, 199
Brexit, 32, 35, 56, 60, 105, 134, 175, 177
brocialism, 7, 25
business unionism, 64, 66, 85, 86

C

capitalism, 7, 8, 10, 11–14, 19, 24, 25, 29, 32–35, 38–40, 47, 50, 51, 62–64, 66, 68, 70–72, 74, 77–80, 82, 83, 89, 94, 96, 99, 101, 102, 104, 106, 108, 109, 111, 118, 136, 146, 159, 184, 189, 196, 197, 200

climate change, 8, 12, 15, 19, 62, 182–184, 190, 194
colonization, 8, 11, 72, 74, 79
communications decency act, 133, 146
conservatives, 2, 7–10, 18, 22, 26, 30–33, 35–38, 46, 48, 49, 51, 53, 55–59, 62, 63, 69, 71, 77, 78, 91, 94, 96, 98, 104, 106, 108, 111, 114, 125–127, 129, 132, 135, 137, 138, 149, 150, 152, 159, 168, 169, 176, 178, 181–189
conservativism, 33, 119
conspiracism, 194, 197, 200
conspiracy theory, 33, 187, 193–200, 203
contraception, 4, 24, 150–152, 154–157, 159, 164, 168, 170, 171
contrarianism, 129, 138
courts, 2, 10, 14, 18, 36, 56, 64, 79, 104, 149, 150, 152, 154, 158, 168, 184, 191, 192, 204
criminal justice, 16
culture, 25, 34, 45, 47, 53, 68, 73, 78, 79, 101, 114, 116, 118, 119, 126, 127, 132, 135, 175, 185, 201
cyber
  bullying, 124
  harassment, 120, 124
  mobbing, 121, 122, 182
  organizing, 114, 131, 133

D

democracy, 33, 35, 45, 53, 55, 56, 58, 110, 113, 126, 131, 136, 185, 201
  illiberal democracy, 56
Democratic Party, 12, 61, 91, 93, 94, 98–100, 102, 109, 152, 170, 196, 197, 198

democrats, 1, 6, 37, 54, 56, 68, 76, 93,
    97, 98, 100, 102, 109, 110, 169,
    171, 185, 187, 203, 204
derailing, 100, 128
dialectical, 3, 14, 30, 35, 39, 45, 63,
    70–72, 79, 80, 137, 138, 141,
    151, 159, 174, 183, 200, 201
discrimination, 19, 24, 50, 75, 84, 97,
    103, 119, 142, 152
domestic violence, 8, 12, 15, 141, 142,
    164, 166
double standard, 15, 27, 21–23, 51, 128
doxxing, 104, 116, 121

E
economy, 6, 10, 11, 55, 61, 64, 67, 68,
    72, 81, 196
education, 13 19, 21, 27, 45, 64, 69, 73,
    81, 82, 86–89, 99, 119, 141, 161,
    170, 176, 178, 197
e-libertarianism, 4, 114–116, 126.145
evangelicals, 152, 156, 186

F
Facebook, 5, 6, 26, 58, 86, 87, 92,
    94–96, 114, 120, 133, 134, 146,
    147, 183, 186, 187, 203
fake news, 4, 60, 174, 175, 184–189,
    196, 197, 199, 201, 203
false consciousness, 2, 41, 91
family, 9, 12, 20, 47–49, 58, 67, 73, 79,
    83, 88, 91, 119, 121, 123, 124,
    141, 142, 151, 155, 164, 167,
    169, 171
fascism, 1–4, 7, 18, 29, 30–38, 41–44,
    46–51, 53–57, 60, 92, 101, 111,
    115, 128, 138, 140, 172, 196
fathers' rights movement, 141, 142, 144
feminism
    conservative feminism, 8–10
    Marxist feminism, 7, 13
    neoliberal feminism, 8, 9
    postmodern feminism, 7, 10–12

socialist feminism, 1, 5, 6, 10–13,
    15, 29, 30
third wave feminism, 7, 8
fetal personhood, 149, 151, 152, 154,
    155, 156–159, 161, 163,
    165–168
free speech, 115–118, 121, 123, 125,
    128, 142, 191
Freedom of Information Act (FOIA),
    182, 183
fundamental attribution error, 68, 69

G
Gamergate, 122, 123, 138, 139
gaslighting, 127, 129
geek culture, 118, 119
gender, 5–8, 10–15, 19–29, 32, 46–48,
    62, 69–71, 73, 79, 81–85, 88, 89,
    95, 106, 108–111, 120, 124, 129,
    130, 141, 143, 154, 175, 181
globalization, 34, 35, 40, 58, 65, 66, 99,
    136, 185, 196

H
healthcare, 86, 159, 169
heteronormativity, 24
homophobia, 27, 47, 50, 60, 62, 90,
    101, 111, 113, 114, 121, 124, 130,
    132, 134, 145, 180

I
identity politics, 3, 4, 12, 26, 62, 65, 70,
    85, 90, 96, 106, 107, 109, 135
immigrants
    detention of, 43, 67
    undocumented, 15, 197
immigration, 8, 32, 46, 48, 49, 67, 68,
    80, 84, 116, 135, 183, 196, 204
incels, 115, 141–145
internet, 26, 31, 46, 57, 58, 60, 113,
    114–118, 120–125, 131–134,
    137, 143, 146, 160, 173, 174,
    195, 198

J

job
gig, 81, 83
manufacturing, 40, 65, 70, 83, 84, 175
minimum wage, 65, 102, 107
part time, 66, 82, 83
public sector, 83, 84, 104, 151, 159, 168, 169
retail, 81, 83–85
service industry, 20, 69, 70, 83, 84, 168
temporary, 82, 83
journalism, 3, 28, 46, 114, 123, 174, 187, 190, 192

L

labor, 6, 9, 10, 12, 13, 15, 19–21, 24, 33, 34, 39, 40, 41, 62, 68, 70–75, 79–86, 89–91, 119, 145, 146, 151, 182, 185
LGBTQI, 1, 9, 50, 59, 67, 89, 108, 138
liberalism, 9, 32, 35, 38, 45, 46, 49, 50, 56
libertarianism, 4, 57, 114–116, 126, 127, 136, 140, 145

M

manosphere, 4, 115, 133, 141, 142, 144, 145
mansplaining, 25, 26, 128
Marxism, 3, 7, 10–12, 25, 36, 70, 110
media, 1–4, 21–26, 31, 32, 35, 37, 42, 44, 46, 51, 55–59, 62, 65, 80, 83, 89, 92, 94–97, 99, 101, 191–193, 197, 201, 204
meme, 31, 46, 62, 63, 76, 81, 96, 106, 127, 131, 185, 204
Men's Rights Activists (MRAs), 141, 142, 144
#MeToo, 6, 16–18, 86, 98, 170
middle class, 5, 6, 38–40, 61, 66, 69, 70, 73, 74, 76, 81, 83, 92, 127, 132, 140, 142, 167, 169

minorities, 1, 4, 18, 27, 33, 40, 42, 43, 46, 56, 60, 61, 64, 68–71, 74, 75, 80, 82, 84, 86, 88, 89, 97, 103, 108–111, 113, 114, 116–119, 121, 122, 124, 125, 128–130, 135, 138, 145, 146, 166, 181, 192, 197, 201
misogyny, 1, 3, 18, 19, 26, 27, 29, 35, 48, 57, 60, 89, 111, 115, 117, 119, 123, 124, 130, 133, 139, 141, 142, 164, 204

N

nationalism, 33, 40–41, 57, 60, 64, 95, 106, 139, 142, 163, 166, 181, 201
neoliberalism, 23, 32–35, 38, 40, 56, 63–68, 81, 99, 103, 104, 108, 109
neo–Nazis, 118, 135, 139
neutrality, 118–120, 124
normies, 139
North American Free Trade Agreement (NAFTA), 68, 73, 102

O

objectification, 15, 23–25, 124, 151, 159–161
occupy movement, 93
online harassment, 26, 121–124

P

patriarchy, 11–14, 63, 79, 141, 143
Pickup Artists (PUAs), 141–144
political correctness, 46, 65, 118, 129
populism, 1–4, 7, 18, 29, 30–36, 38, 41, 42, 44, 47, 50, 51, 53–55, 58, 60, 61, 64, 65, 73, 77, 87, 89, 91, 95, 99, 100, 104, 109, 111, 115, 140, 172, 203
authoritarian populism, 1–4, 7, 18, 29, 30, 32–36, 38, 41, 42, 44, 47, 51, 53–55, 64, 65, 77, 104, 109, 140, 172
right-wing populism, 31, 87, 91, 100, 104, 111, 203

pornification, 23
postmodernism, 8
poverty, 19, 20, 26, 62, 64, 65, 67–69,
    75, 78, 79, 161, 170, 180
proud boys, 131, 132, 135, 139, 142
pseudoscience, 42, 175, 179–181, 183,
    184, 201

Q
QAnon, 198, 199

R
race, 7, 11, 12, 14, 20, 25, 34, 43, 51,
    59, 63, 64, 70–77, 79, 81–83, 85,
    89, 94, 106–111, 118, 124, 130,
    132, 136, 139, 142, 151, 161,
    175, 180, 181
racism
    colorblind racism, 71, 74–77
    reverse racism 50, 75
rape, 8, 10, 12, 15–18, 25–28, 48, 123,
    141, 144, 145, 149, 153, 154,
    156, 160–163, 170
redpilling, 143
refugees, 5, 34, 36, 43, 64, 67
religion, 59, 89, 139, 152, 155, 183, 184
reproduction, 10, 12, 27, 82, 83, 150,
    151, 161, 169
reproductive rights, 3, 5, 6, 8, 22, 96,
    102, 103, 141, 144, 149, 152,
    154, 159, 161, 163, 168, 170, 171
Republican Party, 51, 53, 64, 67, 69, 91,
    100, 134, 153, 171, 174, 182, 188
ressentiment, 138
right-wing
    backlash, 66–69, 106, 138
    organizing, 133, 135, 137, 138

S
science, 4, 45, 92, 99, 118, 119, 130,
    131, 136, 139, 153, 155, 156,
    173, 175, 179–184, 186, 187,
    194, 196, 197, 201

secular, 13, 32, 55, 127, 156, 181, 184
segregation, 9, 71, 73, 75, 76, 152
sexism, 2, 3, 7, 12, 14, 15, 18, 19, 21,
    24, 25, 27, 41, 48, 62, 63, 88, 89,
    95, 101, 105, 108, 110, 111, 113,
    114, 121, 130, 132, 134, 145, 180,
    184
sexual harassment, 6, 12, 14–18, 20, 27,
    29, 84, 86, 108
sexuality, 6, 7, 11, 14, 23–25, 50, 89,
    106, 108, 110, 111, 149–151, 156,
    161–163, 169
single mothers, 20, 64, 69
social class, 7, 22, 34, 41, 108, 156
Social Justice Warriors (SJWs), 118
social media
    analytics, 92
    economic model, 92, 134
socialism, 11, 12, 32, 57, 63, 91, 92, 96,
    102, 103, 107, 110, 178
sockpuppets, 134

T
tankies, 28
teachers' strikes, 86, 87
technology, 45, 70, 113, 118, 119, 133,
    170
#TimesUp, 6, 16, 17, 86
tone policing, 129, 171
translocal whiteness, 136
trolls, 124–130
Twitter, 22, 26, 94, 95, 114, 120, 123,
    124, 126, 131, 133, 134, 142,
    146, 183, 184, 187, 194, 195, 199

U
union, 39, 40, 63, 64, 66, 73, 74, 82,
    85–88, 185, 196
Unite the Right Rally, 132

V
violence, 5, 6, 8, 12, 15, 22, 27–29,
    32, 35, 40–47, 49, 50, 53, 59, 60,

70, 77, 113, 114, 116, 117, 121,
141, 142, 144, 145, 149, 164, 166,
167
voting, 10, 22, 23, 54, 62, 67, 83, 91,
96–99, 101, 197

W
the wall, 67, 137
welfare, 33, 40, 46, 50, 54, 64, 67, 69,
70, 72, 73, 75, 80, 82, 110, 168,
169
whataboutism, 28, 77, 105, 203
White(s)
 men, 9, 10, 17 18, 26, 28, 47, 61, 62,
70, 74, 96, 113, 119–121, 125,
131, 137, 145, 201
 nationalism, 33, 40, 57, 106, 139,
181
 poor, 77, 78
 rural, 63, 67, 71, 76, 77, 80
 suburban, 76, 83, 111

supremacy, 8, 11, 33, 42, 48, 57, 63,
71, 72, 89, 106, 107, 111, 116,
125, 132, 136, 138, 139, 141
 women, 9, 10, 28, 40, 73, 74, 76, 86
whiteness, 10, 61, 63, 71, 72, 108, 114,
136, 142
women, 1, 4–29, 40, 48, 49, 56, 73,
74, 76, 86, 89, 90, 150–154, 170,
191–193, 201, 203, 204
women's march, 5, 86, 90, 170
working class, 1, 3–6, 8, 12, 13, 15, 21,
22, 30, 35, 38, 39–41, 48, 61–66,
70–77, 80–83, 85, 86, 88–90,
105, 109–111, 142, 150, 151, 153,
159, 161, 163, 169–171, 204

X
xenophobia, 3, 42, 57, 62, 90, 181

Y
Yellow Vest protests, 62, 88